FEMINIST THEORY TODAY

FEMINIST THEORY TODAY

An Introduction to Second-Wave Feminism

Judith Evans

SAGE Publications

London • Thousand Oaks • New Delhi

First published 1995

SAGE Publications Ltd
6 Bonhill Street
London EC2A 4PU

SAGE Publications Inc
2455 Teller Road
Thousand Oaks, California 91320

SAGE Publications India Pvt Ltd
32, M-Block Market
Greater Kailash – I
New Delhi 110 048

British Library Cataloguing in Publication data
A catalogue record for this book is available
from the British Library

ISBN 0 8039 8478 2
ISBN 0 8039 8479 0 (pbk)

Library of Congress catalog card number 95–068523

Typeset by Mayhew Typesetting, Rhayader, Powys
Printed in Great Britain by The Cromwell Press Ltd,
Broughton Gifford, Melksham, Wiltshire

Contents

Acknowledgements   vi

1 Introduction   1

2 Equality and Difference in Feminist Thought   13

3 Early Liberalism: Feminism's First Equality   28

4 Essential Tensions? Liberal Feminism's Second Stage   47

5 Radical Equality: the Early Fire   62

6 Cultural Feminism: Feminism's First Difference   76

7 Woman's Kindness: Cultural Feminism's Second Face   91

8 Socialist Feminism: from Androgyny to Gynocentrism,
   Equality to Difference   108

9 The Postmodernist Challenge   125

10 The Legal Challenge   143

11 Conclusion and Afterthoughts   160

Select Bibliography   169

Index   179

Acknowledgements

I wrote this in troubled times. I am the more grateful to the people who helped me through. Among them are remarkably dedicated and skilled members of what remains of the National Health Service. We all stand in their debt.

Two people supported me throughout. At York, David Edwards encouraged and consoled me, and convinced me I could finish the book. Without him, it might not have been written. And at Marist, JoAnne Myers emailed almost daily with words of comfort, comments on theory, and news of The Biggest Cupboard In The World. David's and JoAnne's greatest feat was to restore laughter to my life. Both have given far more than conventional notions of friendship suggest. I owe them a massive amount.

The Political Studies Association Women's Group has been an important, if occasional, part of my life and work. Of its early members I thank especially Sally Jenkinson, Elizabeth Meehan, and Ursula Vogel. They have shown me the warmth anyone who knows them would expect, and listened with patience as I wandered the highways and byways of feminist thought. They bear no responsibility for views expressed, crimes committed, here.

I have known also the kindness of strangers. From the streets, cafes, and shops of York to as far as the Internet runs, people have come to my aid. They are harbingers of a better way of life. Not only I, I hope, know that.

Sage make publishing a pleasure, insofar as that can be done. Patiently they endure my belief that I am the only author in the world. They have worked like a collective on this book, and I thank them all.

There are communities, social strata, milieus, whose women do not study. Certainly they do not study for years, with no end in view. My mother stood with me through the uneasy laughter; she supports me still. This book is for her.

Bishophill, York
March 1995

1

Introduction

In 1972 the United Nations declared 1975 to be the . . . International Year of the Woman. Among the world's women . . . reaction was not all good. Was this . . . an admission that everything else was the Year of the Man?[1]

Through the centuries, women have endured the Year of the Man. Ever, some have rebelled. If feminism is a protest against women's oppression, there is no confining its story, by country, culture, or time. We know of the suffragists who campaigned for the franchise. Do we remember Emily Davison, who died in its cause? Do we recall those arrested time after time, brutally force-fed, that we might vote?[2]

It may be, we do. Do we know of the Indian women who have for decades fled patriarchal laws and led gangs of bandits; famous among them, released in 1993, Phoolan Devi, the 'Bandit Queen'?[3] Or the Chinese women who fought in rebel armies; and to the end of the nineteenth century, fleeing foot-binding and other cruelties, formed roving bandit gangs? Though few could escape, so strongly were they held in submission, except by death at their own hand.[4] The women of Muslim Central Asia, forced to give birth in squalor, subjected to innumerable other cruelties, spied for the Bolshevik invaders of the 1920s, to gain a better world. And their reward? The defeated men joined the Bolsheviks: women were subjugated once more.[5]

This book is born of a different and mainly later history, much of which is nonetheless unknown, or partly hidden, now. It is not only the story of the unhappy housewives of the best-known early books, like *The Feminine Mystique* and *The Captive Wife*.[6] It also tells of those who fought for socialism in the 1960s Left in the US, Germany, and the UK; women who denounced their male comrades for preaching liberation for all the peoples of the world: all except women. This is a story far milder than those above. But there are analogies, for, as Robin Morgan said, a woman of the New Left 'could be declared uptight or a poor sport if she didn't want to be raped', while a leading black militant announced that 'the only position for women in [the Student Non-Violent Co-Ordinating Committee] is prone'.[7] And the story, once more, tells of promises broken, a contract unfulfilled.

My book is not a biography of these women, or a political or social history of feminism's Second Wave, which they began. Rather I address Second-Wave theory, which is not, early writings apart, necessarily the 'movement' voice. For feminist theory has become an enterprise all of its own. There is a gulf between activism and the academic writing that emerged; a gulf that has widened with time.[8] The reasons for and consequences of this are not my topic here.

The writing I address ranges from 1963 to 1994; beginning with the publication of *The Feminine Mystique*, and covering Second-Wave feminism's first thirty or so years. I do not attempt to discuss it all; that is impossible, given the amount and range of feminist thinking now. Nor is there a generally accepted – and certainly no ideal – way of deciding what authors and texts to include, and how they should be grouped. So I have had to make difficult choices.

I chose writings in two ways. First, I decided to study 'schools' like liberal feminism and within them, to focus on significant texts. This raises the question, which ones? I do not want to suggest I tried to include all the major works, or even the most important writers. I do not even want to say I chose the writings most representative of a given school, though of course I would have liked to do that. Formidable problems of definition and classification ruled it out. Second, I chose, when reading these texts, to concentrate on two concepts which have been central to feminism more or less throughout: the concepts of equality and difference. These have of course normally been taken to mean sex equality and difference. But they are more widely employed than that, and will be used more broadly here.

I suggest that there is a tension between these concepts that runs through the schools, and exists within individual thinkers, too. Though I do not expect to show this in every case. It may not be the same tension, given that the concepts are used in various ways, and have given rise to more than one dispute.

In the remainder of this chapter I introduce the meanings of difference encompassed here: between the sexes; between groups of women; between individuals and 'within woman'. I then explain in more detail how and why I have structured the book by 'schools' of feminist thought, and the problems that can result. I note that various of the writings are neither conventionally 'theoretical' nor specifically concerned with the debates, so I have had to tease their views of equality and difference out. Finally I address the problem of language within feminist writing, of for example the over-inclusive 'we' that overrides the differences feminist writing seeks to grasp; and how I have tried to cope with that.

I begin by outlining aspects of feminism's 'equality–difference' debate, which concerns equality of, and differences between, women and men.

The equality and difference debate

> feminism means that we seek for women the same opportunities and privileges the society gives to men, or . . . that we assert the distinctive value of womanhood against patriarchal denigration. While these positions need not be mutually exclusive, there is a strong tendency . . . to make them so. *Either we want to be like men or we don't.*[9] [italics mine]

The sex equality–difference controversy is key to my book. It is what these concepts tend to evoke, that is, when feminist thinkers hear the terms together, they normally think of that debate. I outline it briefly here.

In its most basic form, the argument concerns women's similarity to or dissimilarity from men. That, though, is not its starting point; that is, it is not its primary motivation to find out what sex differences, beyond the most basically biological, there are, and how they are caused. Rather, in its origins at least, it concerns the quest for equality of the sexes – equality of rights and of opportunities, and more radically, of condition.

Equality and difference are counterposed here because of the view that women can only be equal if they are the same as men, though clearly, 'same' is not 'identical' and means, say, alike. Hence the stress on, for example, IQ test and examination results, and on finding non-biological reasons for any differences that emerge. Though as time has gone by, as the debate has become formalized and cast as a dispute among feminists, as well as between them and their opponents, matters have become more complex.

Feminists are so used to the debate that, disagree violently over the issues though they do, they may not see the immediate problem it poses for newcomers to the field. That is the problem of its name. Those new to feminist thought might well think that 'equality–inequality' would be the more appropriate opposing terms. However these would be misleading, initially at least, as they could be taken to imply first that we know what equality means, and second that there are 'inequality feminists' who favour a situation in which women are regarded as men's inferiors, or held subordinate to them.

'Sameness–difference', which some feminists employ, might be a better axis, even though there is no doubt that equality is in some way involved in the debate. For 'sameness' feminists undoubtedly seek equality with men:[10] they ask to be treated as men are, and justify this on the grounds of sameness, though 'likeness' might be a better term. So they ask, for example, for equal entitlement to consideration for jobs. To a suggestion of sex differences which ruled that out, they would reply that there are none, or rather that they are small in number and size, trivial in type, and irrelevant to the equality of women and men.

I continue the 'sameness–difference' discussion as if the two formed an axis, and equality was placed with sameness as though they were automatically linked. However, before moving to difference, I note that we might want to ask whether equality *does* necessitate sameness. For there are some who would say not. We might then want to see 'equality', 'sameness', and 'difference' as forming not a continuum, but, three corners of a triangle. Then the notion of 'equality in difference' enters in. (This is the idea that we merit equal though not identical treatment; equal in the sense of 'equally good, and more appropriate to us'.) Though so does 'equality through difference', as opposed to 'equality through sameness':[11] my 'sameness' category above.

These ideas have implications for what we think equality is. One is this: to treat people equally, it is not necessary to treat them in exactly the same way. To treat people as equals may *require* that they not be treated the same way. This is a difficult point, and I delay discussion of it until later in the book. I shall first deal with what might be called more basic views of equality, beginning, in detail, in Chapter 2.

The equality–difference debate generally implicates 'sameness' feminists in a male world. A strict equality feminist would not wish to change that world; and for her, 'as good as men' means 'the same'. Her harsher detractors – 'strong difference' feminists – would tend to regard this as bad in itself, believing men's qualities whether innate or not to be a force for ill, and a 'man-made world' to be inimical to more than female advance. (Of course, there are various positions between these extremes.) I want to consider a point made by such detractors here, though it is mainly relevant to Chapter 10.

'Sameness' is shorthand for women's sameness, for purposes relevant to women's advance, with men; as opposed to men's sameness to women. This point may sound odd. Are not these identical? Certainly 'sameness' feminists would think so. But their view is thought by others to leave them open to attack.

What have 'sameness equality' feminists failed to see? Why is asking whether men are the same as women different from asking whether women are the same as men? Difference feminists would say this: to compare women with men, to be concerned with the way *women* differ from *men*, is to write not only difference, but inferiority, or at best, deviation from a social standard, into the question itself. So whatever the answer, its implications – that women are the ones who are different, deviant, even abnormal – are decided in advance. And the notion, if not indeed the fact, that men are the standard, that 'man' indicates and defines 'human', is entrenched.

Such feminists would add that society is ordered according to what men need, or are thought to need, and that this is seen as the normal and rational state of affairs. To order society so as to cater for women's needs, too, requires 'special arrangements'. This is because those who see the current position as natural think providing for men is catering for people; providing for women is adding something else. To exaggerate their view somewhat: men simply ask for their rights, women for affirmative or compensatory action. Women are given to 'special pleading'. That is how feminist demands for fair and indeed equal treatment are seen. Or so one type of 'difference feminist' indictment runs.

I am not going to take a stand here on these ideas. I shall however quote a feminist lawyer who rejects equality *and* difference, as the terms are used now; Catharine Mackinnon:

> Men's . . . needs define auto and health insurance coverage . . . their perspectives and concerns define quality in scholarship, their experience and obsessions define merit . . . their image defines god, and their genitals define sex. For each of their

differences from women, what amounts to an affirmative action plan is in effect, otherwise known as the structure and values of American society.[12]

The 'values of . . . society', she and others say, are geared to men. To grasp this view is to see how great the stakes in the argument are. Even within the 'equality–difference' or 'sameness–difference' debate – as opposed to the broader question of how these concepts are employed by feminists, and their general consequences for feminist thought – massive implications lie. Here is a discussion that latently, anyway, goes far further than the extraordinarily difficult task of achieving parity of the sexes in society now; or even gaining it by revolutionary means by which the general oppressions perpetrated by our system are overthrown.

For here we move towards a declaration that our entire value system is male. And we will see in Chapter 10 an argument – whose premises are not the same – that the very terms of the debate are, too. Clearly at some stage along the way to the wholesale rejection of culture as man made, the question arises whether women and men can communicate adequately, let alone 'equally', at all. Here, conventional means of analysis are of little use. I give this section's end to a poet.

> some men would rather see us dead than imagine
> what we think of them/
> if we measure our silence by our pain
> how could all the words
> any word
> ever catch us up
> what is it
> we cd call equal?[13]

Beyond sisterhood? Other women, other groups

> The oppression of women knows no ethnic nor racial boundaries . . . but that does not mean it is identical within those differences . . . . To deal with one without even alluding to the other is to distort our commonality as well as our difference.
> For then beyond sisterhood is still racism.[14]

Above, I pointed out that there is a problem of terminology in the equality–difference debate: the dichotomy seems incorrect. Only if we link sameness to equality does it begin to make sense. Many feminists seem not to understand this point. I do not mean that theoretical naïvety is involved, undertheorized, within feminist thought, though 'equality' is. We have become used to the name of the debate, and some part of us simply 'knows' what it means, at least, to us. Also, I believe that 'equal' has come to appear to mean only one thing. At times I am inclined to add, 'and not very much'. But when people of my ethnic background, 'race', and occupational grouping make comments like that, it is time for difference, in the sense of difference between women of various groups, to enter in.

One oddity of 'difference', both within the debate and elsewhere in feminist thought, is that it would appear to be endlessly invoked, but again, often is not defined. Writers silent on equality are voluble on difference. But what do they mean? Even that within the debate 'different' means 'from men', is not that simple a point. I move to other meanings, now.

There is a lesson feminists have been slow to learn: that there are variations between groups and categories of women[15] and that at the very minimum, one group does not speak for all. Middle-class white hetero-sexual women do not a movement make. Or rather, we might. But it would not be *the* feminist movement. Some indeed would doubt whether it can be *a* feminist movement at all.

'Difference' in this sense has been seen, perhaps because of its supposed association with black and lesbian feminists, as equivalent to identity politics, that is, a politics anchored securely in an identification with, for example, one of these two categories or groups.[16] I discuss identity politics in Chapters 8 and 9. Here I note that I reject the proposed equation in part because it assumes, say, that a feminist who is a lesbian is also a 'lesbian feminist', and that she identifies with lesbianism as a group.

There is another reason for my rejection, related – how closely, I am not sure – to the first. I feel that such equating over-homogenizes the 'groups': it can exacerbate stereotypes, too. Though viewed another way, identity politics can be seen as crucially necessary for those we have the gall to name the 'different'; and solidarity via that politics, regarded as conferring strength. I raise points like this in Chapter 9, via the writings of lesbians and black women.

My rejection of this particular proposed equivalence is also linked to a view that it is always the member of an underprivileged group who is taken to need an 'identity' and thought to belong to a school of feminism based on that, and even on that alone. We blithely speak of 'black feminism' and 'lesbian feminism'. Is there a book whose index lists 'white feminism'? Is a feminism unqualified, reserved for us?

I do not find it easy to hear, let alone to forward, these points; I have seen this form of difference as sundering the movement. I have been forced to see that sisterhood has to be earned, and that it may not be for me to decide when. Nor do I suggest that I have yet learned enough.

Feminism is divided by the sex equality–sex difference debate. It is riven by this second difference too. I want equality, and justice. I do not believe these to be 'Western', or 'white' or 'male'; certainly not inherently or irremediably so. I want unity within the movement. However, I think I have come to accept that feminists will have to live with a sundering for a long while yet, and that we may have to live with the knowledge that the sundering was done by 'us'. And I have also come, belatedly, to see that to live with this is to live by the founding tenets of the movement, the beliefs of the radicals among the early Second Wave, which I address in Chapters 2 and 5. More, it is little to ask that we see that 'though all women are women, no woman is only a woman'.[17] Indeed, that is especially incumbent on those of us who have sometimes, anyway, insisted that we were, and were 'worth', more, while ignoring the very existence of women from less advantaged groups.

I move briefly to the 'third difference', postmodernism's in part, most fully addressed in Chapter 9.

The last difference? Can woman there be?

This approach, whose more technical aspects I address later on, has been variously construed. I aim to capture its original meaning, insofar as that is reflected in British and American thought. I see the term as employed in two major ways. The first, which is not postmodernist, but which I will for the moment treat as such, emphasizes the differences between women within and across groups. Its import is less that it views women as entirely different one from another, than that it reminds us forcefully that we are not reducible to the groups to which we belong. Thus it has implications for identity politics, at least if they propose that one 'identity' or affiliation is paramount, it may be, regardless of a woman's views or choice.

A variant of this first idea emphasizes differences between women to the point, it is said, where we cannot use the notions of women or gender in our thought. I assume the belief is that the differences outweigh what we might have in common, but that they are individual and not group differences (though obviously groups will enter into the account).

The second notion, which is highly complex, I would call 'full' post-modernism. It threatens to explode the category of 'woman'; I do not mean to suggest that it says women literally do not exist, though there are readings on which it might. Its views are difficult to convey, though perhaps I think that because I do not find them easy to grasp. I am here merely going to suggest one way of looking at the questions raised, paralleling the discussions above: via the notion of the fragmented self.

We all understand that there are various facets to our 'selves', that most of us have a nationality (or more than one), a family of some kind, friends made at stages of our lives, some gone. We may be in waged employment. If not, that may not be by choice. We probably have what are called 'outside interests' or 'leisure pursuits', and there can be a very wide range of these. We all have one or more ethnic origins, though people often speak as if 'ethnic' means 'not-white'. We have sexual preferences. And so on. Some of these are more important to us than others; or perhaps we think they are. Their importance may change over time, or we may choose to focus on one at a given moment, or drift into doing that.

As I wrote this, my mind moved to my Dutch ancestry, though I am only in small part Dutch. Day to day, this rarely comes to mind. If I could go to Holland often, I might think about it more. Currently, I think mainly about my job. And while I have been working on this book, I have left most other interests – other parts of myself? – aside. My feminism has been with me throughout, though in different ways. My writing brought the early days of the movement back. For a while, that was hard to bear.

All this really says is that I am like most people and different from them at the same time. I am like other people, in part, because I am different from them: we all have our interests, and they will not be the same.[18] But that supposes there *is* an 'I', a self. I change, but there is a self to change.

'Full postmodernists' argue, or try to, that there is more to it than that – though I shall give in to temptation, and say, also, 'less'. For them, at the extreme, there is no 'self'.[19] The individuality and the changes I have discussed, are for some people evidence of this. It follows that there could be nothing called a 'woman'. I shall explain the argument, and offer a critique, in Chapter 9.

Feminism's 'schools'

I have divided this book into the following 'schools' of feminist thought: liberal, 'early radical',[20] 'strong cultural' (or 'cultural radical'), 'weak cultural', socialist, and postmodernist. A mixture of tradition and practical concerns has dictated my choice. Insofar as it is tradition, however, I have broken with it, in part via my simultaneous analysis of equality and difference, in part by emphasizing the heterogeneity within these schools.

Some will think my classifications wrong; others, a division into schools not only narrow and old-fashioned, but totally inappropriate now. Marianne Hirsch and Evelyn Fox Keller,[21] for example, think it best to speak in terms of issues and debates. And it is true that if we do that, we see the schools 'split'. If for example we looked at pornography, we would see no united front within my 'ideological' groups. However, that is part of the point I want to make. I do not believe, because that is so, that feminists have transcended the (always somewhat faulty) standard classifications of political groupings and views. But further, the fact that the groups remain will have an influence on our thought, too important to deny by employing new categorizations when we write.

That is: 'liberalism' and 'liberal feminism', say, are inadequate constructs in various ways; in particular, for me, because they may do violence to the nuances of a writer's thought. But many people think of themselves as, for example, liberals, and socialists; and the fact that they do may interact with the beliefs or other factors that led them to choose that affiliation at the start. There is a relationship between affiliation, attitudes, and behaviour, and it includes, for example, 'I am a socialist, and so I should not do this'. So these labels, problematic as they are, 'represent' overlapping views as they may do, nonetheless constitute part of our social reality; and of identity, some would say. It may be too soon to give them up.

A standard way of presenting liberal feminism, for example, is to produce a definition of liberalism and examine liberal feminist thinkers in relation to that. This is problematic in various ways.

Liberalism is normally defined via the work of men.[22] A framework of ideas is produced, and is called liberalism. It is then customary to say that liberal feminists will hold certain views – those already articulated – and their work will be read with that in mind. If they do not hold them, it will be said that liberal feminism differs from liberalism.[23] We have become so accustomed to this way of proceeding that perhaps we have not seen its flaws. I point to them first via an eloquent protest by Joanna Hodge.

Hodge attacks the way postmodernism is conventionally understood and defined: like the other schools, via the work of men. Women postmodernists such as Julia Kristeva and Hélène Cixous are, she points out, 'feminist postmodernists' (if not, indeed, non-existent) according to this way of thought.[24] 'The (real) postmodernists' are the male writers in the field, and – I would add to Hodge's complaint – entire books on 'postmodernism' can be written without mentioning a woman's name.

My method here springs from agreement with Hodge.[25] I have not, however, taken the step of defining, for example, liberalism by the writing of women, or, to go further on the attack, via the feminist texts,[26] tempting as these ideas are: they are every bit as illogical as defining liberalism by the works of men – though, no more.[27] Rather I have singled out ways of looking at equality that seem to me to be liberal, and tried to locate them within feminist work.

I do not pretend to have solved the problem of categorization by doing this. For how did I gain an idea of 'liberal equality'? But it seems to me preferable to the alternative of, in effect, first ignoring a writer and then classifying her against the background of men's ideas: an alternative that helps perpetuate the odious distinction between 'real' and feminist theory. That can have various bad results. It can stifle innovation as prudent feminists produce Theory. Or, ironically, it can move feminists away from the mainstream, strengthening the kind of view which calls that 'malestream' and wants feminist theory to be different from non-feminist or 'male' thought.

Some feminists would disagree less with what I have just said than with the idea that 'postmodernism' (for example) necessarily incorporates its allied feminist writings. For 'feminist postmodernism' differs from (most) 'postmodernism', they say,[28] and an assimilation of the two would be wrong.

While the former point may well be true – though I suspect that both in its postulation of a gulf and in its suggestion that there is 'a' feminist postmodernism, or a 'feminist' postmodernism, it assumes too much – I do not see that it can answer the basic challenge to, and charge of, the 'writing out' of women's work.

Given its importance and its applicability to other schools, I shall take the point further now. First, to say that 'feminist postmodernism' is different from postmodernism is I believe to cede the terrain without a fight. Is postmodernism, 'real' postmodernism, which men write about without mentioning even *one* woman author, then the standard from which feminist or women's postmodernism diverges? Or should post-modernism comprise both sets of works? If not, is one to be called men's, or even 'masculinist', postmodernism? Why is men's writing the measure? Are writers within a school to be classified by gender? or by mode of analysis, topic, and style?

This kind of question affects more than one of the feminist 'schools' I discuss. And it parallels a major issue of the book, discussed mainly in Chapters 8 and 10. For questions about addressing a 'school' of thought, and classifying an individual author, are questions about how we think of groups and individuals, too. That is: who comprises a school, or a group? Is it heterogeneous or monolithic? To what school, or group, does a writer, an individual, belong? How do we know that? Are we diminishing the writer, the individual, if we say they belong to a school or a group? Are we ignoring aspects of their texts, of their 'self'? Are we forcing them into a straitjacket, adversely affecting their personality and their thought? Do we misrepresent their characteristics and their views? These comments are about theory. They are about political, cultural, and social differences between people(s), too.

Theory inferred

The writers I have chosen to discuss are, of course, not necessarily consciously engaged in the 'equality–difference debate'. And even though there is in almost all, I believe, an important element of the usages of equality and difference commented on here and in Chapter 2, they may offer no definition of the terms. Further, the early writers will not address 'difference' as it is known, and discussed, now, so I shall infer their views on certain points from their texts. I shall attempt to locate their concepts of equality and inequality, and their views on sameness and difference. And I shall try to say how they think equality is to be gained; and what the future will bring.

I am discussing major writers within the 'schools', via their most important works, or, ones that seem most relevant to me. Most authors would employ, many readers prefer, a more synthetic approach. However, as Patricia Collins says, that might well over-homogenize the schools.[29] This is an important consideration, but there are others that affect my choice.

Feminist theory has reached the stage where more or less any analysis, though especially a textbook like this, could become a summary of com-mentaries on commentaries on major articles and books. While there is a place for that kind of writing, it distances a reader from, and affects their reading of, the original work. Of course, any reading, any interpretation, does that. I am not claiming any particular insight, nor do I say an especial ability to avoid imposing a framework on the literature inheres in my approach. But I focus on, if possible adhere to, the first text. In choosing this path, I shall omit some outstandingly good writers who have offered critiques of various kinds. I regret that.

There is another reason besides the problem of piling interpretation on interpretation why I chose the approach. It applies in particular to the earlier works I discuss. It is common now, though possibly more so in the US, to discuss feminist theory either in a 'historical' manner that ranges back to the nineteenth century at least, or by employing mainly contemporary work. I do not want to adjudicate either between these, or between them and an issue-based approach. However my reading has convinced me that there is a particular history we have to recover, whose theories and values we do well to recall. It is the history of feminism's second wave. And so I have framed my book.

'What Language is it?': conventions used here

There is forever in feminist thought a problem of what terms to employ when speaking of, say, women. I have chosen to say 'they' except when referring to white middle-class (and sometimes heterosexual) women; then I shall say 'we' or 'us'. When I talk about an author's discussion of this group of women, I shall say 'they'. But I have found it almost impossible not to say 'we' meaning 'you who read this, and I'.

The use of 'women' (or 'men') is problematic. That will emerge at various stages below. I know that there will be times when I say 'women' without meaning 'all women'. It is impossible to qualify, adequately, each time the word is used.

Speaking of feminists poses a similar problem, which I have not been able to resolve with ease. I use 'we' more or less as I do in the case of women; 'I' in giving my views; 'they' where I obviously cannot speak for the feminists concerned. But I know inconsistencies will appear.

These are, ensuing chapters will, as 'difference' follows 'difference', show, not the only problems of wording I encountered as I wrote this book.

Notes

1 Gloria Steinem, 'Houston and history', in *Outrageous Acts and Everyday Rebellions*, 1985, p. 279.

2 Rebecca West, 'The life of Emily Davison', 1913, in Maggie Humm (ed.), *Feminisms: A Reader*, 1992, pp. 30–1.

3 Mala Sen, *India's Bandit Queen: The True Story of Phoolan Devi*, 1993.

4 Elisabeth Croll, *Feminism and Socialism in China*, 1978, pp. 36–7.

5 Gregory Massell, *The Surrogate Proletariat: Moslem Women and Revolutionary Strategies in Soviet Central Asia*, 1974, *passim*.

6 Betty Friedan, *The Feminine Mystique*, 1982 (first published 1963); Hannah Gavron, *The Captive Wife*, 1966.

7 Robin Morgan, 'Goodbye to all that', in Leslie B. Tanner (ed.), *Voices from Women's Liberation*, 1971, p. 273; Stokely Carmichael quoted by Jo Freeman, *The Politics of Women's Liberation*, 1975, p. 57.

8 bell hooks, *Talking Back: Thinking Feminist – Thinking Black*, 1989, pp. 35–41.

9 Iris Young, 'Humanism, gynocentrism and feminist politics', in *Throwing Like a Girl: And Other Essays in Feminist Philosophy and Social Theory*, 1990, p. 85.

10 I am here using 'equality' in a fairly undifferentiated way, and as if its meaning were clear.

11 See Sibyl Lipschultz, 'Social feminism and legal discourse, 1908–1923', in Martha Fineman and Nancy Thomadsen (eds), *At the Boundaries of Law*, 1991.

12 Catharine Mackinnon, *Feminism Unmodified: Discourses on Life and Law*, 1987, p. 36.

13 Ntozake Shange, 'Some men', in *A Daughter's Geography*, 1985, p. 44.

14 Audre Lorde, 'An open letter to Mary Daly, in Cherríe Moraga and Gloria Anzaldúa (eds), *This Bridge Called My Back: Radical Writings by Women of Color*, 1983, p. 97.

15 My rough distinction is that a group is something one joins, a category something to which one is deemed to belong.

16 They are of course not mutually exclusive. It is for clarity that I hold them apart.

17 Elisabeth Spelman, *Inessential Woman*, 1990, p. 187.

18 I am not talking here about anything remotely like the idea that politics, or 'life', is about the pursuit of our own interests at others' expense.

19 As we will see, they find it difficult to be consistent on this point.

20 I do not mean that radical feminism has gone, nor that 'cultural radical' feminism is its current dominant form.
   My understanding that this is not so has been greatly aided by the views of Pauline Bart.

21 'Introduction' to Marianne Hirsch and Evelyn Fox Keller (eds), *Conflicts in Feminism*, 1990, pp. 1–5.

22 It is not my point that it is wrong to assess women by 'male standards'.

23 See for example Alison Jaggar, *Feminist Politics and Human Nature*, 1983; Rosemarie Tong, *Feminist Thought*, 1989.

24 Joanna Hodge, 'Feminism and postmodernism', in Andrew Benjamin (ed.), *The Problems of Modernity*, 1991, pp. 86–7, 101ff.

25 Patricia Collins, *Black Feminist Thought*, 1990, takes an analogous but more radical view: pp. xii–xiii.

26 Here I distinguish between liberal women and feminist liberals.

27 There are of course historical reasons why the latter has been done.

28 Sandra Harding, *The Science Question in Feminism*, 1986, p. 194.

29 Collins, *Black Feminist Thought*, pp. xiv–xv. Collins though rejects a 'major writers' approach; hers is issue orientated: p. xiii and *passim*.

2
Equality and Difference in Feminist Thought

Early second-wave feminism was a feminism of two forms of equality. The first began with the Presidential Commission of 1960, and *The Feminine Mystique*;[1] the second emerged from the 1960s New Left, and that decade's movement for black Civil Rights.[2] The first I shall call liberal, the second 'early radical'. The first begins with a claim of 'adequate similarity', that is, of no differences that could justify discrimination on the grounds of sex. Where differences other than the biological at their most basic are said to occur, this school sets out to disprove their existence, or to show that they are the products of socialization by families or schools, or by, for example, medical experts, or the mass media, in later life.

Liberal equality feminism, then, asks for equality in the sense of sameness of attainment, and therefore treatment, and justifies it via sameness, 'androgyny'.[3] It says: we deserve to be equal with you, for we are in fact the same. We possess the same capabilities; but this fact has been hidden, or these abilities have, while still potentially ours, been socialized, educated, 'out'.

Here I distinguish between a claim of equal capability now, hidden by stereotypical beliefs held about women, and a claim of potential equal capability, taken away from women by the social arrangements that have made them 'second class'. These feminists profess one of the two. This is not then a politics that denies difference, though it would either eliminate or reduce it, or argue that instances of it were both rare and minute. Or it would say they were produced by socialization, were not innate.

So such feminists would claim that any differences found lacked relevance to women's advance towards the status of men. But they would argue it – contrary to writers we will meet below – on the grounds of the paucity, and potential transience, of both sources and instances of difference by sex. Thus they would normally be called 'sameness' thinkers. However, the greater the emphasis on socialization, the more they approach 'difference' thought; to the extent that we may think the axis I spoke of in Chapter 1 is indeed a genuine continuum, and the sides of my 'triangle' are continua, too. There are, that is, a variety of beliefs about equality, sameness, and difference. I am fairly convinced that is correct. But I shall speak of dichotomous thinking, here: of the 'opposite poles' and sides.

Proponents of sameness have devoted much time and energy to showing that psychological, behavioural, and linguistic differences between men and women are few. However, so resistant are many feminists – and others – to this thought that approximately thirty years after the movement began, writers like Cynthia Fuchs Epstein are patiently, wearily, repeating the very points concerning, or emerging from, their empirical research, first made so long before.[4]

Objections to such research run more or less throughout this book, though very few are overt. As Susan Okin has said, certain philosophers assume that they need not offer proof of their statements:[5] these would be theorists of difference.

The second 'equality school', early radicalism, discussed in Chapter 5, consists of radical egalitarians who believe that both men and women have been damaged by capitalism and patriarchy, though patriarchy is the crucial force. They have been materially damaged, and their characters warped. Equality of the sexes, and for some writers, justice for both, demands these systems' overthrow. Thus Shulamith Firestone's *Dialectic of Sex* seeks and predicts a revolution that will bring full equality and abolish oppression in all its forms. Hierarchy, exploitation, subjugation of any kind at all, must and will disappear.[6]

That is how I would distinguish, on the issue of equality, between for example Firestone and the early Friedan; though of course there are many other differences between these writers, and more than one representative of their 'schools'. Both are 'sameness' feminists in their belief that now or eventually, men and women are or could be the same, and equal or capable of being equal once stereotypes are changed or barriers removed. But the divergence in their views of what a society in which men and women were equal would be like is massive.

Meanings of equality

What does it mean to say that feminists seek equality of women and men? Is it true? Why have I called both liberals and early radicals equality, and 'sameness equality' or androgyny, thinkers? Why is equality contrasted with difference rather than, as seems logical, inequality (the unlikely prospect of a group consenting to be called 'inequality feminists' aside)? These issues pervade my book. Here I begin to depict the theoretical arena where the debates take place.

Equality and androgyny are disputed terms. Equality here must mean at a minimum some form of equality of opportunity for the sexes, if simply in the procedural sense. That is, there should be, in for example selection procedures, no pro-male bias. (As the existence of equality of opportunity tends to be judged by an equality of result, it may of course mean more.)[7] And androgyny must mean not merely the ignoring of difference. It must mean an absence of differences relevant to full participation in the structures that exist now.

These issues are more complex than my account suggests, and I discuss them more thoroughly in Chapter 3 and later on. Here I offer brief introductory accounts, beginning with equality.

I take it to be definitive of a liberal feminist that she believes, at a minimum, in equality of opportunity in the sense given above. That in itself implies that there is something women must have an equal chance – equal with men – to do. Does it also imply that resources – occupations, particularly 'careers', education, especially beyond a certain level, and so on – must be scarce, though to different extents, so that we are talking about some women having an equal chance, in competition with some men, of obtaining the asset(s) they need or seek?

For liberal feminists, I think it does. Therefore, they seek equality of opportunity with men in a hierarchical society like ours. They may be seeking procedural equality, that is, equity, fairness of treatment, or they may want more; though the most they can want, I shall suggest here, is parity, at all existing ranks and levels, with men.

This is a standard way of viewing the issue. It might be truer to current feminist thought to say that almost all contemporary equality feminists would tend to see parity at the various levels of society as the goal, but that they differ on what methods could be used, and in particular on how far the state can or should intervene in their cause.

For them, a greater equality cannot entail that all women be treated equally. For all men are not. And indeed, this has been a charge brought against liberal feminists: that lacking interest in equality for all women, they are not 'feminists'. There are two things the claim can mean, and they may have become confused. The first is that liberal feminists cater for white middle-class women alone. While I am not sure that was ever completely true, I see the point of the charge. The second follows from my comments above; it concerns the notion that women should be equal, one with another. I give an answer to this when I propose conditions for a feminist ideology that would work to bring about women's equality in that sense (see Chapter 5). The liberal feminist stance itself will be discussed in Chapters 3 and 4.

My wording suggests at the very least a positive relationship between sameness of the sexes, in the sense of their possession of certain joint qualities, and equality, in the sense of being treated in the same way.[8] Do women have to be the same as men, to attain equality? If we are the same, why are we not already equal? Why has our sameness been ignored? Where does difference enter the discussion? Why is it counterposed to equality? These issues will be addressed at various points in the book, though mainly in Chapter 10.

Early radical equality differs from the liberal aim, in that it consists of a rejection of hierarchy, and oppression in all its forms. Certainly if we take Firestone as the exemplar of this type of thought, this is so. Women's and children's oppression are the most basic, and they must fall. The aim though is broader; to lift 'The double curse, that man should till the soil by the sweat of his brow, and that woman should bear in pain and travail';[9] to gain an equality of condition once seen as the socialist aim and spirit, so either all possess the same amount and are treated identically, or there is some form of allocation of goods according to need. This is generally thought to apply, of course, to the ending of economic exploitation. That is not always explicit in these writers, perhaps because of the very different emphasis of the New Left until shortly before its end.[10]

Radicals sought also, obviously, the eradication of discrimination by sex and race: not 'after the Revolution', this time around.[11] Indeed it can be said that the eradication of sexual oppression is primary in more senses than one. It may be the oppression from which all others spring. Or it may be that, given the history of rebel and revolutionary movements, women feel they must be included now, and prior – or adequate – importance accorded them until their liberation is ensured. However, the relevant point here is this: this is not a matter of advancing women in society as we know it now, or even marginally changed.

Therefore not only is the radical type of equality different, but also the way in which it will be reached. It is impossible to discuss either of these at the same length as equality of opportunity and means towards it: the relevant secondary feminist and mainstream writings are few. Further, early radicalism has no one view of the exact nature of the good society, or the means by which oppression will fall.

For example, not all such writers emphasized revolution to the extent that they spurned reforms. Rather, they would work for them in the context of final political aims that were not reformist, and insofar as they fulfilled the criteria they set up, Charlotte Bunch's first criterion being, 'Does it materially improve the lives of women and if so, which women, and how many?'

> All women are oppressed, but some have more privilege than others . . . .
> Material reforms should aid as many women as possible and should seek to redistribute income and status so that the class, race, and heterosexual privileges that divide women are eliminated.[12]

While Bunch speaks of 'material reforms' and 'income and status', she mentions heterosexuality too. It is a characteristic of early radicalism to address oppression within, and as caused or exacerbated by, the existing structure of sex. The emphasis was to become a major reason for attacking this feminist strand.

Firestone, again, was prominent among such writers, though unusual in her emphasis on love and romance. Indeed we find among her attacks on these as they are now an appreciation of the pleasure of the erotic, though, allied to a belief that it is bought at massive social cost. But we further find, I believe, in her comments on love between two equals, a vision of the gaining of equality within love itself.[13] Is her suggestion feminism's last frontier? Is there, that is, love after equality? Can they co-exist? Are our views of what love is a product of the oppression we have known? These are questions taken up in part, though in part alone, by those nearest to 'early radicalism' now: the radical feminists who combat 'sexual liberalism' and heterosexuality as it presently exists.[14] I shall return to such topics in Chapters 10 and 11.

A place for difference?

An understanding of difference in the sense of a proper appreciation that 'woman' or 'women' or 'we' were not terms that could be used without caution; that subordination was not uniform; and that it was not for one group of women to speak for another, came later, insofar as it has come at all. However, at a very early stage, as bell hooks has said and as the collections of early pamphlets and speeches show, feminists knew of differences and inequalities between groups of women, and in particular, perhaps, those of race and class, loosely defined, while believing in a commonality in the sense of mutual support.[15] Further, as early as 1969 some were aware that all was not well within the movement:

> HOW WOMEN ARE DIVIDED: Class, Racial, Sexual and Religious Differences.
> If sisterhood between women were a fact, it would not be necessary to hold this conference.[16]

Whether while at one level knowing this they also believed that in a sense all women suffered equally and in the same way, is virtually impossible to assess. Though the wording above suggests an awareness of divisions, a belief in assimilation, rather than an understanding of the position of different groups. It would of course have been strange, given the New Left or Civil Rights milieu from which so many – for example Firestone – emerged, if they had; if they had not at least been aware of some heterogeneity of oppression.

It is hard, for example, to believe that women who had worked for black voter registration in the American South were not aware of the situation of black women; though given the tendency of activist groups to be male dominated,[17] they might not be. In any event, this is not the sense of difference feminists have come to know.

Indeed, ironically, early radicalism's sense of difference might well best be called an overly inclusive awareness that would lead to the universalist usage of 'patriarchy', and to a movement torn apart by the concept itself. This is a point I have not been able to develop here. However, I turn to an expression of it at this chapter's end.

Hooks regards only that very early movement as accepting black women, and documents the racism that overtook the movement so soon.[18] (I do not mean that she believes the whole movement, or every white feminist, to be racist now.) Indeed she refuses to say '*The* feminist movement' because of that. The first major change I discuss here, the first form of 'difference', has been said to be linked with, and be something of a reaction to, the challenge from black women the racism of the white movement evoked.

This change, which occurred around the mid-1970s, is said by Eisenstein to stem from lesbian writing earlier in that decade.[19] It comprises the move within radical feminism[20] from androgyny and equality to what has variously been termed cultural feminism, the 'woman-centred school',[21] and 'gynocentrism/gynandry', though the last is a socialist term.[22] This is a feminism that emphasizes the differences between women and men which Friedan regards as a myth; it normally 'revalues' and celebrates them. 'Classic ecofeminists' like Andrée Collard probably represented cultural feminism at its separatist and 'woman-culture' extreme.[23]

As cultural feminism has grown, 'equality and difference', in the sense of differences between the sexes, have become crucial factors in Second-Wave feminist thought. They cannot, given the various usages of 'difference' and equality, comprise but one axis around which feminism can be organized, though they may well form the strongest and most enduring one. From them emerges a train of thought that has run through Second-Wave feminist thinking and remains a tension at its heart. It exists not only between, but also within, the usual 'schools', and on occasion, within the writings of individuals, too.

Feminism has probably always known 'different and better' arguments within its campaigns and thought, as during its First Wave, and from the granting of the franchise until now.[24] And from the very beginning there was an association of women and peace, and a perturbation about that.[25] As the dispute among radical feminists over the action at Greenham Common shows,[26] a concern about that linking, and the implications of celebrating or emphasizing gender difference, is – the massive ascendancy of cultural feminism despite – with us still.

The 'different and better' arguments have until fairly recently been of roughly two kinds. One seeks to gain some form of equality of treatment, or esteem, via an assertion of complementary virtue, while the other will rebut, refuse, attack, ignore, that which is perceived as man-made, or as male. I shall call the first liberal, problematic though that is,[27] the second, 'strong cultural', though basically *faute de mieux*.

Very few members of this particular school are essentialist in the full sense of the term. Very few, that is, say that from a shared biology other characteristics, normally regarded as unchanging, spring. They believe, rather, in a certain universality of and commonality among women, overriding other concerns. Essentialism would take a stronger stand on what stemmed from the commonality, and on its being biologically based, than this. Though Elizabeth Grosz views essentialism as entailing a shared character, but one not necessarily based on biological 'facts'.[28]

Cultural feminists also tend to claim that women, by virtue of their closeness to the body, to nurture, and to nature itself, possess qualities superior to men's. Mary Daly and Adrienne Rich are commonly cited in this context, and as rejecting rationality, reason, and humanism as male. I am unhappy about these claims, particularly in Rich's case, as I later explain.

Cultural feminism is broad in its scope and range. Only at its most minimal is it concerned to argue for the existence and desirability of differences between women and men, or, better, female and male: difference is not necessarily permanent, let alone biologically caused. Though it will tend to favour 'female values'. It can be construed as ranging all the way from a 'strong essentialism' to what I have elsewhere called 'a thinly- or tactically-gendered self'.[29] However, it does on the whole tend to believe that female qualities are superior; hence its 'tactical' use.

In the First-Wave feminism of the nineteenth century, this view was akin to what I have called tactical, in that 'cultural' feminists believed female values could be deployed to make the public world a better place, as they argued in the suffrage campaign. This tendency seems to have faltered, now, before the appeal of a *women's* culture, and/or an abhorrence of all that is said to pertain to the public world, viewed as irremediably male.[30]

So for cultural feminists of the 'stronger' variety the idea that such qualities should be used outside the family; that they were a reason for women 'leaving home'; that they justified women's entry into the public world not on a basis of equality or equity, but of superior or complementary character, fell. In their place came the view that while certainly women were possessed of better qualities than men, these had been denigrated by the patriarchy, and persistently and systematically devalued, and women cast down. Rather than either emulate men, or add women's complementary qualities to a mutual male–female cause, cultural feminists would revalue womanhood, celebrate difference, and change language or reclaim it for their own.

Thus rather than accept dualism, as liberal feminists are said to do, rather than transcend it, as early radicals, in the end, might, cultural feminism both embraces and inverts it. It values 'nature' over 'culture', revalues motherhood, suggesting that nurturing values are present in all women whether they are mothers or not; seeks a love 'surpassing the love of men',[31] and asserts womanhood in triumph. While 'weak' cultural feminism, as we will see in Chapter 7, exalts what are viewed as womanly qualities of caring and care.

But what is this except a renewed, if not strengthened, acceptance of the subjugation we have known? What is the virtue of qualities born of oppression? Can we afford to forget the early feminist charge that motherhood is among the 'more precarious ventures on which to base a life'?[32]

According to Ann Snitow, equality feminism came under attack because of its tradition of equality for separate independent individuals, and its emphasis on their acting in the public sphere; and because therefore it strengthened the public–private split. Further, it ignored differences between women. And its ethos of neutrality could only be a pretence, in the face of inequalities of gender, race, and class.[33] I am not entirely convinced by this. Early radicalism was not associated with such ideas, and it fell. And liberal equality might have come under attack more because the burden its aims placed on women was perceived.[34]

I am not querying Snitow's historical account. My view is based on a belief that equality feminism is being conflated into one school; that is, I have suggested, wrong. That it was cultural feminism that rose may be part of a more general move towards a belief in male and female characteristics as extant and enduring; a turn which can be seen in liberal feminism too. However, I am unsure. For Echols, its success was based on its 'vision of a global sisterhood . . . [which] seemed to offer an escape from the debilitating discourse of difference', in her view widespread by 1973: her suggestion is that it enabled certain feminists to evade the charges brought by, among others, blacks.[35]

It has been said – on the basis of the emphasis on 'women's' qualities and values, and even more because of the turn to asking what 'woman' is – that feminists have opted for ontology rather than epistemology. But the position is rather more complex than this. What is perhaps true is that at various points ontology has been made to bear rather too great an explanatory burden in the analysis of women's character and lives.[36]

But far from leaving epistemology aside, feminists have issued challenges to more or less every form of 'male concept' and 'male reasoning' there is, and have produced a flourishing body of thought. Their attacks have stretched. as far as natural scientific endeavour; though I know of no successful feminist attack on basic scientific method *per se*.[37] At another level from most such writings, and metaphorically, what I take to be the aim and belief of many such feminists was put by Lorde: 'We cannot use the master's tools to dismantle the master's house.'[38] For the contention is not simply that such methods are inimical to equality and aid the oppression of women, because they are in the hands of men or are put by men to that use; but that they are in themselves, importantly, gendered; inherently to the advantage of men. The tactical answer to this has been given by Firestone; by Rich;[39] and more recently, most forcefully, by Mackinnon:

> We do not trust medicine, yet we insist it respond to women's needs. We do not trust theology, but we claim spirituality as more than a male preserve. We do not abdicate the control of technology because it was not invented by women. . . . If women are to restrict our demands for change to spheres we can trust, spheres we already control, there will not be any.[40]

Mackinnon might well have added, I do not believe this is a just society, I do not think our legal institutions are fair, but (and this is why?) I teach and practise the law.

Difference and identity politics

More or less at the same time, though not necessarily as part of the same process (indeed the two would seem to be antithetical, though this is not quite correct), came not so much an understanding as a renewed awareness of differences between women. Primarily, this meant differences between groups of women, and these mainly by sexual preference, and by race, ethnicity, and country of birth. The process would seem to have begun as a series of charges against the (mainly white and heterosexual) movement, and to have become what is known as 'identity politics'. It is that tendency I introduce now.

First I summarize certain charges brought against white feminism. Of late, African-American and Third World women have posed feminism a question that, given the issues of cross-cultural understanding and the culture-laden meaning of womanhood, has come to the forefront of many debates.

White feminists, it is said,[41] very early radicalism apart, ignored the existence of black women, or over-homogenized 'women's experience' derived from white experience; and tended to see black women mainly as helpless victims. Moreover, the practices of non-white communities (though this would refer mainly to, say, Africa or India, not the US), whether or not they were ones feminists should condemn, must be seen in the cultural context within which they took place: their indigenous meaning should be understood.

Further, comments like 'feminist theory must take differences among women into consideration' imply that there is *a* feminist theory, *one alone*, and that only the views of certain writers matter; statements like 'we need to hear the many views of women' evoke the question, who has the right to say, to be, 'we'? Who are the speakers only, and who both speaks, hears, and understands? (And interprets, and writes the books . . . .) Who speaks of and for 'women'? Who represents them – in the manifold meanings of represent? Gayatri Spivak is a writer who has pondered her own 'location', as an Indian born, working and writing in the US. She is more aware of such points than most.[42]

It is for a lack of awareness, and worse, that hooks attacks white feminism. She charts its racism,[43] and comments on the type of writing different groups are expected to produce: black women will give of their 'experience' while whites provide 'theory' and decide which account of 'black experience' is correct.[44] This is an interesting parallel, of course, to the usual expected theoretical contributions of women and men.

Where cultural feminist is not essentialist, it can be presumed to be universalist, though this does not hold for all writers in the field. And yet its founding 'universalism' would be based on the experiences of women who were white. Thus it is as flawed as the male universalism other types of feminist impugn. And so it might ignore or attack this form of difference,[45] as would poststructuralism and postmodernism, though in a different cause. The latter would tend to attack a fixity this form of identity politics could be said to induce, in that 'identity politics limit and constrain the cultural possibilities that feminism is supposed to open up'.[46]

Difference recognition in this second form does not, and may not intend to, rule out an ideal of the unity of women, or indeed, of a coalition of women and other oppressed groups.[47] At least, it does not say that it does. And it does not do so for ever. It does entail that to attain either, a considerable amount of hard work will have to be done. And this puts it mildly.

From this form of critique of the white (and later, heterosexual) movement there followed a move towards 'identity politics', that is, basing an activism, a political viewpoint, and a sense of selfhood on, say, religious practice, ethnic identity, or sexual preference. Why?

> A paradox confronts anyone who tries to understand the perplexing and persistent phenomena of 'race' and racism in Europe today . . . in genetic terms, the physical and biological differences between groups defined as 'races' have been shown to be trivial . . . . And yet . . . it is all too clear that racism still remains a widespread, and possibly intensifying, fact of many people's lives. Reiterating that 'there's no such thing as "race"' offers only the frail reassurance that there *shouldn't* be a problem.[48]

Thus groupings that are not materially different and can prove it, and have pleaded their case via equality, have to face the fact that the 'reasonable', 'equality', 'equity' approach has largely failed. Evidence that there are no differences whatsoever relevant to the general treatment of persons, and certainly none that could justify the occupational, educational, and social disparities so apparent now, confronts a legal system unable to enforce the most basic rights these findings should confer, let alone redress the balance in full.

To explain properly what occurs as a result, we would have, I think, to look at the history of the 1960s US Movement for Civil Rights; and its journey from an emphasis on legal rights, and integration, to a Black Power stance. I do not mean to draw a comparison between the position of 'women' and 'blacks'. I have in mind, more, the way various parts of the movement changed from integration and a notion of rights within the system, to secession and outright attack; and to a certain concentration on identity politics, now.

I shall return to 'identity politics' in Chapters 8 and 9, focusing on black politics and the politics of lesbian liberation, given their crucial political and political-theoretical importance, and the part they have played in emancipatory thought. And I shall in Chapter 8 also address what I take to be the rather different idea of group politics and group representation discussed by Anne Phillips and Iris Young.[49] I turn now to postmodernism and poststructuralism, and the forbidding concept of *'différance'*.

Différance and difference: the influence of poststructuralism and postmodernism on feminist thought

Finally, though the dating is difficult to give, came postmodernist and poststructuralist *différance*, the most complex-sounding form of 'difference' we will see. This in its English and American version is of course mainly derived from French thought, which will not be discussed in the original here, the points to which I now turn apart. It is, even so, virtually impossible to proceed without using a vocabulary inimical to some. I shall avoid that as much as is consistent with not warping the ideas I discuss. I begin with Jacques Derrida and Jean-François Lyotard, as it is their wording I shall employ below.

Derrida's notion of *différance* is not in any sense a direct equivalent of the English term. I shall not attempt to explain any of his concepts here, but rather say what part *différance*, together with deconstruction, might play in the political realm. I say 'might' because such writings are used more by literary critics and writers in cultural studies than in works of political and social theory such as this. Therefore the abolition of the 'author', the view that all 'readings' are equally valid, and the emphasis on the 'text', are ideas whose relevance must be in doubt. Despite this, the notion of a fragmentation of the 'self', the dissolution of the knowing, thinking, and acting agent and subject, and the relativism whereby all views are equal, have entered social and political science of late.

Différance and deconstruction would, as I understand it, be employed to attack hierarchies, dichotomies such as the dualisms mentioned above, and fixed identities; and to fight against 'closure', which means something like a premature cutting off of options; and purely 'politically', to ensure that the hierarchies did not arise again. Further, after Lyotard,[50] the follower of postmodernism will call the grand narratives, the all-embracing ideologies and world views, dead. (This applies to any such narrative – also called totalizing – and is not aimed at, say, Marxism or liberalism alone.)

Postmodernism is a relativist creed, that is, basically, it holds all views equally good. Why then should feminists, who would proclaim women's wrongs, want to link up with postmodernists at all, even if only via an eclectic appropriation of what they say? Why, that is, should they adopt a world view within which there is no way of judging between 'Women are innately inferior', and, 'Women are the equals of men'? It has been suggested that they gladly embrace a view that writes into prehistory the grand narratives that have ignored them (though should this be regarded as a problem of grand narratives *per se*?); that all other schools of thought suggest some kind of human 'essence', fixed now or no, whereas it is a fluidity of the self feminists seek; that postmodernism brings – presumably by its refusal of closure – new options 'not only of genders and bodies, but of politics itself'.[51] Further, the new cultural and political pluralism, in part by its abolition of the primacy of class, gives 'women', *prima facie*, a greater chance of gaining ground.

I shall not list further comments by the supporters of postmodernism here, nor summarize the charges brought against it. Rather I select a couple of critiques particularly salient to my theme. The first concerns vocabulary, though only in part. I have said that the 'new pluralism' could be seen as aiding women. But where the politics of identity makes it difficult to say 'women' as it may be asked, '*Which* women?', postmodernism's deconstruction will, it is said, make it difficult if not impossible to say 'women' in that the category has been definitively deconstructed, more or less infinitely so.

This would seem to abolish feminism's project, particularly given the notion of the social construction of 'woman' herself. Hence Spivak's view that while '[we] take a stand against . . . essentialism . . . *strategically* we cannot',[52] essentialism here meaning, as I think it does, being able to say 'women' in front of both 'male humanists' and the postmodernist gaze. Finally: relativism, while somewhat two-edged, which is I assume why those battered and bruised by 'male knowledge' embrace it, will make it impossible for feminism to assert its claims. If I am right, poststructuralism and postmodernism would rob feminism of its female constituency, and the intellectual basis for its claims of truth: *a* truth, perhaps, in the sense of part of the truth, but true nonetheless.

Challenges

At the end of this book I shall be presenting what I regard as challenges to the equality–difference axis and dilemma, construed as a male–female, sameness–difference, axis only. I shall also be asking what, if anything, they have to say about the various other equality–difference issues discussed here.

First I shall address poststructuralism and postmodernism as such a challenge, though not in relation to its deconstructive tendencies alone. Second, I shall outline the 'legal challenge' of Carol Bacchi and Mackinnon.[53] Their contention is not only, or even primarily, that the proper antithesis is between sameness and difference, equality and inequality, as many might conclude: a conclusion that will be queried here. For Bacchi, women have been forced into fighting for equality on the grounds of sameness, when this could be detrimental to their cause. And for Mackinnon, both 'equality' and 'difference', and the causes and cases fought around them and on their grounds, are manifestations of (male) dominance, and the former two, its construct.

These are powerful ideas. I leave them aside, pro tem, to recapitulate this chapter's views.

Summary

There are within Second-Wave feminism, I have argued, two forms of equality feminism, and three of difference; though this may be a straitjacketing of the relevant ideas, that will not hold. Further, these variations on the concepts 'split' each conventional 'school' – liberal, radical, and socialist – and, I shall say, beginning in the next chapter, individual writers too. What is the significance of this tension, and this split? Is it a dichotomy feminists can transcend? For we have not gone beyond it, yet.

One aim of this book is to remind feminists of the strength of our intellectual and political past, and argue, perhaps tentatively, that it is with us still. Have we forgotten much of what we knew about feminism's ideas, goals, and problems? Do we know what feminism was, once?

> There is a difference between a society in which sexism is expressed in the form of female infanticide and a society in which sexism takes the form of unequal representation on the Central Committee. And the difference is worth dying for.[54]

This speech, key to a major radical and socialist feminist dispute, refers to societies' varying treatment of women. It refers also to an aim of improving women's lives. Can 'difference' come to mean that, once more? Or will feminism remain sundered by difference, as it has been, time and again?

I first discuss early liberal second-wave feminism, the school which seems *prima facie* to be concerned with equality between men and women above all else. In following chapters, I try to say how much of the idea of this form of difference we have lost. But before we can say this we have to begin the neglected task of asking what equality is, and what views of the concept different feminist groups hold.

Not only feminists have neglected properly to investigate this topic. However for us, as for other subordinated groups, the failure to interrogate it may signal that the hope of attaining radical equality has been lost. It is a different notion, or type, of equality – one that has been theorized, if only to an extent, and is more readily capable of being so – I next discuss. That is a notion held by early liberalism, to which I move now.

Notes

1 Betty Friedan, *The Feminine Mystique*, 1982 (first published 1963).

2 See for example Jo Freeman, *The Politics of Women's Liberation*, 1975; Alice Echols, *Daring to be Bad. Radical Feminism in America 1967–75*, 1989.

3 I use the term, at this stage, in the sense of 'sameness'. Its definition is a complex task.

4 Cynthia Fuchs Epstein, *Woman's Place*, 1971; *Deceptive Distinctions*, 1988; and other works.

5 Susan Okin, 'Afterword to the 1992 edition', *Women in Western Political Thought*, pp. 325–9.

6 Shulamith Firestone, *The Dialectic of Sex*, 1971, *passim*.

7 On the radical implications of the notion of equal opportunity see Susan Wendell, 'A (qualified) defense of liberal feminism', *Hypatia*, 1987, and Onora (O'Neill) Nell, 'How do we know when opportunities are equal?', in Carol C. Gould and Marx Wartofsky (eds), *Women and Philosophy*, 1976.

8 This can again be divided into equal treatment in the sense of being granted the same goods; less radically, being paid the same salary for the same post; or – the sense most at issue here – being given equal opportunity in the 'market'.

9 Firestone, *Dialectic of Sex*, p. 274.

10 Lyman T. Sargent, *New Left Thought*, 1972.

11 Robin Morgan, 'Goodbye to all that', in Leslie B. Tanner (ed.), *Voices from Women's Liberation*, 1971; pp. 268–76.

12 Bunch, 'The reform tool kit', in 'Quest', *Building Feminist Theory: Essays from 'Quest'*, 1981, pp. 196–7.

13 Firestone, *Dialectic of Sex*, pp. 145, 175.

14 This is no more unified a group than any other. Indeed, it may be the most split.

15 bell hooks, *From Margin to Center*, 1984, pp. 6–7; Bunch, 'The reform tool kit'; various essays in Robin Morgan (ed.), *Sisterhood is Powerful*, 1970.

16 Morgan, *Sisterhood*, p. 273.

17 The history of black women's activism in the Civil Rights movement now begins to be reclaimed. Vicky L. Crawford et al., *Women in the Civil Rights Movement: Trailblazers and Torchbearers, 1941–1965*, 1993.

18 bell hooks, *Ain't I a Woman: Black Women and Feminism*, 1986, pp. 142ff., 188ff.

19 Hester Eisenstein, *Contemporary Feminist Thought*, 1984, p. 48ff.

20 Some would say 'from radical feminism'.

21 Eisenstein, *Contemporary Feminist Thought*, *passim*.

22 'Womanism' is employed by black feminists.

23 Andrée Collard with Joyce Contrucci, *Rape of the Wild*, 1988. Some would say, simply, ecofeminist; but there are ecofeminists who hold very different views from this.

24 John Carrier, *The Campaign for the Employment of Women as Police Officers*, 1988.

25 Barbara Ryan, *Feminism and the Women's Movement*, 1992, pp. 137–40.

26 Brenda Whisker et al., *Breaching the Peace*, 1983.

27 See Chapter 4.

28 'Conclusion: a note on essentialism and difference', in Sneja Gunew (ed.), *Feminist Knowledge: Critique and Construct*, 1990.

29 Judy Evans, 'Ecofeminism and the politics of the gendered self', in Andrew Dobson and Paul Lucardie (eds), *The Politics of Nature*, 1993, *passim*.

30 For a somewhat different discussion of the retreat from 'politics' see Lynne Segal, *Is the Future Female? Troubled Thoughts on Contemporary Feminism*, 1987.

31 This phrase is of course Lillian Faderman's; *Surpassing the Love of Men*, 1981.

32 Juliet Mitchell, *Women: the Longest Revolution. Essays in Feminism, Literature and Psychoanalysis*, 1984, p. 33.

33 Ann Snitow, 'A gender diary', in Marianne Hirsch and Evelyn Fox Keller (eds), *Conflicts in Feminism*, 1990, p. 26.

34 See Chapter 4.

35 Echols, *Daring to be Bad*, p. 11ff.

36 We can think, for example, of generalizations about women's views, ways of thinking and frameworks of knowledge, said to derive from motherhood and/or the capacity to bear a child. And see the massive literature on essentialism, in particular Elizabeth Grosz.

37 See Sandra Harding for the best overviews of writing in this field, Helen Longino, Evelyn Fox Keller and Donna Haraway for major contributions. Sandra Harding, *The Science Question in Feminism*, 1986; Helen Longino, 'Can there be a feminist science?', *Hypatia*, 1987; Evelyn Fox Keller, *Reflections on Gender and Science*, 1985; Donna Haraway, 'A manifesto for cyborgs: science, technology and socialist feminism in the 1980s', in Linda Nicholson (ed.), *Feminism/Postmodernism*, 1990.

38 Audre Lorde, *Sister Outsider*, 1984, p. 102.

39 Firestone, *Dialectic of Sex*; Adrienne Rich, *Of Woman Born*, 1986.

40 Quoted in Wendy McElroy (ed.), *Freedom, Feminism and the State*, 1991, p. 53.

41 I am here compressing statements made by various writers over a number of years.

42 Gayatri Spivak, 'Criticism, feminism and the institution', in Sarah Harasyn (ed.), *The Post-Colonial Critic*, 1990, pp. 1–16.

43 hooks, *Ain't I a Woman*, p. 142ff, 188ff.

44 bell hooks, *Talking Back: Thinking Feminist – Thinking Black*, 1989, pp. 35–41.

45 Ignoring the importance of, say, black identity is the more likely prospect. See Audre Lorde, 'An open letter to Mary Daly', in Cherríe Moraga and Gloria Anzaldúa (eds), *This Bridge Called My Back: Radical Writings by Women of Color*, 1983. However, an attack on identity politics as divisive is possible, too.

46 Judith Butler, *Gender Trouble: Feminism and the Subversion of Identity*, 1990, p. 147; see also her 'Contingent foundations: feminism and the question of "Postmodernism"', in Judith Butler and Joan Scott (eds), *Feminists Theorize the Political*, 1992.

47 See Sandra Harding, *Whose Science? Whose Knowledge?*, 1991, ch. 8ff.

48 James Donald and Ali Rattansi (eds), 'Introduction' to *'Race', Culture and Difference*, 1992, p. 1.

49 Anne Phillips, *Engendering Democracy*, 1991; Iris Young, *Justice and the Politics of Difference*, 1990.

50 Jean-François Lyotard, *The Postmodern Condition*, 1984.

51 Butler, *Gender Trouble*, p. 142.

52 Spivak, 'Criticism, feminism and the institution', pp. 11–12.

53 Carol Lee Bacchi, *Same Difference. Feminism and Sexual Difference*; Catharine Mackinnon, *Feminism Unmodified*, 1987, *Only Words*, 1994, and other works.

54 Barbara Ehrenreich, quoted by Batya Weinbaum, *The Curious Courtship of Women's Liberation and Socialism*, 1978, p. 6.

3

Early Liberalism: Feminism's First Equality

In this chapter I discuss liberal feminism in its sameness/equality mode. Equality, I have said, is undertheorized. Its neglect, I suggested, may signal that a quest for radical gender equality has gone. Here are writers who never, anyway, sought that. They tend to forward, if not consciously or explicitly, an equality of opportunity case. Some would espouse procedural fairness, some ask for more. Also they tend to sameness, and androgyny in my sense of the term, though this too is not spelled out. This relatively homogeneous group, however, differs internally, like other schools.

I omit writers who are primarily concerned either to demonstrate a lack of sex differences, or to show, by for example socialization studies, how such differences are produced; even though that may well be how the vast majority of liberal feminists proceed. For liberal feminist theorists are scarce, while empirical writers, apparently of liberal persuasion, abound.

There are three reasons, I believe, for the paucity of such writers and the theoretical underdevelopment of liberal feminism, compared with other schools of thought. First, given its major aim – equality between men and women in our society, more or less as it is now – it makes sense to argue a lack of sex differences, and document disparities at the elite level – though not that alone – and assert or imply that these are unfair. This has been seen as largely an empirical task. Second, liberal feminists, by no means necessarily less concerned with theory, may have less reason to articulate it, given the alleged general acceptance of 'liberal' views on women's advance. Third, though, the very different suggestion put forward by Harding (concerning women who employ a 'liberal-empiricist' methodology) has the ring of truth. They, she argues, are choosing the only feasible path, given the male power structure in the academy of science, to gain 'respectability' in its eyes.[1]

Liberal feminists share these tenets of conventional scientific and social scientific inquiry.[2] Their complaint is that they have not been upheld. Such inquiry is in theory rational and objective; and it could be, but it is not. Women will bring these qualities to science. The immediate problem here, of course, is how. If these critics hold the tenet that the identity, for example gender, of the scientist is irrelevant, how can they change science? If women and men are the same, why should there be change? Why should we assume, as certain feminists apparently do, that women would not have produced the hydrogen bomb, and do not work on biochemical weaponry now? If there are sex differences, but they are socialized, would not entry into the world of science change them? Whether or not, that is, that world is 'male'?

I call the writers discussed below liberal equality feminists because of the kind of equality they seek. I assume also that they believe in androgyny, and that their claims are made on those grounds. I make this assumption because while it is a liberal tenet that gender should not affect the way we treat a person – that liberalism is 'gender blind' – feminists are asking for rather more than that. For 'gender-blindness' refers to an attitude to a person, all else being equal; but the liberal feminist case is precisely that while male and female capabilities have been equal, all else has not.

Androgyny and equality

Both androgyny and equality require definition. Neither can be explained fully, here. I shall however give as much detail as is needed to situate and appraise the writers I address. I begin with androgyny, which I defined in Chapter 2 as 'an absence of differences relevant to full participation in the structures that exist now'. That is also the view of women presented in *The Feminine Mystique.*

Many writers define androgyny in a way nearer to its linguistic origins ('neither man nor woman'), speaking of an alliance of the 'good' qualities of each sex. They think of allying complementary differences: when these are combined in one person, they say, we have an androgynous world. But it seems to me that Anne Phillips is right to suggest – if I have read her correctly – that a similarity of the lives and lifestyles of men and women is entailed, too.[3]

These definitions are problematic. The major weakness of mine is not, for present purposes, the fact that it is tied to current systems and structures, though that charge could indeed be brought. Rather, I may be asked what qualities are relevant in a given case, and confront a stipulative definition of what is required, that targets such differences as exist. And my definition may evade, to an extent, the general issue of sameness or difference.

So I might plead for equality in admission to study engineering by arguing that there are no differences between women and men relevant to the discipline's study and practice. One retort to that would be, then you do think there are differences: what are they? To what *are* they relevant? Should I simply assert similarity? Without, that is, the qualification I give? On the empirical evidence we have, I am almost prepared to do that, for it shows virtually no differences between women and men.

The weakness of the second definition lies in a certain capitulation to difference and to stereotypes held now. Androgyny theorists of the 'duality' kind may be accepting what they should attack. Certainly, the characteristics they would ally are (some of) the ones we are told we have, and clearly, ones of which they approve. They have no interest in a marriage of traits that would unite the less endearing qualities of the sexes, assuming they believe these exist. They also tend to assume that the characteristics they discuss are both complementary and capable of enduring 'transportation' or transplantation to another realm; insofar, that is, as they think that structures and practices would not have to change, massively, too.

These thinkers cannot be essentialist, or the characteristics to be allied, innate; inborn qualities of one sex cannot be combined in women and men. Learned or taught qualities, though, may not be sufficiently strong to endure. If they are imported into spheres where other values have ruled, how will they survive?

In maximizing on difference, such feminists also face the problem that it might be used against them. The resulting harm might not only be short term. (Among other problems, presumably androgyny itself would be delayed.) As we will see, the fear of invoking difference, of its being used against women, is highly prevalent among sameness feminists; a relatively small, but important, group. It is a fear based on more than historical precedent for such use.

There is an element of false universalism in discussing the issue of sameness and difference like this; as if it were a matter of all men and all women being the same or not. The empirically based sameness argument, and dismissal of (relevant) difference, does not necessarily argue that. Rather it concerns research results that amount to a series of findings of little or no sex difference, on various measures, in that they point to there being more variation within the sexes, than between. Their political import is this: that it makes no sense, even if it were humanly acceptable, to treat a person adversely on the grounds of sex alone.

The suggestion that equality is a goal raises another distinction: between those who seek equality for women within the hierarchies of society as it exists now, and those who want more. The first group are, in theory at least, committed to equality of opportunity. In practice this means, for most, an equality of result in the sense of equality of *condition* of men and women *within* each of the strata that now exist. Though the group divides, again, into those who would attempt to enforce equity of procedure, those who would remove barriers to this kind of equality, and those who would take more active steps to promote it. The final group includes those who seek a more general equality of condition within society. They may well view the attaining of sexual equality as premised on or related to the transcendence of our system. I discuss them later on.

Given that liberal feminists characteristically speak of equality of opportunity rather than condition, then it might be said that they uphold an unequal society and simply want to advance women within its ranks. To be more precise, they want to advance women to what is conventionally regarded as equality with men, within the various hierarchically ordered groups. This seems to me, on the whole, to be a true characterization of the school.

That there might have to be change in institutions like the family and the school, to realize the liberal feminist project, I agree. The change might be massive. But liberal feminists do not, on the whole, seek it. Insofar as they do, either they accept what has already occurred, or is clearly emergent, as does Friedan in *The Second Stage*,[4] or they posit a means to an end. The liberal feminist quest concerns *equality for women*: no less, and no more. That point is not in doubt. And for a majority it has been procedural equality, 'weak' equality of opportunity, that was sought. (Though I here speak of 'classical' rather than 'social' or 'welfare' liberals, a distinction I discuss below.)

I am going to define 'weak equality of opportunity' in its two forms, using the analogy of a race. Procedural equality requires that it is correctly conducted, and monitored carefully throughout. Does that ensure that the 'best runner' wins? Most feminists, I think, would say not, being all too aware of the importance of training and access to the track. 'Weak' equality of opportunity then turns to 'starting-gate' or 'first hurdle' equality. All are 'equal', have 'an equal chance', as the race begins. 'Strong' equality of opportunity enters in if — the overwhelming numbers of winners still being men — feminists demand that there be help in the sense of quotas or, to maintain my analogy, that women be given a head start.

The race, that is, must indeed be to the swift, the battle to the strong. One sceptical feminist question, however, has been, how do we know who is the most swift, if some are excluded from the race? And an even more sceptical one, not on the whole put forward by liberal feminists: why do we value so strongly, speed and strength? Indeed, why should we want a race?

The metaphor is unhelpful too, unless we know where the starting-gate — where all should be equal, whence winners emerge — is, the following points apart. It alerts us to the fact that this form of equality is 'acceptable *inequality*'; and that the starting-gate could be moved. That suggests a possible danger for women: who has the power to position, to move, the gates? But it also implies that such a form of equality could have very radical implications indeed: a point I address now, via the comments of Onara O'Neill (Nell).

O'Neill's argument is that a genuine equality of opportunity will have two results. The first is its placing of the notion of 'equality' on the agenda. The second concerns its social results, and their political effect. If, hypothetically at least, members of all groups not only had equal chances of gaining the higher places in the economy but did attain these, then those who had previously taken preferment by birth for granted, would have an incentive to move towards a greater equality in the sense of a lessening of income differentials for all.[5] We might then see the notion of equal opportunity as liberal feminism's Trojan Horse.

Susan Wendell's point differs greatly.[6] She argues that socialist and liberal views of equality are more alike than might be thought, in that socialists too believe there are certain assets – some occupations, some scarce goods – that cannot be handed out equally, that is, to all. Therefore a qualified hierarchy, a certain meritocracy, would be common to both schools of thought.

So for these writers the fact that liberal feminism adheres to equality of opportunity, rather than condition, does not necessarily mean that it supports the hierarchy and elitism we know now. I take it that the debate would then hinge on how many objects and occupations, and of what kind, are regarded as inevitably scarce, how they are valued or rewarded, and on what terms they are given out. Though we might also want to say that there are assets that are scarce, that we would sacrifice for everyone, could we obtain equality for all. (I do not refer to forced seizure or destruction of such goods.)

I shall not discuss Wendell's characterization of socialism, except to say that she describes but one kind. I do suggest that there is another sense in which equal opportunity can become a radical stance. What are the substantive conditions for it? How far back (or forward) is the starting-gate? What does it mean to have an equal chance? How long is that chance to be maintained? How much equality of condition must there be before opportunity really is equal? Pushed to its limits, the suggestion of equality of opportunity becomes very radical indeed.

For the opponents of a greater equality encounter problems as soon as they begin to concede that all should be equal at some point. (I take it that 'having an equal chance' must imply this.) At what point will they draw the line? When does the 'real race' start?

Equal opportunity could, then be liberal feminists' radical stance. In fact they call for the advancement of 'women' within the framework of non-discrimination as conventionally construed, for example in the case of applicants for a given post that is scarce and must be 'won'. Thus they retain the notion of an unequal, stratified society, and, *a fortiori*, are not concerned with the advancement of all. Their radicalism, shown in the work of O'Neill and Wendell, is latent. That the project of liberal feminism remains radical – if not, indeed, a millennial dream – shows to what extent pluralist democracy has broken the liberal contract in relation to a group that otherwise, in the manner of no other disadvantaged group, spans its strata and its range.

Certain liberal feminists including Friedan were, while asking more from liberal democracy than I suggest here, to renounce the radicalism of this challenge. I show that in Chapter 4. There and later we will see the strength, endurance and allure of the feminine mystique, and the extent to which it acts to hinder women's advance.

Was the problem of liberal feminists that they strove to be 'like men'? That they strove to be as certain, perhaps most, men are in most societies as we know them now? And what are the other options? Much feminism since the early days has been an attempt, if latent, to answer my third question.[7] But I turn to the 'sameness equality' feminists of early second-wave liberal thought, of whom it is said, they indeed want to emulate men. For the kind of claim I quote has been construed that way, and been seen as grounds for attack.

> 'Should a woman be treated as a human being, and if not, why not? . . .
> The word 'feminism' . . . might well be summed up in one sentence addressed to mankind: 'Recognize our full humanity, and we will trouble you no more.'[8]

The mystique that enslaves: the early Friedan

Friedan's pioneering *Feminine Mystique* charts a decline in the position of women in the United States following the Second World War. It is somewhat unusual for a liberal work in not merely depicting women's secondary status, but also postulating an overarching, though not sole, cause. This is an ideology. It produces a false consciousness that misleads us as to our real interests, in telling us that

> the highest value and the only commitment for women is the fulfilment of their own femininity . . . the great mistake of Western culture . . . has been the undervaluation of this femininity . . . *so mysterious and intuitive and close to the creation and origin of life that man-made science may never be able to understand it.* But however special and different, it is in no way inferior to the nature of man; *it may even in certain respects be superior.* The mistake, says the mystique, the root of women's troubles in the past is that women envied men, women tried to be like men, instead of accepting their own nature, which can find fulfilment only in sexual passivity, male domination, and nurturing maternal love.[9] [Italics mine]

Friedan's analysis of the 'mystique' has relevance beyond this chapter. Here I am primarily concerned to outline and assess her remarkable book in the light of the concepts of equality and difference, arguing that it is a 'sameness equality' text.

Not only does Friedan, in the words I quote, assert most powerfully that women are potentially equal to men in the sense that their 'nature' is the same. She points to an ideology to the opposite effect, which, her argument runs, has held us in thrall. It is not for her a static ideology; nor has it always held sway. It has sprung up to serve the needs of the economy, and of men; it is in their interests that the contemporary inequality of women was brought about, and sustained.

For Friedan is discussing an inequality created: but also re-created, and renewed. She discusses how the gains of the inter war years were lost. She charts a retreat, aided and abetted, if not forced, and now maintained, by the mystique; as men returned from the Second World War. And in so doing she names and indicts the groupings that have contrived the retreat, and peddled the image that sustains it, showing for example the manner in which women's magazines changed personnel, editors in particular, as men returned from the war; and their content changed too.[10] Her case that women have been virtually indoctrinated into returning to or staying in the home[11] via a change in education, psychoanalysis and psychologists' views of proper mothering, magazine features, and a deluge of advertising; all buttressing if not indeed creating the mystique, is made with force.

Thus second-wave feminism's first major text seeks an equality based on sameness, a sameness masked by an alleged difference between women and men, promoted to turn women to, retain them within, the 'private realm' of hearth and home. It is concerned to expose, and explain, the myth foisted on women, which has not merely held them back but produced massive though little- or ill-voiced distress. This was, I argue, the 'early liberal' view. It is, within explicitly theoretical writing, very much a minority stance. And we see its very obverse, now. For Friedan's 'mystique' remarkably prefigures later feminist definitions of what a woman is.

As Friedan charts the decline in the position of women, she further protests their internment in suburbia and articulates 'the problem with no name': their loneliness and inchoate unease while confined to the private realm. The unhappiness caused by this role is found by her among the working class, not simply her famed suburban mothers. Nor is her discussion of the damage done to children by 'overmothering' necessarily class bound.[12]

Nonetheless this powerful and distressing book, unconventional for its time in its plea for women to find fulfilment in work, is premised on an appeal to 'able' and 'educated' women, 'women' on occasion being employed as if such a perspective spoke for all. So Friedan fails to take account of differences between groups of women. As critics commonly say, she speaks primarily of and for a specific group: white middle-class married women, who might in earlier parts of the decade have entered professional careers.

But to say that should not be to disdain the book's gender politics, to ignore her depiction of the situation later more vividly described in, for example, novels by Fay Weldon and Marilyn French. Such women were, these writers say, blatantly via advertising, but in other ways too, told that their destiny and joy lay in being smiling servicers of men, and that alone.[13] It is all too easy to forget this aspect of Friedan when emphasizing the limitations of her work.

Friedan's remedy is not conceived of as changing the system, in a revolutionary way. For she wishes – and here it could be pointed out that the analysis is liberal in its assumptions about action and responsibility – women to take their (individual) fate into their own hands by seeking education and careers (though facilitating mechanisms would be set up). Housework she regards as something of a manufactured problem, which need not take up the time that it currently does.

Friedan's is not an explicitly liberal-theoretical text. She charges that liberal/pluralist democracy has not treated women as it should, has, in their case, broken its contract. (She does this by implication: she would never so phrase the point.) There are, however, the makings of a far more radical analysis in her work, in the causes of the growth of the mystique. And we can add: if the mystique is as powerful as Friedan suggests, why should it be possible for women to remedy the situation simply by choosing to go or return to college, and work? What vested interests might oppose this? What barriers might women meet? In the next chapter we will see Friedan decide that solving the problem of the suburbs was not as simple as it seemed in 1963.

Rossi: liberal elitism?

Rossi depicts much the same kind of situation.[14] Her proposed solutions are of note, as she begins where Friedan ends. Indeed, there are moments when she begins not to sound like a liberal feminist at all. Her notion of equality is theirs; but we see a different view of androgyny here.

Rossi's equivalent of the mystique has been produced by a variety of factors, which explain why women have accepted their incarceration in the home; and should they work for wages, the double shift.[15] Here I single out the individualist ethos in US society, which, combined with the prevalence of therapy and analysis, tends towards self-blame and guilt. Women have been made to see marriage and the family as all: both the married and the never married feel they have failed.

> It is this sense of failure as a woman that lies behind the defensive and apologetic note of many older unmarried professional women, the guilt which troubles the working mother . . . the restriction of the level of aspiration of college women, the early plunge into marriage, the closed door of the doll's house.[16]

For Rossi, earlier feminism faded because it relied on legal change, and this alone cannot rescue women from imprisonment in the home, or, misery and guilt. To ensure sex equality requires equal participation by women in the public and private realms.[17] This would seem to suggest that men, also, take part in both spheres, but this will not come about. Instead there will be changes in child care, housing, and education, to ease the woman's role. Who will do the necessary work?

Current 'helpers' are not necessarily those best qualified to care for children and home, thinks Rossi. However, the job could be upgraded, its holders trained. (It is difficult to see this group as more than helots with certificates; though my reading may be unfair.) Eventually there would be child-care centres, which might even be government run.[18]

Even if women seem to be content, the changes should be made.[19] This suggests that Rossi perceives the implications of an analysis that incorporates the notion of an ideology better than Friedan. For such a view requires a willingness to say, at the very least, that some women have a mistaken view of their needs, and that it may be necessary to overcome that. This entails that Rossi knows better than they do what they 'really' want, what they are 'really' like. However, any feminist must hold some such view. It is, simply, not normally regarded as liberal. I am inclined to suggest that these writers give us the chance to admit we all think like that.

Full-time motherhood, Rossi points out, is new. She regards it as unnecessary, and even dangerous. Here homophobia appears to enter her work, as she lists the 'ills' that the smothering mother has produced, and will, from one generation to the next.[20]

Women will enter careers, of course. But Rossi believes it possible for a woman to avoid competing with her husband, as they are usually found in different parts of the occupational structure − now why, one wonders, should that be? − but in any event, feminist advance, like all aims, entails costs.[21]

There are though costs Rossi will not pay; she prepares for others to avoid them, too. Changes must take place as early in life as possible, in schools; and both sexes should learn housemaking. But this is to enable them to complement each other, not compete. Here Rossi notes Bruno Bettelheim's view that complementarity leads to 'sexual adjustment' within marriage, and that it is *girls* who must learn to act as the complementary partner. (Presumably it is girls who 'adjust'.) The loss of a male partner, or even, a painful confrontation with a man, a risk of such loss, is the price Rossi − with other women also in mind − will not pay.

For Rossi, equality is 'socially androgynous'. Her meaning combines the definitions given above, though it seems to lean strongly to the second view. Occupationally, and in suchlike areas, she thinks, the sexes are 'equal and similar'. Where physical differences enter into the account, though, they are complementary. The good qualities of each should be cultivated in the other: 'achievement need' in women, 'tenderness' in men:

> rather than a one-sided plea for women to adopt a masculine stance in the world
> . . . the enlargement of the common ground on which men and women base
> their lives together.[22]

Even in Rossi's first, 'equality' piece, therefore, she differs from Friedan, moving towards the 'mystique'. And I believe that her comments here, taken as a whole, betray a tension between equality and difference. They may also expose − I am sure a radical feminist would say they do − where the proximate (if not, indeed, ultimate) origins of woman's subjugation lie. They lie in relationships with men, and the perceived need for these.

Women of reason: *The Sceptical Feminist*

Janet Radcliffe Richards is, it seems, a true liberal feminist.[23] She sets out in more theoretical and philosophical mode the kind of account given by Friedan. And she too is a 'sameness equality' feminist. For her feminism is the belief 'that there are excellent reasons for thinking that women suffer from systematic social injustice because of their sex'. And 'anyone who accepts [this] . . . [is] a feminist'.

For a book written in 1980, this seems a little mild. But we must take Richards's aims into account. She seeks to make a reasoned philosophical case that women are not treated equally with their male peers, that this is wrong, and that change is required. However, she also wants her argument to be plausible and persuasive, as the feminist movement's, she thinks, is not. She wants to distinguish between feminism as she defines it, and 'the movement', for she wants those who have been deterred by the latter's image, expression, and behaviour to accept her case.[24]

Richards employs this definition, then, because she believes it to be correct, but for tactical reasons too. It is more persuasive, more acceptable, she would say, than other accounts, and therefore more likely to gain support. She knows that prejudice lies behind opposition to feminism. We can only assume that she believes her choice of argument, and way of pleading, will win through. However, if she believes that a possible reason for rejection of the feminist case, one to which she must cater, is that 'people . . . just don't like unfeminine women',[25] then I think we have to ask how rational argument is supposed to overcome that. Indeed, we might well ask what kind of feminist case is being put, that can incorporate such comments, and whether we want to endorse it. It should though be pointed out that this is no necessary part of liberal feminism: that is not at stake here.

Of Richards's preliminary substantive points I shall mention her view that feminism cannot be a movement to support women unconditionally, since justice is involved. That is: it may be that as a matter of justice, in a particular situation, we should support a man. And if a woman is treated unjustly, if women are, it is feminism's concern only if the treatment occurs on grounds of sex, and could not have happened to a man. For 'it is far more reasonable to ask people to support a movement against injustice than a movement for women'.[26]

Unconditional support for women is rarely a feminist aim, though I cannot prove that. However, feminism is about the advancement of women. It is a movement 'for women', in that sense. I might have many reasons, including justice, however that is conceived, for supporting a man. There might be a feminist reason for supporting a man. But among these would not be what it was 'reasonable to ask people to support'.

If a man is treated unjustly, that is wrong. I hope I would oppose it. But I would not normally oppose it on feminist grounds. Legal maltreatment, unfair treatment, of a man is not a feminist concern, one, admittedly significant, point apart. Feminists who put their faith in justice[27] will, for their own sake and the sake of all women, want structures of justice, a culture of the just, upheld. But that does not mean that it is a feminist task to combat injustice wherever and whenever it should arise. Nor is the promotion of justice *per se* an issue on which feminism *qua* feminism is necessarily best employed.

Richards wrote this book while first teaching feminism. It may express a transitional view. Certainly she changed her opinions during that time. It is as a result of her conversations with students then that she, while opposing separatism in general, favours women-only consciousness-raising groups. For, she says, 'if women are less good at reasoning than men that is hardly surprising, since men have always taken very good care that women should never have the chance to learn'. And further:

> it can quite simply be dangerous for a woman to assert herself with a man, because men still commonly hold so many sorts of power . . . . If there is to be any hope of winning in the long run, much of the early work of feminism must be done among women.

Richards is, we can see, an androgyny feminist. But these quotations show more. Here are militant words, and perceptive. There is a case for saying that while there is in part in Friedan a radicalism of macro-analysis, Richards, who is the more conformist at that level, points nonetheless to the bases of the sexual politics both would deny.

The analysis in *The Sceptical Feminist*, taken as a whole, is reasoned. But that Richards should both attack and support 'movement' feminists and their practices is strange, given that the attacks are, some would say, offensive, and certainly extreme. It is not though illogical, given the framework of 'rational persuasion' of non-feminists within which she writes. But there is a disjuncture between her view of men and of the way women have been, at minimum, cast down, and her wish to win non-feminists over by reasoned argument. Would men listen?

Toward a just society? Susan Okin

The motive force of Okin's *Justice, Gender and the Family* is poverty among women and children in the US. It is children, in particular, with whom she is concerned. She is not addressing 'children's rights' *vis-à-vis* adults or the state, but saying how failure to tackle the poverty of certain, especially female, parents, affects the young. Though she seeks justice, and social and political equality, for women too.

Okin is a liberal equality feminist. She believes that women and men should be equally placed at all levels of our society as it is structured, or more or less as it is structured, now.[28] (Though on occasion it appears that it is the higher echelons, and in particular those who govern, with whom she is concerned.) It would seem to follow that she is an androgyny feminist in the sense of believing that there are no differences between the sexes that might rule a case for equality out. And indeed she says this, if not explicitly, towards the beginning of her book.

Musing on justice and gender difference,[29] Okin rejects the kind of argument put forward by Carol Gilligan, to the effect that there are sex or gender differences in reasoning about issues of moral concern.[30] The content of such differences is said to be this: men will judge a moral issue in an abstract, rule-bound, 'justice' way, while women will consider the welfare of individuals, in a 'contextual' and 'caring' mode. These supposed differences are normally called the ethic of justice and the ethic of care.

Okin rejects Gilligan's and similar views for four reasons. First, it is unclear that gender-specific modes of moral thinking, of deciding moral issues, exist: the evidence we have, I take Okin to be saying, does not adequately support the claim. Second, if we believe they exist, we cannot be sure what form they take. Third, again assuming the traits are there, their cause is not known, so nor is their status and malleability. Would they disappear, given social change? Further, Okin states that in a gendered society we cannot know whether they exist or not. And finally she comments on 'The capacity of reactionary forces to capitalize on the "different moralities" strain in feminism' as a danger we must not ignore.[31]

So just as Friedan attacked the feminine mystique, Okin argues that there is no clear evidence for differences or, insofar as they exist, for their source; acutely she adds that in a gender-structured society there cannot be (though this point is, as we will see, two-edged). Last she points to our knowledge of the tactical and strategic dangers of proclaiming difference.[32]

I have called the penultimate point acute. It is also a strange comment for a liberal (and one who deploys empirical evidence, to some effect) to make. For it is not commonly thought of as liberal to regard inquiry as 'androcentric', let alone to suggest that all facets of society, including social scientific inquiry, are so 'gendered', so affected by a 'man-made world', that researchers cannot discover whether sex differences exist or not.

But we do not have to discuss such points to see whether we can live with Okin's statement. It is, as I said, two-edged. If we accept her comment, then we cannot produce evidence for differences, and nor can anyone else. If they do, we can rebut them with her words. However, it follows that we cannot demonstrate a lack of difference. Or so I would assume. Okin has, for reasons unclear, talked herself into an impasse.

Okin begins to diverge from liberal equality feminism here. In the following chapter I shall address what I believe to be the difference element in her work.

Bluestone: equality to the limit?

Natalie Bluestone would have no truck with ideas of benevolent difference, one point apart.[33] She believes that empirical inquiry could reveal what natural sex differences, if any, exist. Thus she could not agree with the notion that a gender-stratified society produces ways of thinking and means to 'knowledge' that prevent our finding the truth of a gendered self. Theoretical and scientific inquiry are for her only contingently gendered, and not always so, though she would not phrase the point that way.

If such inquiry located differences that were antithetical to the feminist project as she sees it, to advancement for women in society basically as it is now,[34] she would simply accept that. If women are found to be 'inferior', to be unsuited for the higher places of life, so be it. And if we put our faith in certain canons of inquiry, this is a line of thought we might have to accept. Alternatively, we could adopt one of two more sceptical and radical stances towards the problem. The first says that difference entails that qualifications for those places be changed. The second decrees – though for other reasons, too – that we want a society where no 'higher places' exist.

However, Bluestone argues, on the whole, for a preponderance of evidence of sameness; and in particular that women can reason like, and as well as, men. There can be no doubt that she believes in androgyny in the sense of sameness now.

Bluestone says: 'the question still remains of what arguments justify the statement that it is wrong *in itself* to deny women equal rights',[35] thus grasping what I shall call the 'sameness equality dilemma'.

This dilemma may explain pleas for equality which do not rest on claims of sameness and appeals to justice alone, but import, appeal to, some notion of complementary difference. It may be that Phillips is correct when she says that this is because of '[their] canny eye to the limits of moral persuasion'.[36] But we have seen movements campaign for a considerable length of time, and gain much, by arguing precisely on the grounds of sameness and the equity which should then accrue. Perhaps the possibility, and perceived desirability, of an appeal to complementary difference varies with the group.

Is the problem of the 'equality appeal' that the dominant are little moved by notions of what is fair and just? Or is some other factor involved? Appealing on the grounds of difference can of course mean asserting women's superiority, moral or not. We have seen that gambit played straight back, rebutted by arguments that women should guard their finer qualities by remaining safely outside the morally abhorrent public world of men.[37]

If we rest our case on 'the same capacities' and 'identical skill', certainly we make ourselves candidates for certain posts, if we want them. The 'equality problem' Bluestone points to, I suggest, is this. If women are as well qualified as men, then men are as well qualified as women. So, why appoint women? Hence, the difference case?

The question then arises, what the aim of the demand for equality is. It becomes even clearer than before that this sense of equality rests, again, on the notion of hierarchy, and inequality, and even on disparity and inequity of reward. Does this mean that a demand for equality with men rules out an equal society in a broader sense? I give an initial view that it does not, and the criteria for believing that, in Chapter 5. Here I address liberal feminism's 'street-fighters', via the sameness segment of an inspiring strand of theory, US feminist legal thought.

The politics of equality feminist law: trying equality out

It is the overall project of US feminist lawyers of the mainstream to make gender, like race, an 'inherently suspect' classification under the law.[38] As various cases show, this is far from being the situation, now. If anything, 'men and women are ... not similarly situated' is the reasoning behind the judgments in the 'hard cases' of *Rostker* v. *Goldberg* and *Michael M.* v. *Sonoma County*, which I move, via the work of Wendy Williams, to discuss.[39] *Prima facie* it would seem that it is difference that feminist lawyers who seek justice for women must combat. This is by no means agreed.

Within feminist legal theory, Williams represents sameness equality, 'equal treatment' feminism in this context, at its extreme. Before further discussing her views I note that given the necessity to plead cases in court, sameness and difference stances in law will be ideological, obviously, but tactical, too.

I am employing 'sameness' directly here, as the equality lawyer's goal is, indeed, to win equality by pleading that; or at least by opposing general beliefs about sex differences, and with reference to what a given case requires. The broader aim, we have already seen. If that were gained, those who defended a given law against an allegation of unconstitutional discrimination would bear the onus of proof. A 'heavy burden of justification'[40] would lie on the defendants in a sex discrimination suit.

Williams's point is not that the courts are the only motor of change; far from it. But if equality cannot be won wholly within them, yet the cases are 'a focal point of debate about the meaning of equality'. Feminists, she believes,

> are at a crisis point in our evaluation of equality and women and ... perhaps one of the reasons ... is that having dealt with the easy cases, we ... are now trying to cope with issues that touch the hidden nerves of our most profoundly embedded cultural values.[41]

Williams does not mean, by easy cases, 'cases that are easily won'. By 'hard cases' she means here, as my quotation suggests, those which 'concern themselves with ... perhaps more basic sex-role arrangements' and in which 'a sex-based classification was upheld by the Court'. What, she asks, can they tell us 'about the cultural limits of the equality principle'? The cases discussed are *Michael M.*,[42] in which the California statutory rape (under-age sexual intercourse) law was upheld, and *Rostker*, which maintained the provision that only men be required to register for the draft.

Rostker was brought by men who argued that the law was unconstitutional. They were supported by various feminists, and the National Organization for Women (NOW) filed an *amicus curiae* (friend of the court) brief. The Court decided that it was not unconstitutional to restrict the draft to men given that its purpose was to raise combat troops, and women are not combat troops.[43] According to Williams, the first point is demonstrably empirically incorrect. But this is not her main theme.

Michael M. faced a law that made under-age intercourse illegal: 'statutory rape' for him, but not for the woman. A plurality of the court accepted the state's argument that the law was intended to deter teenage pregnancies: a woman would be deterred by fear of pregnancy. A legal sanction was required to deter a man.[44]

Williams regards both findings as foregone conclusions, and the judgments as rationalizations. She believes they reflect deeply held cultural beliefs about sex differences. The cases have been discussed by others, and feminists disagree strongly on both. Before continuing with Williams's analysis I want to point out that while there is factual disagreement on the draft case, it is immaterial to her views. The disagreement on *Michael M.* poses more of a problem. Perhaps this is inevitable in a 'real' case rather than the *Rostker* type of suit. Williams cannot argue a hypothetical case if she wants to comment on the Court as opposed to the framing of the law.[45] While obviously I cannot know precisely what occurred, certain accounts suggest that we cannot view this case with equanimity as a matter of equality of, and equity between, the sexes. That is particularly so as the law in question is, as I understand it, not normally enforced.

US feminists tended to take one of two views on the male-only draft. Some held it indeed to be unconstitutional: this would emerge from a sameness equality view. Others, in a 'difference' and cultural-type feminist mode, posited a 'female ethic of nurturance and life-giving' as opposed to 'a male ethic of aggression and militarism', asserting that to support the *Rostker* plaintiffs was a betrayal of womanhood, and support of what was least endurable in the 'male'.[46]

Williams's final reply to this point is that

> *Rostker* never posed the question of whether women should be forced as men now are to fight wars, but whether we, like them, must take the responsibility for deciding whether or not to fight, whether or not to bear the cost of risking our lives . . . or resisting in the name of peace.

And of the cases in general she says:

> do we not, by insisting upon our differences at these crucial junctures, promote and reinforce the us–them dichotomy that permits [right-wing judges] to resolve matters of great importance and complexity by the simplistic, reflexive assertion that men and women 'are simply not similarly situated?'[47]

Here we see the fear of difference, said to be so much more common in the US than the UK, especially pertinent to feminist lawyers who do not want to plead a case on those grounds. The specific fear is that, as Williams suggests, differences or alleged differences will be seized upon to deny equality of opportunity in, say, employment. We will see in Chapter 10 that they have.

Liberal feminist equality

Whether equality under liberalism requires sameness depends on what equality means. If it is a somewhat minimalist and formal concept of respect for persons, then it does not matter what differences there are, and may not matter what differences are said to exist. Liberal feminists want more. And so they have tended to postulate sameness, or to attack, or seek to eliminate, difference.

Thus Friedan assails the feminine mystique, and thus Okin argues that on the whole, differences cannot be shown to exist. Richards suggests that apparent inferiority is socialized. Bluestone argues for a preponderance of evidence that women's reasoning is similar to and as good as men's. And Williams argues against judgments that stereotype women, for a legal understanding that the sexes are, for all material purposes, the same.

So these writers, in works ranging from 1963 to 1994, propose the equality of men and women in the sense of a lack of significant and relevant difference. Accordingly, women should be treated as well (or – though only Bluestone faces this squarely – as badly) as men. Most tend to speak of 'men' and 'women' as homogeneous groupings. Liberal feminists like these base their claims on 'adequate equality'; I have pointed to the problems this might cause.

Their other proposals vary. Friedan's individualist solution tends to place the onus on women, and makes it unclear how equal with men, in terms of condition, they will be at the end. Bluestone's argument for parity of men and women combines with her description of day-care centres – let alone servants for middle-class women – as 'gardens of privilege for a privileged species in a privileged portion of the globe'.[48] Okin wants, from a concern about poverty and its effects on the children of the US, radically to change the institutions of family and work, or rather, the relationship between them;[49] though not, I think, the present social structure of the US.

I assume that these writers would agree with Okin that 'A just future would be one without gender.'[50] Though she falls short, I believe, of the early radical wish, which we will encounter below, to abolish gender as it is now.

Before leaving sameness-equality feminism, let us invert Okin's comment, and say, 'A future without gender would be a just one.' Would it? If feminism is about justice for women, it does not follow, despite my qualifications, that it is about justice *per se*. If it is about equality for women, again it does not follow that it is about equality *per se*. 'It would be arbitrary to work for *sexual* equality,' says Sabina Lovibond, 'unless one believed that human society was disfigured by inequality *as such*.'[51] Is that the case? It sounds as if it should and must be correct. I have my doubts.

Certainly we could not care about equality for women, whatever exactly we mean by that, unless we possessed some idea of the concept of equality:

whether we were able to articulate it or not. I do not see why that logically or empirically entails a more general concern for the unequal of this world. The feminism I have discussed is about the advancement of (on occasion, perhaps, only some) women and, I think, women alone. I believe that is what feminism is. We may or may not like this. The advancement of women may logically entail the advancement of others, whether or not we particularly care about that.

In this chapter I have on the whole discussed liberal feminists as equality/sameness proponents, aiming for equality of opportunity with men and pleading it on sameness grounds. We have seen difference as non-existent, and as the product of a 'mystique'; as existing but to be overcome by education (though we have to wonder how 'equal' Rossi's women would be); and later, especially in the field of legal activism, to be denied, not to be employed in a plea, lest it be seized upon by the opponents of women's rights.

But we will see liberal feminists, though not all, change from seeking equality of opportunity of a kind that entails purely procedural change, to demanding the facilitation of the development of women's equal capabilities, and perhaps even more. We will see liberal feminism forsake in part Friedan's initial statement that equality is merited, to plead for a kind of equality of result via a notion of female difference; a difference that springs from women's environment, can therefore (usually) be held by men too, but could – and here is a formidable problem – be changed.

So various liberal feminists have turned to difference, if, that is, it was not in their writing, in tension with equality and sameness, all along. And I now turn to that.

Notes

1 Sandra Harding, *Whose Science? Whose Knowledge?*, 1991, pp. 111–15.

2 Hereafter 'science', etc.

3 Anne Phillips, *Engendering Democracy*, 1991, pp. 7–8.

4 Betty Friedan, *The Second Stage*, 1983; see Chapter 4 below.

5 Onora (O'Neill) Nell, 'How do we know when opportunities are equal?', in Carol C. Gould and Marx W. Wartofsky (eds), *Women and Philosophy*, 1976.

6 Susan Wendell, 'A (qualified) defense of liberal feminism', *Hypatia*, 1987.

7 See in particular Valerie Plumwood, 'Women, humanity and nature', in Sean Sayers and Peter Osborne (eds), *Socialism, Feminism and Philosophy: A Radical Philosophy Reader*, 1990; and Ynestra King, 'Healing the wounds', in Alison Jaggar and Susan Bordo (eds), *Gender/Body/Knowledge: Feminist Reconstructions of Being and Knowing*, 1989.

8 Vera Brittan and Winifred Holtby, 'Why feminism lives' (1927), in Maggie Humm (ed.), *Feminisms*, 1992, pp. 40–1.

9 Betty Friedan, *The Feminine Mystique* (1963), 1982, p. 38.

10 Ibid., pp. 47–50.

11 Though she is fully aware that at the time a large number of women worked outside the home.

12 Friedan, *The Feminine Mystique*, p. 24ff.

13 Marilyn French, *The Women's Room*, 1986; Fay Weldon, *Praxis*, 1993.

14 Alice S. Rossi, 'Equality between the sexes: an immodest proposal', *Daedalus*, 1964.

15 This term has normally been employed to describe women of the former Soviet Union, given their exceptional dual burden of work inside and outside the home.

16 Rossi, 'Equality', p. 613.

17 Ibid., pp. 609, 610.

18 Ibid., pp. 630–3.

19 Ibid., p. 614ff.

20 Ibid., p. 621.

21 Ibid., p. 625ff.

22 Ibid., p. 608.

23 Janet Radcliffe Richards, *The Sceptical Feminist*, 1980.

24 There are passages in Richards that have aroused feminist ire. I am not going to parade them here. They detract from her argument in precisely the way that she would allege 'the movement''s actions do from an acceptance of theirs.

25 Richards, p. 3.

26 Ibid., p. 5.

27 I do not mean by this, 'who believe in, who support, the legal system as it is now'.

28 Susan Okin, *Justice, Gender, and the Family*, 1989; p. 104 and elsewhere.

29 Okin tends to speak of 'gender differences', I assume because she means non-physical ones. But we do know what gender differences are: we see them daily. The question for most is, are these sex differences?
I also believe that when Okin speaks of a society stratified by gender, she means by sex. This distinction, and its relevance, will emerge more clearly when we address Mackinnon in Chapter 10.

30 Carol Gilligan, *In a Different Voice*, 1982, 2nd edn 1993. See Chapter 7.

31 Okin, *Justice*, p. 15.

32 While this is consistent with Okin's thought as a whole – see for example her 'Thinking like a woman', in Deborah L. Rhode (ed.), *Theoretical Perspectives on Sexual Differences*, 1991 – we see her apparently saying something very different, in *Justice, Gender and the Family* itself, in Chapter 4.

33 Natalie Harris Bluestone, *Women and the Ideal Society: Plato's 'Republic' and Modern Myths of Gender*, 1987.

34 There is a side of Bluestone that suggests a desire for more radical change.

35 Bluestone, *Women*, p. 98.

36 Phillips, *Engendering Democracy*, 1991, p. 3.

37 Jean Bethke Elshtain, 'Moral woman and immoral man: a consideration of the public–private split and its political ramifications', *Politics and Society*, 1974, p. 453ff. The reference is to the suffrage campaign.

38 On the differing standard involved see Susan Okin, *Women in Western Political Thought*, 1980 edn, p. 255ff.

39 Wendy Williams, 'The equality crisis', in Katharine T. Bartlett and Rosanne Kennedy (eds), *Feminist Legal Theory*, 1991.

40 Okin, *Women in Western Political Thought*, 1980 edn, p. 154.

41 Williams, 'The equality crisis', p. 16.

42 *Michael M.* (for example), denotes a case, Michael M. a party to it. Legal referencing conventions will not be employed here.

43 Williams, 'The equality crisis', p. 19. (David Kirp et al., *Gender Justice*, 1986, give the ruling as merely: 'men and women simply not being similarly situated' in this regard.)

44 Williams, 'The equality crisis', p. 19.

45 Though even that might raise my problem.

46 Williams, 'The equality crisis', p. 21. (I have rested my discussion very closely on Williams's account.)

47 Ibid., pp. 21–2.

48 Bluestone, *Women*, p. 208, n.2; quoting Sarah B. Hrdy, *The Woman That Never Evolved*, 1981, p. ix.

49 This will be discussed in Chapter 4.

50 Okin, *Justice, Gender, and the Family*, p. 171.

51 Sabina Lovibond, 'Feminism and postmodernism', in Roy Boyne and Ali Rattansi (eds), *Postmodernism and Society*, 1990, p. 178.

4

Essential Tensions? Liberal Feminism's Second Stage

Liberal feminists, we saw, seek equality of opportunity; though in practice that can mean parity, at various levels, with men. They base their claims on 'sameness', or, as I would prefer it, 'adequate similarity', to men. What of those among them who have moved towards difference?

Feminists like these assert that the reason for an advancement of women is that their character is complementary to, and possibly better than, men's. However for them, as opposed to certain of the difference feminists I discuss later, it is learned, or absorbed from a context such as the home. So perhaps the real distinction between them and the sameness-equality feminists who want to eliminate difference is that they view it positively. Why have they chosen this path? Does it make them a different form of liberal? Is it related to the 'welfare liberalism' to which, it has been suggested, Second-Wave liberal feminism has in large part moved, in particular, over say the last fifteen years?[1]

According to Carole Pateman, who refers to feminism's First Wave, such thinkers remain equality feminists in that they too seek equality with men; the distinction lies in the reason they give for deserving it.[2] And that makes sense to me. However, they may not avoid the 'danger of difference'. John Carrier noted that in the feminist campaigns for the recruitment of more women into the police forces of the UK, the 'good Christian ladies' who posited complementarity won. Their victory, he argues, had a detrimental long-term impact on the kind of work women police officers were allowed to carry out.[3]

Welfare liberalism has a long history, and one related to feminist thoughts and campaigns. It is on occasion hard to remember this, so used have we become to definitions of liberalism as concerned with a minimal state, and liberal feminism as some kind of offspring of liberalism of the 'classical', individualist kind. If 'early liberal' feminism moved, to favour welfare, what would the change mean?

My question is whether there is a relationship between our views of female qualities and character and what we think should be done to ameliorate women's condition, and/or enable our advance. Would 'difference' thinkers support, for example, greater intervention by the state? (This is not the same enterprise as the work of equality lawyers, even though they may seek legislative relief.) If so, do they want both 'welfare measures' to aid women in poverty, and, say, affirmative action in employment? Are the two types of policy linked?

There are among the writers I address no classic celebrants of difference: here there are equality feminists who have changed their minds in part, or with respect to one aspect of their analysis, appear to 'slip'. The texts I discuss nonetheless renounce Friedan's early assumption that there was nothing wrong with 'trying to be like men', and that to seek equality was to unveil the sameness hidden by the mystique. In disclaiming equality feminism could be said to become potentially more radical, though only if we view 'being like men' as having some association with the hierarchical society we know now, as many feminists would. They begin to laud the qualities, however acquired, of the female (as opposed perhaps to woman: a point I shall clarify below). They may then regard male and female qualities as complementary, and wish to retain both.

This *rapprochement* with difference takes more than one form. Again, I shall first discuss Friedan, whose *The Second Stage*, first published in 1981, contains her reflections, analysis, and proposals after roughly twenty years.

The reactive politics of liberal retrenchment? The Second Stage

> The first stage ... did not involve a new mode of thought. Once we broke through the feminine mystique and said that women were people, *we merely applied the abstract values of all previous liberal movements and radical revolutions, as defined by men*, to protest our oppression, exploitation and exclusion from man's world, and to demand an equal share of its rewards and powers as previously wielded and deployed by men.[4] [Italics mine]

These words of Friedan's are not those of an equality feminist, but of one who rejects equality as previously defined, and supported by her in the past. If we had only these comments by which to judge we would call her a cultural feminist, possibly of an extreme kind. (I refer in particular to 'as defined by men'.)

For she speaks of a new way of thinking, a way that is – by powerful inference – not men's; she attacks the demand for an equal share in their world; importantly, she adds that the 'demand' meant also the world as appropriated, and ruled, by them.

Basing anything on this, or indeed on any one passage or quotation is even more than usually problematic. For the *The Second Stage* is so diverse as to admit no one interpretation of its views. However, Friedan tells, I believe, one central and coherent story, presented as feminism's failure, to an extent; I follow it here.

Feminism advanced, despite male opposition and the general hostility aroused, in her view quite reasonably, by the actions of the 'sexual politics' branch, the politics of the radical wing, and NOW's failure to condemn them.[5] Women indeed returned to college and careers, and made (as they have since) massive occupational and financial gains. (Of course we must add, 'some women', and note that genuine occupational and financial equality is, even so, rare.) Steps towards the aims of *The Feminine Mystique*, then, had been made. Equality feminism had made considerable headway, in its own terms. But with the gains had come costs for the women involved, leading to Friedan's reappraisal of the feminist cause.

This first advance brought with it what I have called the 'double shift'; and if we think of the time it takes to 'be a woman', and the propaganda on appropriate clothes for career women, 'in the office', at leisure, at home, more adventurous *and* more healthy cooking, and so on, we begin to see a 'triple shift'. Part of this, Friedan perceived, though vaguely. What she did not do was draw one of the possible sets of logical conclusions, all of which entail far more change than she called for, or would. Faced with the 'superwoman syndrome', with career women who were lonely and/or overworked, she did not scrutinize a system and structure where middle-class married women who did not work were isolated and unhappy yet occupational and financial advance seemed more to kill, than cure. Instead she blamed the movement. And she did so in the words quoted above, in virtual antithesis to her definition of the feminine mystique.

Did she, then, renounce her earlier analysis? Did she opt for difference? Castigating 'sexual politics' – that is the radicals' focus on sexuality as institutionalized now – as part of the feminist malaise, she invokes the 'biological relationship between woman and man ... the reality of woman's open sexuality, her childbearing, her roots and life connections within the family'.[6] While this suggests a certain belief in difference, it does not necessarily 'celebrate' what it depicts. A more overt suggestion of pride in difference appears in her account of women cadets at West Point.

There are ambiguities and ambivalences in Friedan's account of these soldiers. However, she finds it pleasing that when the proportion of women was sufficiently large, they could ignore male role models and aid one another in maintaining their own, 'women's', traits.[7] Here Friedan ignores a somewhat obvious point. A very small number of women probably would find it easier to adopt the habits of men in order to be seen as 'good soldiers', 'officer material', and so on. A larger number could more easily bring their own mores to the Academy. But that says nothing about the relative desirability of these qualities. The Friedan of *The Feminine Mystique* would, I assume, have regarded both as the outcome of socialization – as indeed her discussion here suggests – and to be overcome.

Further she approves of the comment that women's skills, rather than men's, would be appropriate for future wars.[8] But she then sees the danger: the problem, for an equality view, of

> assuming women's moral superiority ... greater sensitivity to the values and needs of human life. That, after all, is the rationale of those who say women should not be exposed to combat duty, or even drafted, in the next war.[9]

Here we see the classic threat and dilemma of gender difference. (It would not normally be invoked in this particular context, of course. War and the draft are not a popular 'equality' cause.) Can Friedan find a way out?

Her answer, ironically, is based on difference. Just as women no longer had to change, she argues, men could. They might be able to adopt the traits and values of women: those needed, in a technological era, for war. Thus there could be no argument that women should not fight side by side with men.[10] She reaches this view via a direct inversion of the politics of the *Mystique*. Here, women will be the standard by which (an aspect of) society is run.

Friedan often speaks of *assumptions* about men and women. But there is no doubt that she believes there are sex differences that materially affect the conduct of occupations and behaviour, socialized and changeable though they are. For later she talks of Alpha (male) and Beta (female) leadership styles, while making it clear that they are not to be thought innate.[11]

So whether or not we regard this as a difference text, it is not a sameness-equality one. It adopts a 'deferred' or 'potential androgyny' model: one of complementary characteristics of women and men. Though it remains alert to the perils of proposing difference, it appears to assume all too easily that we can find a way of overcoming these.

For Rosemarie Tong, Friedan moves towards androgyny, in the sense of male and female characteristics that can be combined.[12] For me, she moves towards it in one sense only, and with a certain eye to the dangers of such a move. These differing judgements rest on two views of what androgyny is.

Tong also thinks liberal feminists have moved towards welfare liberalism. And indeed Friedan moved substantially and strongly from her early views, arguing (in a time of recession, and when state sector spending was being cut) that women did not *choose* to work;[13] that parents should be aided, possibly by vouchers; that from various sources, including the corporate sector, there should come flexitime, child care, and parental leave.[14] Financial aid for abortion should be available for the poor.[15]

Much of the impetus for change, Friedan believes, comes from economic necessity, and the humiliating ending of the Vietnam War. But also, some men are simply tiring of the 'rat race' women once sought to join. There will be a move towards a new, humane mode of life and work. Here again a middle-class perspective appears, though Friedan does recognize the economic needs of the less privileged.

Has Friedan become a welfare liberal, as opposed to the individualist she appeared to be before? On the whole, yes. If so, then difference and welfare liberalism, equality and gender-neutral laws may be related, if in this case weakly. That is: we cannot point to differences, and proposed measures, and say that they are linked. But if so, she gives a hostage to fortune, in that 'the solutions may come not necessarily because of or for women . . . but from converging causes . . . that add up to profits or other benefits for the men and institutions involved'.[16]

I do not mean that I want changes to entail yet more weary struggle. (Feminism has brought costs, as well as gains. There will be more.) But this somewhat determinist conclusion is open to the query: and what when the economy, or a regime, again requires a retreat?

To say this is not to condemn social liberalism as a feminist tendency, tactic, or goal. It is to point to a problem. US feminists are especially accustomed to the concern, given the way abortion and other policy has been made and unmade. In the spring of 1994 they prepared to lobby for a feminist or at least 'feminist-friendly' nominee to the Supreme Court, though it was a woman Justice many sought.

Taken together, *The Feminine Mystique* and *The Second Stage* well illustrate the point that liberal feminism seeks not to change the present system/regime in a revolutionary manner, but to advance the cause of women, and normally, some women, within it. Equality means equality of certain women with certain men, in a society that will remain unequal, itself. The welfare proposals that appear in the second book, do not change this. Numerous critics have made this point, if not in these precise terms.

The feeling I gain from *The Second Stage*, furthermore, is that Friedan's attachment to the liberal democratic society of the US, whatever discrete criticisms of it she may have, runs so deep that in her disillusion, and perceiving others' disaffection and distress, she can respond only by thinking that feminism has in some way erred. Close as her phrasing is to certain other viewpoints, her policies will pin their faith on conventional political activity, broadly construed. Thus she will never be radicalized to the point where she would propose a system completely different from the one we know now.

Friedan is enabled to conclude, for example, that part-time working by both sexes is an end to conflict, by the economic climate of the time. She can find reasons totally independent of the women's movement (her criticisms of radical feminism apart) for the reaction she laments,[17] the changes she views with optimism, and the ones she wants.

Do we not, though, see Friedan now entrapped by the feminine mystique? This aspect of the retreat cannot, given the character of other writers who have adopted it, be caused by her ties to pluralism and liberalism. It could however be argued that it is linked to the deformation of liberalism, of liberal society, that has ranged so powerful a series of forces against women that equality is the hardest choice of all.[18]

Nonetheless, we owe Friedan a massive amount. *The Feminine Mystique* brought feminism to hundreds of thousands of women. And despite the passages I have quoted from the *Second Stage*, she will be remembered as an equality theorist. Will Okin?

Okin: difference for justice's sake

Okin is an equality feminist, and an androgyny feminist who rejects the notion that the sexes differ in their psychological traits. She is not, however, totally consistent here. In *Justice, Gender and the Family* she accepts and employs the view she initially rejects. Though she speaks of sex differences not in an essentialist manner, but as originating in a context; or so I believe. Conceivably, nonetheless, they are universalist: that is, they apply to all women. Why does she support a view that goes against the grain of the rest of her work?

We have seen that she rejected writers like Gilligan. Yet it is Gilligan that she endorses, and her greatly influential work on a gendered psychology of thinking about justice.[19]

Gilligan, a psychologist whose work has begun a massive debate in various fields, including political thought, discusses moral reasoning, positing a male 'ethic of justice' and a female 'ethic of care'. It is I suppose because Okin is writing on justice (and in the end, perhaps, care), that she singles this work out. Having specifically dismissed it, she moves to acceptance, saying that she regards the distinction between the ethics as overdrawn.[20] There seems reason to believe that she would attempt to combine them. I infer that from the final chapter of her book.

Okin presents a problem of summary and interpretation given the extent to which her project either is, or departs from, a discussion of male theorists' views. Certain of her comments are not entirely intelligible outside that context. The chapter in *Justice, Gender and the Family* which seems to me the crucial moment of the move to difference, and which also explains, I believe, why Okin moved, is a critique of *A Theory of Justice* by John Rawls. It is furthermore the chapter on which Okin seems to rest much of the remainder of her book.

It is not my purpose, here, to assess either Rawls's remarkable work, or Okin's influential critique; but to extract from the latter what seems to me to show her as some form of difference feminist, ill though the stance sits with her general views.[21]

The grounds for Okin's critique are Rawls's neglect of women; his failure to perceive that gender[22] is a crucial social fact which must be taken into account. This leads her to launch an attack which, in its final form, is characteristic of difference feminists of various kinds. She attacks Rawls, that is, for a particular form of universalism and abstraction. An 'ethic of justice', in this version of the argument, is worthless unless it incorporates an ethic of care:

> The best theorizing about justice . . . has integral to it the notions of care and empathy, of thinking of the interests and well-being of others who may be very different from ourselves [it] . . . is not some abstract 'view from nowhere', but results from the carefully attentive consideration of *everyone's* point of view. This means, of course, that [it] is not good enough if it does not, or cannot readily be adapted to, include *women and their points of view as fully as men and their points of view*.[23] (Final italics mine)

I have chosen this quotation because it seems to me to illustrate most clearly the 'difference' aspect of the discussion in her major work.

Why does Okin take this step? What is her justification for the emphasis on 'women and their points of view'? Why does the need to consider 'everyone' lead to a stress on a category of certain 'ones'?

Okin's major illustrative argument is a cartoon of three old, male, and very pregnant judges, one saying, 'Perhaps we'd better reconsider that decision.' She links this to various recent '"gender-neutral laws"' 'that in effect discriminate against women'. Here she highlights the Supreme Court statement in *Geduldig* v. *Aiello* that exclusion of pregnancy from a disability benefits plan '"is not a gender-based discrimination at all"'[24] having previously noted that the Court explained that the distinction was between pregnant women and '"non-pregnant persons"'.[25]

We may well find the idea of this cartoon amusing, and the decision of the Court bizarre. But what is really strange here, given Okin's illustration, and her annoyance, is that she herself does not support universal paid maternity leave. Rather, she would instate a system whereby illness during pregnancy would be covered by such a plan.[26] Given this, her reaction to the judges' refusal to regard pregnancy as sex-related seems, while commonsensical, somewhat strong.

Okin believes that the cartoon serves to show that female judges would think differently, adding, strangely perhaps, that the justices 'can, in a sense, imagine themselves as pregnant' but may not be able to 'imagine themselves as women'.[27] This helps found her views on the composition of the US judiciary too. Though, as we will see, female judges contribute more than an ability to see themselves as women.

At this point Okin approvingly cites Gilligan, and various writers who have pursued the theme of 'maternal thought'. If there is a uniting strand in the 'motherhood' thinkers it is that they believe parenting should be jointly carried out.[28] And this is Okin's conclusion too. I note her *rapprochement* with them, for they are thinkers of difference.

I give here but one critique of 'motherhood thought', Elshtain's critique of Dinnerstein, which, despite Dinnerstein's beliefs,[29] is aimed at liberal feminist thought. She asks why it should be the good characteristics of the private realm that are retained and infused when men 'parent', rather than the bad values of the public realm that they import when coming in from the cold.[30]

I suggest that Okin is keeping strange company here. The problem is not that she believes in socialized attributes; liberals do. It is rather that she would found a politics on so fragile a base. And fragile, for her, it must be.

I turn to another entry of the voice of difference into her work:

> *in a gender-structured society* there is such a thing as the distinct standpoint of women . . . . The formative influence of female parenting on small children, especially, seems to suggest that sex difference is . . . likely to affect one's thinking about justice . . . a fully human moral or political theory can be developed only with the full participation of both sexes.[31]

The (qualified) belief in difference – in 'thinking about justice' – is apparent here. What concerns me more is 'standpoint'.

Standpoint theory in its original form – and this could be what Okin means – is a worrying position for a liberal feminist to endorse, for it posits a separate and superior female knowledge and means of knowing, derived from oppression.[32] It postulates a female viewpoint more accurate than that of males, derived from women's experiences of subordination. I imagine that Okin is in fact employing a mild and non-technical version of the argument, which nonetheless suggests that all women have a viewpoint that differs from that of all men.[33] Therefore she is not taking account of differences between women. Whatever opinion we happen to hold of 'difference' in that sense, I think we have to accept that belief in 'a' standpoint of women is strange.[34]

Okin is I think supporting two separate types of view. The first, following Gilligan, postulates different forms of reasoning by sex, and derives arguments from it that tend to suggest that it will endure and is therefore stable enough to base a policy on. The second postulates a different form of thinking contingently and partially linked to sex, in that it emerges from what I shall term active parenthood. It emerges, that is, from the activity of rearing a child from shortly after its birth.

Neither form of argument is necessarily essentialist – and Gilligan's, despite ambiguities, is almost certainly not – and so neither falls prey to the classic attacks on womanly virtue, biologically based, as leading to the downgrading of women. However the second could, if employed in woman's advance, meet suggestions that values derived from the home mean that women should remain there. I suspect though that both are falsely universalist in their respective assumptions that 'women' and 'mothers' will think in a certain way, and exclusionary in their view or implication that men and non-parents will not.[35]

Okin should not, as a liberal, endorse this view. Alternatively, she should endorse it to the point where it can have no implications for the way people are treated. That it does is shown, albeit on the whole implicitly, in her policies outlined in the final chapter of her book. They include – admittedly as second-best – what is in effect a 'Wages for Housework' policy, which has of course been subject to devastating attack.[36] And it is shown further by her stress on the crucial importance of replacing the present elites, who are

> men . . . or women who have . . . forgone motherhood . . . or hired others . . . [they] make policy at the highest levels – policies not only *about* families and their welfare and about the education of children, but about the foreign policies . . . that will determine the future . . . for all these . . . . Yet they . . . almost all . . . gain . . . influence . . . in part by never having . . . [nurtured] a child. This is probably the most significant aspect of our gendered division of labor . . . . The effects of changing it could be momentous.[37]

It is not that she suggests that others should be excluded – though nor does she say we will not – but rather, there is a distinct suggestion of the value of views that presumably could not be ours. (I speak here for all who have not, will not, cannot, for whatever reason, bear and/or rear a child.) Of course she could be correct. Or she could be totally wrong, less in her assessment of the existence and value of such views – though I admit to scepticism – than in her belief that they are homogeneously distributed among mothers, relate so directly to policy, and can so easily be transferred between realms.

Okin's two possible acceptable societies both appear to intrude into private life to a degree that a liberal cannot accept.[38] So I read her willingness to compel fathers to support their children fully whether they are married to the mother or not,[39] a measure that has been strongly attacked by feminists in the UK. Whether her emphasis on parenting as a qualification for making decisions should also cause us concern is another matter. Not only is it exclusionary. It tends to suggest a lack of knowledge of the dark side of motherhood, as described by Flax.[40]

Is Okin's invoking of difference allied to welfare liberalism? This is difficult to judge, but I would say not. What I have referred to as her version of 'Wages for Housework', confined to women living within a stable heterosexual relationship, entails that the man pay.[41] Biological fathers will be made to support their children, in place of support by the state. It is not that in this version of liberalism the state does not enter the private realm. While allegedly it remains outside, in fact it comes thundering in, laying privacy waste.[42] Rather, this can hardly be called 'social', or 'welfare', liberalism at all. But then it is unclear that her policy proposals relate to the difference thinking she (temporarily) adopts.

I earlier quoted Okin's, 'A just society is one without gender'. I am not going to interrogate it in the same way here. Rather I want to say that I think Okin is in fact talking about a society stratified by sex, and whose sexual stratification is related to and overlaid by a system of gender. It is an end to stratification by sex of which she speaks, though gender is involved too. In other words, if we abolished gender, abolished the characteristics to which men and women are supposed or alleged to conform, we would not in my view have attained equality. We would have reached androgyny, in one sense of the term. That is not the same thing. An end to stratification by sex, on the other hand, would bring an equality, of some form, of women and men. Stratification of other kinds – including of course an inequality among women – would clearly remain.

Women, then, are discriminated against because of their sex, though real or alleged gender-related characteristics may contribute to that. While Okin clearly wants the sexes to be more alike in two contexts and for two related reasons, yet in one version of her utopia, at least, and the one she really wants, she says, without arguing the issue through, that she wants more than this. She then faces the question of how fragile gender is.

Bluestone: looking 'facts' in the face

Bluestone seems to be the most hard-line 'sameness' feminist I discuss. Certainly, of all these thinkers, she finds the equality claim the most tenuous. She feels, more than others, that it needs to be justified.

This may sound odd, when it is difference theorists who, in part, renounce equality. But I think it does make a kind of sense. Bluestone's question is this: 'what arguments justify the statement that it is wrong *in itself* to deny women equal rights?'[43]

Here I think we meet the sameness equality dilemma. That is: if women and men are equally good at something, why hire women?

This Bluestone firmly grasps, neatly inverting the usual type of comment that might be made:

> If men and women have the same capacities, and reason with identical skill, then surely there can be no special reason why female philosophers are needed. Men can point out inequities and suggest reforms as effectively as women.

And what is Bluestone's way out of her own trap? Okin appealed to 'empathy', appearing to relate this in some way to women, and in a rather different way to what can be learned from parenting, as a reason why women should advance.[44] The way Bluestone phrases the issue prevents her from saying anything like that. Her answer is this:

> for generations to come women will have a unique connection with all females before them who were condemned because of their physiology .... *For there is no philosophy performed by disembodied souls, and all thought arises out of a particular situation* .... It is we who were confined to household chores, whose sex life was regulated and whose mental capacities were denigrated. We who reason, think, imagine alternatives, weigh the just with the unjust, must keep alive the memory of those inequities.[45] [Italics mine]

Here again, and this time against the whole of the previous content and tone of a book, a liberal feminist argues for equality because of difference, and for gendered thought. But at least it is not a gendered *way of thought*. A memory that arises from the scars of a subordinated sex, and its given gender, seems to me a different kind of point: a remembrance; more acceptable, to me anyway, than some notion that women are 'kind'.

However, my doubts remain. What is wrong with the argument that, since women can reason as well as men, half of for example the posts in philosophy should go to them? Why do we need to import 'difference', give women an additional desirable characteristic, before we can ask for equality? Why do we have to be even better than men, before we can ask for the same things?[46]

So while Bluestone does import difference, she does so in a very attenuated sense. As for welfare liberalism: we do not see it here, although we see a stance that would support it, in my quotation towards the end of Chapter 3. But that is tenuous. Here we cannot relate imported difference and policy stance at all.

Rossi: the sociobiological case

Of the writers I discussed in Chapter 2, Rossi, while perhaps the strongest in pursuit of parity for the middle class, and prepared, as we have seen, to *tell* women feminism was better, was yet the 'complementary features' androgyny theorist. Perhaps then it is not surprising that she changed. The surprise is the type of change she underwent. For she wholeheartedly embraced sociobiology, that is, the belief, which tends to be derived from studies of animal behaviour, that the traditional roles of men and women are 'natural', have evolved for the survival of the species, and cannot be changed.[47]

Rossi's 'A biosocial perspective on parenting'[48] is not what 'An immodest proposal' would lead us to expect. For it positively emphasizes difference. Rossi now believes in significant, role-determining differences, both physiological and psychological, which are transhistorical and cross-cultural too. Her arguments can be quickly put. (More or less) always, and everywhere, she says, women have cared for (newly born) children. And they have prepared the household food. It is not that men are incapable of learning to look after babies, or to cook, though 'as a group they are less apt to show ease in infant handling and food preparation than women are'.[49]

This does not seem a strong case, given the centuries when (most) women have carried out these duties and (most) men have not. (Rossi would throw this point back, using the time scale as her proof.) The two instances, I think, vary. Who has mainly done the cooking for whom is fairly clear, but obviously not the crux. Holding and 'handling' babies really does seem, for many women, to be a learned skill. That they are probably taught by other women, who are more experienced mothers, is what we would expect. Men's ease with babies has probably changed anyway, since Rossi wrote; some, at least, have fulfilled her views, and 'learned'. If, however, her case is that such skills can be acquired, why does she hold such an extreme difference view? She says:

> A biosocial perspective does not argue that there is a genetic determination of what men can do compared to women; rather, it suggests that the biological contributions shape what is learned, and that there are differences in the ease with which the sexes can learn certain things.[50]

But she adds – for she accepts extant findings on within-sex variation – that any occupation that requires very few entrants will find qualified candidates equally among women and men.[51]

It is the evolutionary viewpoint sociobiology entails that makes her not only emphasize reproduction as 'species survival', but see roles, behaviour patterns, and personnel related to it as likely to be innate; childrearing as a mother's task. Interestingly, though in historical perspective not surprisingly, she does not endorse the type of family we have now, without the kind of communal facilities – though as an adjunct: to lessen the isolation not only of the mother, but also, and very much so, of the child – she wanted before. Such facilities are for her unlikely to come – as formerly it seemed they might – from the state.[52]

I find this way of thought problematic. And I find her views on equality so. She suggests that we have wrongly assumed that women must be the same as men in order to be 'socially, economically or politically equal'. In fact, she says, the sexes can be different, carry out different tasks, and still be equal in all these ways. If we reduce the role and expectations of motherhood to handling a baby; if we work out what the role of cook should feasibly mean; we could have one form of 'equality': women could do the same things as men, and a little more. If we massively revalue both, we could have another kind of equality, though, one about which I am sceptical in the extreme, given the history of the 'revaluing of natality', aimed at making women baby-factories. Further, it is based on a man–woman binary opposition that, as I suggested in Chapter 1, does not exist.

For Rossi, it does. Rossi has turned to difference in the sense that she has produced a model that will she says appeal more

> to those who question the desirability of a work-dominated life and to those who see both strength and meaning in the family support, community-building, and institutional innovation in which women have been for so long engaged

though she is aware that this will be seen as a conservative retreat to times past.[53] I see it less as that than as cultural feminism, true difference feminism, discussed in Chapter 6.

Elshtain's 'liberal difference' critique·

Elshtain, too, has focused on difference in liberal feminism.[54] Liberal feminists have, she feels, a dilemma. They want both what they believe the public realm has to offer – say, wealth, acceptance, renown – and a somewhat separate private sphere, a belief in whose virtues they espouse.[55] They cannot, she says, have all this:

> it is impossible to indefinitely have things both ways: to condemn woman's second-class status and the damaging effects of her privatization and, simultaneously, to extol or celebrate the qualities that have emerged within the sphere women are to be 'freed' from.[56]

I wonder where she locates these writers' beliefs in the 'virtues' of the private realm.[57] (I suspect, in 'liberalism' itself.) Her comments do not apply to the writers I have discussed. However, I accept the argument as put here. Such a mixture of equality and difference, simultaneously promoted, would indeed be fairly lethal to feminism's cause. Elshtain would like women to escape the bonds of both, as they are, or can readily be conceived of, now.[58] As we will see below, some feminists have solved the apparent dilemma by fully embracing difference, and some of those by renouncing the public world as the 'world of men'.

I have mentioned 'liberal empiricism'[59] in the context of the paucity of liberal feminist thought. Elshtain's labelling of liberals as positivists (a basically similar position) could be said to lead her to the same view – certainly, there is latent in her discussion a view of undertheorization and more manifestly, a notion of the poverty of liberal thought. But she has chosen to argue, somewhat against the odds, that the fact–value distinction of this type of method and thought means that feminists cannot prove their case. As she herself will, presumably unwillingly, show, it depends what case one wants to put.

> One finds liberal feminists alternating between the 'hard facts' of discrimination and institutionalized sexism and the 'soft appeal' to feminine opinions and values.

and so for her, they 'fail to treat squarely and cogently the problem of "separate but equal" and different, or "not-separate but equal" and the same';[60] an important point, to which I return in Chapter 10.

Elshtain further argues that liberal feminists are basically environmentalists; but they are inconsistent ones. For they believe that women are socialized into their values and beliefs, 'taught' them, or acquire them from their 'home' in the private realm, but that they must if they maintain that those values are good[61] be concerned lest they fall as women enter the public realm and are subject to different pressures, opinions, and views: a process that might be called 'secondary socialization' now.

I agree with much of this. However I think it is probably better suited as an attack on difference theorists, 'weak cultural feminists', on the whole, than on the writers I discuss here. (Though certainly, there are liberal feminists who have not considered points like these enough.) We will meet those writers soon. First I move to Second-Wave feminism's second equality, to 'early radicals', the equality theorists of the Left.

Notes

1 Rosemarie Tong, *Feminist Thought*, 1989, pp. 26–7, 38.

2 Carole Pateman, 'Equality, difference, subordination', in Gisela Bock and Susan James (eds), *Beyond Equality and Difference*, 1992, pp. 17–18.

3 John Carrier, *The Campaign for the Employment of Women as Police Officers*, 1988, pp. 252–3.

4 Friedan, *The Second Stage*, 1983, p. 239.

5 Ibid., pp. 49–50.

6 Ibid., p. 51.

7 Ibid., p. 189.

8 Ibid., p. 182.

9 Ibid., p. 189.

10 Though there is reason to infer that a different, highly technological type of warfare was in any event what West Point had in mind; ibid., p. 172.

11 Ibid., p. 243ff.

12 Tong, *Feminist Thought*, p. 27.

13 Friedan, *The Second Stage*, pp. 72–4.

14 Ibid., p. 262.

15 Ibid., p. 24.

16 Ibid., p. 267.

17 This reaction is both anti-feminist, and more generally reactionary.

, 18 I do not mean to suggest that what we call 'liberal-democratic' societies are particularly culpable. It is part of Friedan's case in the *Mystique*, and a fair one, that the US could be expected to be better than it is.

19 See the discussion of Gilligan in Chapter 7.

20 Susan Okin, *Justice, Gender and the Family*, 1989, p. 15.

21 Susan Okin, 'Thinking like a woman', in Deborah Rhode (ed.), *Theoretical Perspectives on Sexual Difference*, 1991; Okin, 'Gender inequality and cultural differences', *Political Theory*, 1994.

22 Okin tends to use 'gender' when I think she means 'sex'. That is, she employs the term for the social construct that is 'woman', when she means the biological being. This seems to occur throughout her work (though not only hers). See Okin, 'Gender, inequality'.

23 Okin, *Justice*, p. 15.

24 Ibid., p. 102.

25 Ibid., p. 11.

26 Ibid., p. 176; she believes women will have different needs.

27 Ibid., p. 102.

28 Though not all think that. And such is not Gilligan's concern.

29 These are hard to categorize. However, 'radical' seems fair.

30 Jean Bethke Elshtain, *Public Man, Private Woman: Women in Social and Political Thought*, 1981, pp. 286–90.

31 Okin, *Justice*, 1989, pp. 106–7.

32 See Sandra Harding, 'Feminist justificatory strategies', in Ann Garry and Marilyn Pearsall (eds), *Women, Knowledge and Reality: Explorations in Feminist Philosophy*, 1989, pp. 194–8.

33 The 'all women' problem is one of the reasons why standpoint theory has changed.

34 Okin has said she knows there is a problem. But she does not expand on that.

35 See the concern about 'elevating marriage and parenthood above other facts of the private world' in Robert Paul Wolff, 'There's nobody here but us persons', in Carol C. Gould and Marx Wartofsky (eds), *Women and Philosophy*, 1976, p. 142.

36 Tong, *Feminist Thought*, pp. 54–7.

37 Okin, *Justice*, pp. 179–80.

38 The two that can be decided on from Rawls's 'original position' as amended by her, and that do not 'violate such fundamentals as equal basic liberty and self-respect' in their views on gender roles; ibid., p. 174.

39 Ibid., p. 184.

40 See Chapter 7; and also the discussion of Adrienne Rich, *Of Woman Born*, 1986, Chapter 6.

41 Again, this is second-best.

42 I have in mind the ensuing requirement that a woman name the father of a child.

43 Natalie Harris Bluestone, *Women and the Ideal Society: Plato's 'Republic' and Modern Myths of Gender*, 1987, p. 98.

44 Her concern for the number and proportion of US children who live in poverty should not be ignored; though I have suggested that the link she makes between women, parenting, and caring about the issue could be wrong.

45 Bluestone, *Women*, p. 196.

46 Of course I do not mean 'better' in the sense of outperforming men in, say, examinations; though that could also be true.

47 For incisive attacks on such studies and the idea of their relevance to us, see Hilary Callan, 'Harems and overlords: biosocial models and the female', in Shirley Ardener (ed.), *Defining Females: The Nature of Women in Society*, 1978, pp. 200–19; and Bluestone, *Women*, pp. 179–82.

48 Alice S. Rossi, 'A biosocial perspective on parenting', *Daedalus*, 1975.

49 Ibid., p. 4.

50 Ibid.

51 'Equally' is my interpretation.

52 Rossi, 'A biosocial perspective', pp. 21–2.

53 Ibid., p. 25.

54 Elshtain, *Public Man, Private Woman.*

55 Ibid., 1993 edn, p. 240ff.

56 Ibid., p. 248.

57 While Elshtain forwarded a case similar to mine, she mainly addressed *The Feminine Mystique.*

58 This is my interpolation.

59 See Chapter 2.

60 Elshtain, *Public Man, Private Woman*, pp. 240–9.

61 This is my interpolation. Elshtain rather takes it for granted that they do.

5

Radical Equality: the Early Fire

The feminism I discuss now, 'early radicalism' as I call it, is an equality feminism; though it places a greater emphasis on difference, in more than one sense of the word, than liberal feminism does. Also in sharp contrast to the works discussed above, and to their writers' annoyance, if not indeed anger and chagrin,[1] it frequently addresses sexuality and its discontents. In doing this, such writers think, it avoids the real problems that women face, or antagonizes those who might otherwise support the feminist cause. Sometimes, indeed, its analysis is based on a critique of sexuality: sexuality is seen as oppression's cause, in a way that must be anathema to them.

Further, its equality is not theirs: it is not equality of opportunity, to whatever extent. While it perceives immediate problems it must confront, it transcends the most radical interpretation of the liberal stance. For it consists in a rejection of rank and hierarchy, and of oppression in all its forms. Thus, it tends utterly to reject the social, political, and economic systems we know now. What this group has in common with the first – a commonality important for understanding feminism – is that it too protests at a broken promise, and seeks to have that promise fulfilled.

Liberalism broke its contract with women. The New Left spoke of liberation for more or less every group except women. Indeed, it insulted and abused women. Liberal feminists could remain 'within' liberalism, or to be more precise, uphold the pluralist framework with which it co-exists. For early radicals the time had come for socialist men to pay their dues; to live their beliefs, or be abandoned.

The early radicals' goal, then, would differ too. It would be an equality of condition once seen as the socialist aim and spirit, so that either all possessed the same amount and were treated identically, or there was some form of allocation of goods according to need. (This goal is generally thought, of course, to apply to the ending of economic exploitation, and I have inferred it. It is not always to be found explicitly in these writers, perhaps because of the very different emphasis of the New Left, until quite shortly before its end.) Feminist radicals also sought the eradication of discrimination by sex and race, and the simultaneous liberation of all the oppressed. And not only is the type of equality different, but the way in which it will be gained. Not that this is always said; nor that a consensus exists.

It is impossible to discuss the aims of early radicalism in the same way as liberalism's goal of equality of opportunity: the secondary literature on it is sparse, and many of the important pieces are tracts. More, early radicalism has no one view of the exact nature of the good society, or the means by which oppression will fall. And not all its writers emphasized revolution to the extent that they spurned reforms. Some would work for them as necessary interim measures, so long as final aims remained non-reformist and to the extent that they fulfilled criteria feminists set out. Bunch, for example, gave as a first criterion for supporting a reformist act: 'Does it materially improve the lives of women and if so, which women, and how many?'; she speaks of various forms of oppression.[2] (This is a characteristic of early radicalism, as it is to address oppression via the existing structures of sex and love, be they what would later be called compulsory heterosexuality, or sexuality in general, as ordered now.)

That this form of equality existed within feminism seems largely forgotten, though I do not mean that the major writers are ignored. However a somewhat monolithic, untheorized, view of 'equality' seems to be held: one that narrows debate.

Here I discuss early radicalism's divergence from liberal feminism, in the form of equality it sought, related in part to its explanation of the causes of the inequality that was to be overcome and the means by which it would fall. I shall, as before, explain that via the texts, discussing writers one by one. Because of their origins, and also their influence in England, I include among them an early, major, Marxist feminist piece from the UK.

Early radicalism must, for some who would not embrace its tenets, yet be celebrated for the enduring impact of its work. As Michèle Barrett, whose project is Marxist, says, its 'ideas represent an irreducible core of truth and anger which forms the obstinate basis of feminist politics'.[3] Its legacy cannot be overestimated, nor should we forget its force.

This grouping was concerned to overthrow all forms of oppression. The specifically feminist aspect of the programme was presented from within a more general revolutionary perspective, but with a determination that women would at no stage take second place. In major and more fully fledged theory the roots of all oppression were argued to lie in the oppression of women – and sometimes children – so that with their liberation, with the gaining of equality for them, would come freedom and equality for all humankind. Some feminists, of course, had already renounced the notion of benefiting men, except, perhaps, by chance. Like revolutionary schools of thought in general, early radicalism does not say what its end-state of equality would comprise. However Firestone's *The Dialectic of Sex* very nearly does.

So perhaps it can only be inferred – though the inference is strong – that equality of situation, of condition, is what is meant. In one very important, conceivably rather different sense, though, early radicalism was in theory egalitarian to the core. That sense concerns the practices of the movement. It believed that not only should all voices be heard, but all should be given equal weight. So would consciousness be raised; so would experiences be seen to be shared; so would a movement form. Though very early on a small but crucial minority began to voice unease about the implications of procedures like that. I shall discuss a major early text articulating the concern, Freeman's 'The tyranny of structurelessness', below.[4]

Early radicalism is a gender difference school in that it sees both male and female character as marred by society: by patriarchy and by capitalism; by 'the system', as would probably have been said then. But the sexes had been harmed in separate ways, and women the more. In contrast to other feminist analysts, early radicals were, though less than their successors, concerned to point the finger of blame at men; it may be that the notion of patriarchy entails this, though it would depend on how its regime was thought to have begun.

Early radicals believe these differences can and should be overcome, or minimized at least. I infer this from Firestone's account of the genesis and accentuation of character difference; and her later hopes for a new world, as well as her comments on love, outlined below.

So like liberal feminism, early radicalism can be said to be androgynous: it believes there are sex differences, but that they can and should be overcome. Unlike liberal feminists, of course, or unlike 'sameness' liberal feminists, at least, early radicals are concerned not because women have been held back by not being allowed to be like men, in the sense of sharing their characteristics, for men's current characteristics are not desired. But nor are women's. Both are flawed.

Then early radicalism sought androgyny, presumably in one of the two senses given above; though it is difficult to say which. Indeed for Firestone, the human has been sundered by the gender split. But if the radicals do not want to be as men are now, nor do they want equality with men in this society, which is anathema to them: for its poverty, racism, sexism, and hierarchy, and the way it has scarred the self. They want to overthrow society, and create equality so.

I next illustrate these points, initially via early speeches and tracts.

Sisterhood is powerful: the first years

> There is much anger here at Movement men, but I know they have been warped and programmed by the same society that has damn near crippled us. My anger is because they have created in the Movement a microcosm of that oppression and are proud of it. Manipulation and careerism and competition will not evaporate of themselves. Sisters, what we do, we have to do together, and we will see about them. (Marge Piercy, 1970)[5]

This passage is a classic statement of the politics of the New Left from which activists like Piercy came. It stood, in theory at least, for participatory democracy; for treating people as beings worthy of respect, and not as papers to be processed, cyphers or machines.[6] So radicalism retained many of the views of the groups from which it seceded; its aim was to carry them out. Obviously this meant primarily that the liberation preached by such groups should be applied to women too. But the women's movement was to be massively influenced, as this quotation suggests, by the more general failure of that Left to live according to ideals, to which Piercy alludes.

I speak of women; Piercy of 'we'. However at an early stage, as the early feminist collections show, feminists acknowledged differences between female groups. Some of the first writings, nonetheless, focus on 'women' in a way that could bring the same kind of charge levelled at liberals: that it is middle-class white women of whom they speak. (We should of course, when we say this, know that the wording is difficult to avoid.) Others are aware of the oppression of various groups, including black women, and, I believe, of the differential oppression and location of female groups.

The end result at this stage, though, is to postulate an overarching sisterhood that, because of patriarchal oppression, unites them all. This will bring a usage or perceived usage of 'patriarchy', an alleged regarding of all oppression as the same in scope and extent, that will spark the first major rejection of the term: we have seen that in Ehrenreich's speech, quoted in Chapter 2. 'Patriarchy' as an awareness of difference and an obliteration of it, an inclusion of all women and an over-inclusiveness, has its own history. That cannot be told here.

This early movement is concerned, crucially, with the relationship of ends and means, and with a radical egalitarianism as characterizing both. That is, the aim was not only to gain equality of a type that had been envisaged, but unknown. It was also to attain that via a movement whose members' treatment one of another emphasized a notion of equality and egalitarianism, of an equal respect.

I have said that the idea of radical equality, in the substantive sense, has in large part gone. What has not left feminism is the notion that human relationships can be conducted differently from the way they are, conventionally, now, and an attempt to practise that. I say this not from a naïve view that all feminists treat others well: sisterhood was perhaps ever both frail and double-edged.[7] Rather, the early ideal remains.

However, early on there were voices of dissent. I illustrate that via Freeman's 'Tyranny of structurelessness', which addresses the consequences of movement policy then. In theory all voices were equal. No one was to dominate in meetings; there would be no leaders; there would be no permanent speakers for the movement or a group. Feminism would be the very antithesis of what it opposed. There would be no political or theoretical vanguard within the movement; no elite of any form. Women would both on their own and together, that is, through communicating with others but unconstrained by them, come to see that their oppression was shared. But surely while women were thought to arrive semi-spontaneously at 'the' feminist understanding, yet other feminists knew, or thought they knew, what understanding would be gained; what the 'right ending' was.

Freeman's attack is stronger than this. Her powerful comments spring from an immediate engagement with the US movement then. (I do not imply a lack of commitment now.) She believed that the notion of attaining egalitarianism via a lack of structure had failed. For structure-lessness itself was a myth; the question was rather whether formal or informal structures would prevail. And if it were the latter, then power within the group would be hidden from most.[8]

'Tyranny' addresses the issue of elites within feminist groups. Friendship networks, bound to occur, are made more powerful, in her view, by the notion of equality, and the ensuing lack of any mechanisms to make their members accountable for their acts. The fact that group elites emerged from friendships entailed that power was derived from the criteria by which friends were chosen at a given time, rather than commitment and contribution to the feminist cause.[9] Strikingly, in the absence of spokes-persons there emerged the 'Movement Stars', who spoke for no one but themselves.[10] Though it would I suppose be more accurate to say that there was no way of assuring that what they said was what others believed; that they genuinely spoke for the 'movement' or a group.

Phillips agrees with Freeman's points on friendship, arguing that later attempts to cope with the problem made the mistake of trying even harder to avoid hierarchy, 'the risk being that this presented any shortcomings as essentially an individual's fault'. She prefers rather to 'accept that there is always a hierarchy of power, and try to make the leaders accountable to the led', as would Freeman, too.[11] However, she is concerned that mechanisms might be set up and accountability made an issue where the divergent interests that would call it forth did not exist; though as she says, 'The difficulty . . . is knowing when it does matter.'[12] Many, I assume, have thought it best to deploy procedures against the day when it does, for fear of acting too late. But of course there would be a concern about stifling spontaneity then.

Phillips would prefer to fend off Freeman's strictures in the case of small, and movement, groups. And I would like to do that too, though increasingly I lean towards an entrenching of accountability, for fairness's sake. There is a tension in Phillips here; one I feel, too. While it derives from the early Second Wave, one like it will be present, I believe, in any movement that rejects, and rejects utterly, the notion that the end justifies the means; and holds means and end to be linked.

Early radicalism produced not only such, fortunately retrieved and collated, movement tracts. There are also various books key to the grouping and to those years. Because of their greater availability and subsequent higher profile, they have had more effect. I move to possibly the most major early radical writer, in that sense, of all.

Abolishing inequality: Firestone and *The Dialectic of Sex*

... the end goal of feminist revolution must be ... not just the elimination of male *privilege* but of the sex *distinction* itself: genital differences between human beings would no longer matter culturally .... The tyranny of the biological family would be broken. And with it the psychology of power.[13]

For Firestone it is in part from sexual difference that women's subordination sprang, as reproductive biology condemned women to a fearful existence of bearing children, themselves to be oppressed, in squalor and pain. The reproductive bond is not in this account even remotely pleasing. It is wretched. Firestone then takes the logical step that follows from this belief. She proposes freeing women from their long ordeal by means of changes in reproductive technology that would allow the avoidance of pregnancy and birth as they are now.[14] Though as my quotation shows, there is more to the revolution than that; and there are more preconditions for its making than advances in the technology of reproduction, crucial though these are.

Women's and children's oppression are the most basic, and they must fall. The aim though is broader; to lift 'The double curse, that man should till the soil by the sweat of his brow ... and that woman should bear in pain and travail',[15] that we have known until now. Firestone, despite the anger at men that reverberates through her book, is not concerned with the fate of women alone.

Firestone was a 'refugee' from the New Left; this her book most clearly shows. Paradigmatically a radical feminist text of that era in its insistence on male rule and the importance of the concept of patriarchy, it employs a materialist methodology and takes as its starting-point the analysis of Marx. It departs from that to posit the division of labour by sex as the earliest and most basic division and cause of oppression, from which all other forms, including racism and classism, spring. Firestone is a theorist of the causes of sexual subjugation, and causes and maintenance of sexual difference, but she paints on a broader canvas than that.

Is biology destiny? No. Firestone has certainly been read as saying that. Indeed, she is almost always so viewed. But we could comment, part-paraphrasing Marx, that while all hitherto recorded history has been the history of biological determinism, it can and will be overcome. The aim, I add, is less to overcome 'biological fact' than the material practices it has brought about and the cultural meanings it has accrued. When Firestone speaks of the sex 'distinction', she means that.

Firestone seems to be remembered now as postulating a biological determinism qualified only insofar as massive changes in reproductive technology occur.[16] She is recalled too, of course, for an extraordinarily simple solution to the problem of biological motherhood: its abolition, following a seizure of the means of reproductive technology, whose development would offer the possibility, via 'test-tube babies', of a choice whether to bear children biologically or not. However, 'seizure' is misleading, though it is

Firestone's term, given her determinist view of how society will change: by
automation leading, through a somewhat convoluted process, to revolt.
(Not only Firestone, of course, had a vision of automation, and its
consequences, that has never been fulfilled.)

It could be argued that Firestone thinks technological childbirth neither
good nor bad. What she does say is that it might enable 'an honest
examination of the ancient value of motherhood':

> Until the taboo is lifted, until the decision not to have children or not to have
> them 'naturally' is as least as legitimate as traditional childbearing, women are
> being forced into their female roles.[17]

This belief in choice may let us read Firestone's attack on pregnancy and
childbirth now, more calmly than have some.

Firestone's assumption is not that a new reproductive technology will
automatically help women. Her real argument is that such technology
could provide the means to liberate both women and men, if it were
controlled by women and its power wielded by their hands. It is the
desirability and realism of such an assumption and deployment of
technological power that is at issue here. To think otherwise is to allot to
'technology' an existence over and above our powers, and to regard 'it' as
male biased *per se*, as distinct from being almost totally the product of
men. As Firestone says, 'the misuse of scientific developments is very often
confused with technology itself'.

Therefore women must rebel; women must control fertility. Women
must own their own bodies and new technology. And women must control
childbearing and rearing.[18]

Is Firestone a sameness-equality feminist? For her,

> The division of the psyche into male and female . . . was tragic: the hypertrophy
> in men of rationalism, aggressive drive, the atrophy of their emotional sensitivity
> was a . . . disaster. The emotionalism and passivity of women increased their
> suffering.[19]

She is then no theorist of difference as we understand it. The human has
been sundered, rent into two types of character, neither of which she
lauds. Both are clearly born of oppression, and to be overcome. They can
be, for 'revolutionary feminism' may reunite 'the personal with the public,
the subjective with the objective, the emotional with the rational – the
female principle with the male'.[20]

Thus Firestone basically believes in both sameness and equality. The
world she envisages is so different from the one we know that we can
assume equality, sameness, and difference, as issues, will there no longer
exist. Insofar as she here suggests complementary difference, it is a
difference enforced. When equality is gained, the meaning we ascribe to
sexual difference will have gone.

This is not all, relevant to equality, that Firestone had to say.[21] She
outlines the manner in which love and romance have held women
subordinate, oppressed. We see in *The Dialectic* attacks on love and

romance as they are now, but also an appreciation of 'successful' love[22] and the erotic, though allied to a belief that they are bought at massive social cost, and consist in a flight from an inimical world. But we further find, I believe, a vision of the gaining of equality within love itself. Is her suggestion feminism's last frontier? Is there love after equality? Can equality co-exist with love? Can we be equal, without conquering the asymmetry that (heterosexual) love is? Are our views of what love can be a product of the oppression we have known?

'[successful] Lovers,' says Firestone, 'are temporarily freed from the burden of isolation that every individual bears.'[23] In even bleaker vein, she writes of eroticism that:

> Life would be a drab and routine affair without at least that spark. That's just the point. Why has all joy and excitement been concentrated, driven into one narrow, difficult-to-find alley of human experience, and all the rest laid waste?[24]

Here, as in her discussion of sex objects and true beauty, Firestone's express point is that there is a problem in 'attacking the sex class system through its means of indoctrination'. In the case of beauty, the stylized object is a masquerade, itself oppressive, but among such there are the instances of the real; while in the case of the erotic, again there can be genuine joy, but by contrast with the rest of existence; whereas joy should be diffused throughout life.

The implications of her comments are these. When we attack 'eroticism' and 'beauty' we strike, in the first case, at something of an especial and genuine value to all, the more so given the way we live now, and in the second, at something that could be like that. Then the reaction against us could be overwhelming, so near to the heart have our words struck. And her book's thorough debunking despite, not all of society is brutal, not all of the masque is a mask. If we understand this we will not fall into the trap of denying ourselves pleasure now, though we must perceive its cost.

Firestone regards 'revolutionary ecology' and feminism as having arisen independently, though both in response to 'animal life within a technology'. Feminism has a moral imperative to destroy oppression, and now has a chance; 'ecology' has sprung up because of a perceived need to survive. Both however seek 'the original goal of empirical science: total mastery of nature'. Particularly pertinent to the feminist cause, we have seen, is reproductive technology, and the chance to change the way a woman bears a child.

Automation, again, depends on control. Firestone offers, I said, a somewhat determinist account of the processes that might occur, in very different form from her clarion call for women to seize reproductive technology. At first there will be 'new service jobs for women, e.g., keypunch operator, computer programmer, etc.'; they will be transient in character, hence allotted to women. However, there will arise a new technological elite, and both the new women's jobs and housework will erode. As these events occur, so general unemployment and unrest will arise. Social strife will break out and women will be impelled into revolution, creating a new ecology, in the double sense of a saved earth and interaction of person, economy, and environment.

As Second-Wave feminism has grown, the topic of technology has been raised anew, for two reasons: the coming of a feminist interrogation of the nature of scientific inquiry, and concern about technology's effect on women. The issue of reproductive technology has become crucial with the advent of techniques that allow, in particular, surrogate motherhood. Recent commentary on this has not been incorporated here; it covers a vast field. Issues entailed include the nature of contract; our ownership – or not – of our own bodies (a point raised by abortion, too); and the implications for conventional discussions of individual rights, and views of what the individual is, of the relationship between mother and foetus. In discussing this, we would have to consider developments which raise points akin to these questions but are not related to technological change, such as judgments that allow children to 'divorce' their biological parents and decide with whom they will live.

I return to Firestone's discussion. Flawed as her book is, she reminds us forcefully that feminism once was a movement for the liberation of humankind. But the condition for us believing that is and should be so, I argue, is this: that we accept one very central point of the argument that Firestone puts. We must believe, with her, that women's oppression is the most basic, and that from which all other forms spring. Then working for women's liberation is self-evidently to work for the freedom and equality of all. And then revolutionary activity is not a wager, accompanied by self-sacrifice, for the second of which, some would argue, we are born or trained.[25] We do not have to think we must choose, in some extra-ordinarily altruistic manner, to bear the burdens of all the oppressed: as our oppression is conquered, so will be the oppression of all. If it is not, others' will remain.

If we do not believe this we retain (here I paraphrase Firestone) the goal of eliminating the cultural meaning of genital difference. That is liberal feminism's aim, too. It alone is no small task.

A belief in total equality in economic and social terms is decidedly unfashionable, now. It has frequently been considered abhorrent, and still is, because of the total sameness it is thought to presuppose. One image and caricature of it has always been the 'Communist China' of millions dressed in grey. One anti-equality chorus has always been, 'levelling down'. I have known genetic engineering – in this case, cloning – opposed because 'If all horses are as fast as [the Derby winner], it won't be any fun.' And of expansion in Higher Education once Conservatives would have said, as a reflex, 'More means worse.'

The examples I give are hardly sophisticated. They are however real-life instances of a reaction to something that is, I believe, denied and feared. They represent an opposition to greater equality – for it is not, really, radical equality such commentators have faced – from those who are precisely 'more equal than others'. Do they flinch because they are unsure of their ground?

For what I take to be the majority of the Left now, which once sought such an equality, it is thought impossible too. To try to explain that is not my task. I do want to point to a certain gap in feminism. Early radicalism was to fade so quickly that we have no analysis from within it of how the equality *in each and every sphere of life*, which it postulates, was to be obtained, though Firestone's determinist road to her form of the early Marxist dream – a dream more or less as ill-specified as his – gives us a glimpse.

I have discussed Firestone on love. Early radicalism addressed many different points, took various issues up. But radical feminism has been associated with an emphasis on sexuality and sexual politics – though not only because of Firestone – ever since.

The longest revolution? Juliet Mitchell and the Left

In the UK, too, there was an 'early radicalism' that grappled with the Left, though of a different kind. Mitchell provides an example of a similarly disaffected view of the Left to theirs, and those in the US.[26] I discuss a piece that is *sui generis* in that it was published two to three years before the movement in this country began, that is, before even the first – or first vaguely viable – groups were set up. (Though there is a serious problem of lack of knowledge here, it is plain that Mitchell wrote early.) The piece is 'Women, the longest revolution', first published in 1966.[27]

The preface to a later edition locates Mitchell's concern as directly linked to the theories and character of the Left, though there is no direct parallel, here, with events in the US. (However, Mitchell may have been untypical in this respect, given what seems to have been the strength of her position on the Left.) The British New Left was then discussing the possibility of revolution in the Third World: Mitchell was concerned by a '[women's liberation] after the Revolution' attitude in their approach. And women's absence from Marxist meetings gave Mitchell to wonder, moved her to anger.[28]

If 'Women' is a more tightly theoretical, more accomplished piece than the American tracts, that is in part because of Mitchell's academic and intellectual training, in part because of the particular Marxist tradition from which she came, a tradition that allows an emphasis on ideology's role.

For Mitchell, women, who are importantly different from other groups is that they are fundamental to humanity, are nonetheless marginal too. They are marginal throughout the public sphere, in all its forms. Their (waged) work is marginal to the economy as a whole; they are marginal in the sphere of production, where society itself is produced. This is the 'world of men'. Women's place is the family, which is a social construct, as are they.[29]

> It is the function of ideology to present these given social types as aspects of Nature itself. Both can be exalted, paradoxically, as ideals. The 'true' woman and the 'true' family are images of peace and plenty: in actuality they may both be sites of violence and despair.[30]

Women's subordination is maintained and reinforced by a lulling, compelling, but not utterly imaginary 'myth'. Much of what we regard as womanhood derives from that myth. Mitchell is then an equality feminist.

Set in a Marxist conceptual framework, historically grounded, 'Women' can only superficially be compared with the liberal view of Friedan, despite its focus on women in the economy and the attack on the family and on 'woman'. The distinction holds despite the nature of the attack, and the invocation of a 'myth' that is partly true: despite, that is, the return of the mystique. What is interesting about Mitchell's Marxism, among Marxist feminism of the Second Wave, and gives it an affinity with much later and rather different thought, is precisely this view of woman and the family, and of 'reality' as socially made.

There has, Mitchell believes, been a 'counter-revolution' within socialist thought – revolutionary or otherwise – consisting in a comparative neglect of women, and support of the family. This change constitutes a departure from the founding Marxists;[31] though even they she regards as at best viewing women's liberation as an add-on, presumably *ad hoc*, to revolutionary theory, and not an integral part.[32]

While Mitchell writes toughly, she also writes soberly. But she is making the same point as the women who abandoned the US New Left. Socialism has betrayed women; it has betrayed its own ideals of what humanity could become by relegating half the people of the world to the second league (or below). How the subordination of women came about – for the points given above, concerning the economy, are for a Marxist not enough – remains open, given Mitchell's doubts about the position of women in classic Marxist thought.

The theoretical task, the feminist theoretical and political goal, for Mitchell, is to examine the various structures which comprise the complex unity that is woman. This being is not static. History enters here. Woman has been variously produced, constituted, and viewed; and, says Mitchell, *determined*.[33] However, the notion is not one of total determinism, by various structures acting upon women in a mutually reinforcing way. Or rather, it might be, though that would deny the extent to which 'woman' and the 'structures' interact.

Before turning to the structures of which Mitchell speaks, I note that it is difficult to address texts from her school without adopting its language: my aim is to make the discussion intelligible without misrepresenting the world view from which her analysis springs.

The key point about the structures is that first, they are not always, only 'ultimately', subordinate to the economy, and second, that they are separate and autonomous one from another. At one time, they will act in concert. At another time, not. Key to this point is the notion of contradictions more complex than social contradictions as normally conceived. When contradictions are sufficiently reinforcing, the moment of revolution comes. What agency have women? We will see.

The major structures that decide the female condition are production, reproduction, sex, and the socialization of children.

Within production, an emphasis on physical strength, and an ensuing assumption that women were unsuited for rough manual waged work, together with the notion that domestic labour was not 'productive', relegated women to a secondary place. But as Mitchell points out, women have always worked; even if we discount domestic work – whose arduous character is ignored – that is so. Nor has the non-domestic work been physically easy. Historically, culturally, women's work has varied, and does. When women are needed – as in early industrialization – their work will be coerced. 'This is . . . woman's condition'. It is simply untrue that women's greater physical weakness has 'exempted' them from productive labour. Rather, they have been for that very reason prey to the needs of the time.[34] Given this situation, women unlike men cannot even 'create the *pre*conditions of [their] liberation':[35] for in this analysis, those preconditions cannot be forged except by a continual presence in waged work.

The claims of reproduction, too, have kept women from the productive sphere, and so from the road to freedom. It is not childbearing as such that necessitates this, but the whole structure built on and resting upon it, of reproduction, sexuality, and the socialization of children. For Mitchell these are contingently connected; they come together in the 'family', an untheorized entity that appears to legitimize, make inevitable, women's subordination. We begin, she believes, to see a possible change with the coming of the contraceptive pill, which will separate sexuality from reproduction.[36]

The reproductive sphere itself is not a place of joy for women. Mitchell calls it 'a sad mimicry of production'. The child becomes a product and possession. Anything it does is then 'a threat to the mother . . . who has renounced her autonomy through this misconception of her reproductive role. There are few more precarious ventures on which to base a life.'[37]

And of course mother and children are in effect owned by a man. The family home is a place where he can escape the bonds of exploitation, or apparently so, flee the demands of 'work', and recuperate and rest.[38] While Mitchell does not quite say so, it seems that for women there is no such escape.

Women are, in most societies we know, both the bearers and rearers, and so primary socializers, of their children; of a society's young. Precisely because it has been felt that one parent must fulfil what is called the expressive (basically, the omnipresent, caring, and nurturant) role, and that is assumed for physiological reasons to be the mother, they are yet further confined within the home. For Mitchell – who notes with concern that as less of a woman's life is spent in childbearing, more is spent in rearing – this structure is oppressive and must be transformed.

But then, all the structures must change. Of these sexuality has, she feels, the most potential. I do not intend discussing her views on this. For her discussion of sexuality differs from that of the other structures in being a child of its time and, I think, only that: a kind of comment on the 'Sixties Sexual Revolution' which sees it as a subversive force.[39] I am not promoting a return to a lifelong alleged monogamy when I assert that Mitchell's view has had its day.

How will change – revolutionary change, which Mitchell wants – come? Like Bunch – though she puts the point very differently – Mitchell sees a need for reforms, 'immediate demands', as well. Women must enter productive work, but the work must be equal. Education, then, must be radically changed, for it is the precondition for that. And various forms of sexuality, reproduction, and socialization need to be freed from state control and their association – or not – with the family. Mitchell's idea here is, it seems clear, that rather than carry hypothetical banners saying 'Abolish the family', we create the conditions under which it implodes.[40]

Mitchell, like Firestone, cannot entirely specify the future's human bonds, but her picture of varied associations of groups and individuals does not differ that much. Finally: why is women's liberation 'the longest revolution'? We are frequently disillusioned when we return to well-known texts; it is only fair to emphasize how early 'Women' was written, when we appraise the conclusion I give now. Angry with the Left as she is, Mitchell believes that socialism will come first – though after, as I read her, the equality of men and women in society as we know it now: a liberal equality, therefore – and 'the liberation of women *under socialism* will [come] . . . in the long passage from Nature to Culture which is the definition of history and society' [italics mine].[41]

The critical interrogation of 'nature', though not entirely as meant by Mitchell here, is key to liberal feminism and early radicalism. The 'mastery of nature' is crucial to feminism, in Firestone's view. And liberals are accused of adopting a 'male' nature–culture dualism. I move to thinkers who would, on the contrary, recall us to our 'nature' – and some, to Nature – and for whom culture can mean something to do with women, alone.

Notes

1 Betty Friedan, *The Second Stage*, 1983; Janet Radcliffe Richards, *The Sceptical Feminist*, 1980.

2 Charlotte Bunch, 'The reform tool kit', in 'Quest', *Building Feminist Theory: Essays from 'Quest'*, 1981, p. 196ff.

3 Michèle Barrett, 'Introduction to the 1988 edition', in *Women's Oppression Today*, 1988, p. 4. Rosa Braidotti, too, has paid eloquent tribute to the power of these writings: *Patterns of*

Dissonance, 1991, p. 151ff. especially pp. 152–3. See also Joan Cocks, *The Oppositional Imagination: Feminism, Critique and Political Theory*, 1989, pp. 10–11.

4 Jo Freeman, *The Tyranny of Structurelessness*, 1984 (first published in 1970).

5 Marge Piercy, 'The grand coolie damn', in Robin Morgan (ed.), *Sisterhood is Powerful*, 1970, p. 438.

6 Paul Jacobs and Saul Landau, *The New Radicals*, 1967, ch. 6.

7 Sheila Rowbotham, 'Feminism and democracy', in David Held and Christopher Pollitt (eds), *New Forms of Democracy*, 1986.

8 Freeman, *Tyranny*, p. 6.

9 Ibid., pp. 7–9.

10 Ibid., p. 10.

11 Anne Phillips, *Engendering Democracy*, 1991, pp. 133–5.

12 Ibid., pp. 135–6.

13 Shulamith Firestone, *The Dialectic of Sex*, 1971, pp. 10–12.

14 There is of course the option of 'humanizing' gynaecological and obstetric practice. That too has been a feminist cause.

15 Firestone, *Dialectic of Sex*, p. 274.

16 Ibid., pp. 228–9.

17 Ibid., pp. 225–6.

18 Ibid., p. 66.

19 Ibid., p. 18.

20 Ibid., p. 19.

21 Nor is it possible to give all her points here.

22 I am referring here, as is Firestone, to heterosexual love only. Compulsory heterosexuality will be discussed below.

23 Firestone, *Dialectic of Sex*, p. 145.

24 Ibid., p. 175.

25 See Chapter 7.

26 I have on occasion remained close to Mitchell's wording, as to depart too far from her terminology is to be unfaithful to her thought.

27 I here employ the version in Juliet Mitchell, *Women: the Longest Revolution: Essays in Feminism, Literature and Psychoanalysis*, 1984.

28 Mitchell, 1984, p. 17.

29 Ibid., pp. 18–19.

30 Ibid., p. 19.

31 She cites Marx and, more particularly, Engels and Bebel.

32 Mitchell, *Women*, pp. 19–24.

33 Ibid., p. 26.

34 Ibid., p. 27ff.

35 Ibid., p. 30.

36 Ibid., p. 33.

37 Ibid.

38 Ibid., p. 34.

39 Mitchell does think it might have the opposite effect; ibid., pp. 38–9.

40 Ibid., pp. 50–3.

41 Ibid., p. 54.

6

Cultural Feminism: Feminism's First Difference

Early radicalism knew the importance of differences between groups of women; but that knowledge was of a rather rudimentary form, and except for a few writers, was lost. The knowledge of the salience of gender sameness or difference, of course, never was. While both early radicalism and liberal feminism believed the sexes differed, neither saw the distinctions as innate. They tended to view them negatively, though there were certain liberal feminists who wanted to make female values and qualities known, and would even rest a case for advancement upon them. Further, some early feminists would – even if we say this by inference – adopt the attributes of men, while others believed that the current characteristics of both sexes were warped. All these opinions, in my view, entail a belief in characteristics that are not innate, and most, in their being socially produced.

Here I introduce and discuss a distinct attitude towards sexual or gender difference: contemporary feminism's first major engagement with it, and the one on which it could be said to concentrate the most now. The tendency is of course cultural feminism; to be called 'strong' cultural feminism here.[1] It is distinguished from previous difference beliefs, within the second wave, by its insistence that women's characteristics and values are for the good, indeed are superior and ethically prior to men's, and should be upheld. They and certain of women's roles (for various writers, motherhood would be a case in point) have been derogated, devalued, by men. It is part, anyway, of feminism's task to revalue them, to reclaim woman's heritage, or woman's pride.

These writers then believe in neither androgyny nor complementary difference. They have no interest in allying the (good) characteristics of women and men; nor would sameness appeal. They are celebrating *women*; in part, as they could be. For in theory, anyway, and as these writers are normally viewed, key to their stance is that women's virtues have been despised rather than stamped out.

Before addressing these thinkers I shall explain a point crucially important in any event, but specifically for the discussion here and later in the book: the sex–gender distinction, and the implications of using its terms.[2]

Sex of course refers to biological sex, an assumed biological 'fact'; and normally we think in terms of two dichotomous sexes. Despite my qualification below, I shall try to use the term in that way throughout.

Gender is a social construct. Normally we think and speak of two genders, one mapped on to each sex. Again, that is the way I shall tend to speak. I shall return to the distinction between sex and gender, and its importance, in Chapter 10.

Commentators on sex and gender, however, those who dislike 'gender' apart, would differ on various points. For some physiologists and social scientists, sex is a continuum, and gender the dichotomy. Others would disagree, arguing that only on the margin, and among relatively few, do the biological sexes 'merge'. Others employ a wide definition of gender which seems to encompass sexual preference and age. There is a middle view: a notion expressed in Rich's 'any gender'; that meaning, I think, sexual preference.[3] I have an affection for this slightly broader usage, but will not employ it here.

Cultural feminists reject gender as we know it, and endorse a different version of its claims, countering the androgynies, and complementary differences, described above. Are they, therefore, essentialist? Do they believe that women's qualities are in some sense innate, unchanging, and incapable of being changed? That is a difficult judgement to make. However I shall try to say what essentialism – and universalism, on occasion confused with it[4] – mean, by reference to a writer who has made a sustained attempt to define the first term, in the context of feminist thought: Elizabeth Grosz.

Within feminism, essentialism, strictly speaking, means that the characteristics of a group of people (normally women's) are basically static. No outside force can change what is 'essentially' there (though it could be suppressed by force, I assume, or muted by being devalued, or 'masked').[5] For 'essentialist' feminists, women's basic qualities do not vary historically, across culture, race, or class. Further – of course, this does not follow logically – they are benign: women are kind, women nurture, and women care.

It is common for feminists to employ 'nurture' and 'nurturant' as if they were clearly words that implied something good about the character of the person to whom they refer. 'Care', also, is often used like that. In Chapter 7 I argue that the situation is less straightforward. For the moment I say simply that all 'nurture' has to mean is the action of caring for children – and, it seems, men.

Praise of these attributes does not mean that they are complementary to any male qualities; there is no place for that form of androgyny or deferred androgyny in the writings I discuss here. Nor is there a notion of progress towards equality with men. These cultural feminists share with early radicals a strong notion of patriarchy; they lack a vision of its substantive overthrow.

Most essentialist feminists, thinks Grosz, believe in biological causation for female character; though sometimes woman's nature is given by God. Or, she suggests, an 'as it were ontological' existentialist or psychoanalytic view is held.[6] Female qualities, then, are in some sense innate.

Very few of this particular difference school are essentialist in its full sense. What they share is this, they see a universality among women – women having something overriding in common – and diverge from 'earlier' schools in that they endorse it, and more. That is, rather than castigate the feminine mystique they will praise it, revalue traits despised – they say – by men, and devalued by society, exalting motherhood, nature, and all that they associate with these.

This approach is problematic even if we accept its emphasis on culture. It ignores differences among groups of women, or is unable to address them adequately. It faces the danger that female virtue can be used against women, and has been. It may merely echo woman as described by patriarchy, may simply invert the dualisms we know. Further, feminists like these are often regarded as elitists who 'know' what women are, should be, can be, should say: who know what 'woman' can be. And there remains the issue of who decides what bona fide female experience is.

While conventionally thought to characterize 'strong' cultural feminism, these points are not entirely true of Daly, and hardly at all of Rich, despite so frequently being aimed at them. It would make more sense to level certain of the charges at the 'weak' cultural feminism described in Chapter 7. I hope to show their problematic character, when aimed at the writers I address, below.

Universalism, when employed in feminist thought, is distinct from this, though I suspect the two can be confused and 'shade' into each other. It is as I understand it a generalizing about 'women' without taking into account possible differences between groups. No belief about female character, and no specific cause of a given generalization, is implied.

It is a universalist (and obnoxious, and wrong; though very hard to avoid) language and assumption that is exposed in *All the Women Are White, All the Blacks Are Men*.[7] But equally, 'Women strongly oppose nuclear weapons', or 'Women support abortion', would be universalist comments, or would sound as if they were, even though their intent was to say that a majority of women, or a greater percentage of women than men, think this. Both empirical and theoretical writings are bedevilled by this usage. While it is one from which it is difficult to escape, writers should be more aware of the pitfalls involved.

Feminists also employ 'universalism' as it would be normally used: to mean universal as opposed to specific, the differing cultures and contexts in which different groups of women live, not necessarily in mind.[8] So we might speak of 'universal', universally applicable, values of freedom and justice; or of universal truths. While some feminists will argue that it is possible to talk like that, others will say such notions are culture bound. And some go further, arguing that the universalist is a product of the male: a notion antithetical to female and other advance.

Cultural feminism is further marked, diverging in this from, say, 'difference' liberal feminism, by two separatist beliefs. The first is a generally separatist view: women must live and work apart from men.

Most contemporary adherents of this tenet would I imagine accept that total separatism is impossible. This is a simple practical point, which does not affect the fact that they would prefer not to mingle with, will not work politically with, men. They will be as separatist as societal arrangements allow. The second belief concerns the reclaimed values of which it speaks. These values will not – or not in this version of cultural feminism – be deployed to reform the public world, to redress its wrongs. They do not, whatever their source, stem from a context which men could share, so from which they too might acquire them: a point that distinguishes this aspect of cultural feminism from 'liberal difference' views.

Nor are such values, context derived or not, seen as complementary to male characteristics, as capable therefore of contributing to 'androgyny', in the sense in which we will see it attacked below. Women are reclaiming themselves, finding or remaking their culture, by and for themselves. Hence, I suppose, the terms 'cultural feminism' and 'the woman-centred school'. Though it should be added that there is no genuine feminist agreement on, no definitive account of, what a woman's culture or 'woman-culture' might be.

Throughout feminist history, while some have asked for equality on the basis of sameness, some have argued via difference, on the basis that the values and virtues of women could and should be used to better the public realm by woman's entry into public, and more especially political, life. While the second view is still held by some, it seems to have faltered for two reasons. First, as we have seen, there is a form of equality feminism that is said to fear difference, and certainly will not make use of it in its demands. Second, there has emerged the appeal of cultural feminism and/ or, an abhorrence of all that pertains or is said to pertain to the public realm, as man made.

However, the earlier positive view of the merits of deploying female values to the public good has returned in some strength, with the important distinction that the virtues of the female are not always seen as unproblematic and that, in theory at least, essentialism is not involved. Renouncing essentialism has its own, possibly negative, implications for feminism, as we will see.

The cultural feminism reviewed in this chapter sees matters differently. Its major authors believe – or so I suppose – either that there is a separate and benign woman-culture that must remain apart, or that the world of men is irremediably bad. They could believe both. 'Cultural' feminism certainly seems to imply the first, though the question arises of what we mean by culture, here.

My comment does not rest on the idea of 'culture' in one popular sense, as something 'higher' than the 'uncultured'. Nor can the meaning be akin to say 'French culture', that is, to the supposition that a way of life and thought derives from a basic monopoly of territorial space. It is the burden of much feminist literature that women do not have *any* form of 'space' that is their own.

What I say here concerns modern cultural feminism in its early days, and is held to be true insofar as radical cultural feminism can be said to form one school. That matters are not so simple, we will see. But they may never have been as simple as was commonly thought. To illustrate this, I shall discuss works by Mary Daly, Andrée Collard and Joyce Contrucci, and Adrienne Rich.[9]

Mary Daly: naming, renaming, changing the world?

Daly has no doubt that women are oppressed, and that at the centre of this oppression stands patriarchy: in this version, the untrammelled rule of men. Women have been materially, physically, oppressed; but also, women have been psychologically oppressed: devalued and defamed. The very language that describes women is base, and women are debased by it. But more or less anyone could say this, and many feminists have. In what sense does Daly go further than to express our usual dislike of the words that point to women's being feared, hated, and held in contempt? What is distinctive about her analysis of language and its use?

First, Daly singles out woman-hating words, some of which were once prized. Rather than employ other terms, she seeks to recall and regain women's heritage and prime by altering, some would say, inverting, their meaning and use. (Though 'meaning' may be misleading, here.) She is engaged in subverting the male linguistic project by using certain of the names of insult – hag, crone, spinster – with pride. In that sense, her politics is, I believe, a form of identity politics: a politics I address in Chapters 8 and 9. But it is an unusual one; it takes a highly atypical form. Many would regard it as no longer a politics.

The feminist voyage is linguistic, infused with allegory and myth. Or so her account would suggest. It is an inner, a spiritual, voyage. That is the kind of reason why it has been said of Daly, as of this 'school' as a whole, that she turns from politics to mysticism.[10]

That women are indeed supposed to overcome oppression via language, and a voyage of the mind and heart, is shown clearly by Daly's 'Foreword' to an ecofeminist work by a follower of her views, where she renounces any notion of taking part in a movement led by men, of supporting 'female self-sacrifice' in such a cause. Rather: 'I am affirming that those women who have the courage to break the silence within our Selves are finding/creating/spiraling a new Spring.'[11] She embraces the cause to the extent that she does, regards herself as an 'ecologist', only because '*Women and our kind* – the earth, the sea, the sky – are the real but unacknowledged objects of attack, victimized as The Enemy of patriarchy.'[12] Therefore for her, too, feminism is about the advancement of women, and that alone. How it is to happen is obscure; as is what 'equality' might mean, here.

For Tong, Daly inverts the value system of the patriarchs, and so what they consider bad, she will see as good. Further she will see it as good precisely because they see it as bad, or bad because they see it as good. Hence her fondness for, for example, 'hag' and 'crone'.

Certainly Daly opposes the patriarchal value system; that is a mild way of phrasing the point. But she is not saying, for example, 'hag is good', let alone 'I believe hags are good because men think them bad', or, 'Hags must be good; men think them bad.' (I do a certain violence to Tong's analysis here. But I convey the image that part of her work evokes and that remains with me now.) Daly's message is not, 'what you dislike, I commend'. Or not only that. She changes the meaning of say 'crone', both to expose the hatred of women which lies behind the term as it is used now, and to make it a word of pride. There is a sense in which her linguistic project also says to men, 'and I simply do not care what you think'.

However what Daly is really saying – here I recapitulate, in part – is I think this. Language has power over us, though it can also empower. Men have used language – though not only language – to denigrate us. Let us reclaim those words of debasement, words like hag and crone, and bear them with pride.

Daly rejects, has abandoned, androgyny, in either sense of the term.[13] Indeed, very early on she caricatures complementary androgyny as 'something like "John Travolta and Farrah Fawcett Majors scotch-taped together"',[14] and it is precisely that kind of idea she attacks. The very notion of combining alleged good qualities of patriarchs and women seems to her absurd: so much so that rather than waste time and argument on the idea, she sweeps it aside.

Before further discussing what equality and difference might mean in this context, I note that roughly one-third of *Gyn/Ecology*, perhaps her best-known work, is devoted to charting the subjugation of women, their maltreatment, in various parts of the world. Here the project is not a matter of naming, nor does she suggest that the trials women have known can be overcome by revaluation and a 'woman-culture' pride. Though she does not say it explicitly, she knows, physical and psychological torture are no mere devaluation and debasement of woman and the good.

I am saying this in part to rescue Daly from a charge of rampant idealism; from an epistemological stance that, I believe, can say nothing convincing about oppression and its defeat. I want to show that she knows that women are oppressed, as well as defamed. But to point this out is also to show an incoherence at the heart of this stage of her thought.

It is one thing to celebrate a 'spinster' as one who 'spins', as part of the process of weaving the webs of life. It is another to attempt to apply this kind of process to genital mutilation or *sati*. Not that Daly tries. But how would she work for the women so harmed? She cannot say, 'By exposing their oppression.' For does she not think that all women are, though perhaps not equally, oppressed? Why are only some women helped, by cataloguing their ills?

Admittedly Daly faces a dilemma here. For it may be that she should not work for such women. Can she speak of or for them? How adequately does she do either, in this book? Can she address other cultures? How well? It is Audre Lorde's suggestion that Daly has been insensitive, indeed racist, in more than one way. Invoking the Goddesses of the West to show that women once held power, she does not mention those of the East. This omission adds, in Lorde's view, to her tendency to see women of colour only as victims.[15] Further, she says, while of course *sati* and genital mutilation, in particular, must be opposed, Daly should try to comprehend them in the context of the culture of which they are a part.[16]

Daly is a male–female separatist. This is not a tactical move, ceasing when equality is gained, or rather, when oppression is overcome. For equality with men, in any way that we can conceive of that, is not the aim. Equality of women, in one sense, is. Those who join the voyage will find their own ending. I take it, such women will be equal in the sense that they choose their journey's end. These will, Daly's words suggest, differ. Can women then be equal? It may be that within the context of Daly's thought, this question does not make sense. Or it may be that their equality lies in a freedom to find, during and at the end of the voyage, their own self, their own ending, and their own peace.

Who are Daly's sisters? Who can be regarded as her equal? Or worthy of equal consideration? Not simply those who join the 'flight' now. Rather any woman who has helped others – she instances Simone de Beauvoir – is a BeFriender, and so a sister. Then Daly gives women more ideological space than we might expect; accepts more women than we might think, into her Pantheon, and, if in honorary mode only, to her flight. Though by no means all.

Gyn/Ecology is deliberately allegorical and mythic in large part. If such works can be seen as allegories, play the part of myths, be regarded as inspirational stories, then they should not be expected to provide a political plan, need not detract from female advance. For they can politicize, if not in a conventional sense, and awaken the subjugated female self.

Ending the man-made: the ecofeminism of Andrée Collard

Collard's *Rape of the Wild*[17] is a fairly classic cultural ecofeminist work. Collard speaks for those for whom man is the enemy of womankind, and of the whole earth.

Once, says this story, there were women who held power, though not as men do. Once there were matriarchies who worshipped Earth-Goddesses. Such groupings knew no hierarchy. They were overthrown by the rule of men and their gods, and so their values were replaced by the values of hierarchy and self-seeking individualism, and a lust for power.

Women must learn about, and remember, those years. Otherwise they will try to be like men. They will adopt their values and seek 'equality' rather than the 'kinship, egalitarianism and nurturance-based values' that ruled in those times.[18] In the centuries since then, women have been oppressed, as has nature:

> processed in the same way as foods: breaking down, removal of essential parts, replacement with man-made additives, reconstruction into artificial aggregates.[19]
> 'Properly reared pets' have a great deal in common with the well-adjusted women and people of colour whom the white man has conquered/colonised/enslaved.[20]

So are women subjugated; their beliefs and values downgraded. Our interests, and those of the 'natural' world, are denied or ignored.

But patriarchy has not banished women's prior, cherished, link to nature, the good qualities we possess. For women share the experience of childbearing and rearing with 'the rest of the living world', whether we are or have been mothers or not.[21] Here is genuine essentialism, of the kind I mentioned above. For how but through female biology could there be such a link?

Collard gives us an extreme, though not unique, cultural feminist account. For her women are inherently different from, and better than, men. That is a biological matter, and stems from innate ties to the 'natural', to the earth. 'Equality' – on which she does not expand – is for her a male value: though her comments can be construed, and perhaps most fairly are, as seeing it as equality within a hierarchical framework, within which a divisive self-interest holds sway. If she had used my language, that is, she would counterpose some form of equality of opportunity, within a highly competitive system, to radical equality in an egalitarian world.

Is the latter something women can attain? The golden past will not return. However, women can choose a way of life that celebrates closeness to the earth. They can resist technology, refuse non-natural medicine, avoid the products of the tortured animal world. And they can – I mean this kindly – cultivate their gardens and so 'reclaim' part of the earth. I see the appeal of this. But it is a retreat.

Loving like a woman: Adrienne Rich

Rich, too, is concerned with the way women have been oppressed, and women and their activities have been devalued. She emphasizes the difference between the way being a woman, as institutionalized in our society, is, and the way it could be; and between how some behaviour is viewed now, and how it should be. So like the Daly of *Gyn/Ecology*, she addresses both material and psychological oppression. She prioritizes the former, and allies her proposals for coping with both. I argue this in relation to *Of Woman Born*, which discusses motherhood as it is now, and as it could be.[22]

Very near the beginning of her book Rich denies the existence of a nurturing instinct, and so would seem to reject essentialism. Her position appears in some ways to be more materialist than cultural feminist, in that she links women in general to motherhood with the comment that historically all have been related to it in one way or another, that is, as members of extended groups.[23] And these statements are followed by the setting out of a position characteristic of Rich — we will see it also in her writing on lesbianism, discussed below. She distinguishes between motherhood's 'potential', and motherhood as an 'institution', the latter related to, and ensuring, the domination of men.

Motherhood as institution has been crucial to social systems many in number and varied in kind. Although Rich does not say 'all', one feels she means that. Motherhood gives women power. But female power brings male dislike and retaliation; male myths of mother-power, many taking a malignant view of the mother, bring more. Motherhood, then, has been a poisoned chalice. 'If rape has been terrorism, motherhood has been servitude.' However, '*It need not be.*'[24]

Rich's own memories of motherhood are dramatically mixed, the good inseparable from the bad. She visited her mixed emotions on her children and now bemoans the 'waste' of her life and the maiming of the mother–child relationship, 'the great original source and experience of love'.[25] Motherhood so moulded and so experienced, the major source of women's inequality, denies to us also — this is its most powerful aspect, its most fearful, too — authentic love.

For Rich, then, there is nothing 'natural' about the entire complex that is motherhood now, a process with its own history, deep-rooted ideology, of and stemming from patriarchal control.[26] Nor is there anything innate about the behaviour and emotions involved: 'We learn . . . those qualities . . . : patience, self-sacrifice, the willingness to repeat endlessly the small, routine chores of socializing a human being',[27] together with the fierce mixture of love and violence by which a mother would kill for her child (or feels that she would). And yet women, powerless in patriarchal society, may well visit their sense of that lack of power on the only creature over whom they have even a vestige of it, treating a child as the world has treated them. Nor need this amount to 'cruelty' in any generally accepted understanding of the word. It may, anyway, massively damage a child.

That a woman would kill for her children is an integral part of her beliefs. Rich says also, however, that frequently a mother feels, as she has, as have women to whom she has 'confessed', that she would kill the child herself. She charts the years before a mother can say this, and recounts how heart-wrenching it is to admit, even then.

I have mentioned patriarchy, and its different usages, before. We meet in Rich, who mingles generalization and nuance, an attack on Marxist and Maoist regimes, though not on them alone, as part of a universal, though not transhistorical, comment: 'There is nothing revolutionary whatsoever about the control of women's bodies by men. The woman's body is the terrain on which patriarchy is erected.'[28]

Now for the first time,[29] there is a chance of change, an appreciation of 'the *possibilities* inherent in beneficent female power, as a mode which is absent from the society at large, and which, even in the private sphere, women have exercized under terrible constraints'.[30]

How exactly this would come about is not clear. Even bearing a child remains, particularly it seems in the US, literally in the hands of others. And Rich, quoting Suzanne Arms, points out that what a woman brings to the process cannot easily and quickly be changed given the long history of 'ingrained fear, expectations of pain, and obeisance to male dominance'.[31] Nonetheless she wants women who so choose to be able to reject obstetricians' care.

One reason for being sceptical about the Rich of *Of Woman Born* – only one of her works, of course, but major; perhaps her best known – is her insistence that unless the conditions of birth are changed, other changes will mean nothing.[32] Admittedly if birth remains as she describes it, an important part of *some* women's experience will remain submissive, passive, and subordinate. But why should that nullify other change?

I now address an aspect of her language that is relevant to my point above. Rich, in many ways no universalist, yet for most of her work talks as if all women were mothers. But of course she does not think that, nor does she believe that 'non-mothers' necessarily share experiences with those who are, as Collard does.[33]

We must say 'non-mothers' here because Rich sees a variability in 'mothers', too, and a problem of definition. Though she tends to assume that women without children would have borne or reared them if they could, ultimately her view is this. The 'unchilded' are affected by attitudes towards 'the birthing, childrearing function of women'.[34] That statement seems to me to be true, and powerfully so. It is not celebratory in any way; it does not suggest universal 'potential motherhood' links: by the extant form of the institution, by the views held about it, by the very belief that because we can bear children, we *should*, we are all oppressed.

I turn to the Afterword, importantly different from stereotypical 'cultural feminist' views. First, Rich believes that far from boycotting science, and more particularly, forms of science that might be relevant to reproductive change, women must become scientists within those fields (and other women, lay experts who 'monitor' activity, and broadcast the information gained). Second, women must be especially wary of deciding that 'nurturance' is an especial female strength and promoting that as capable of creating a new regime; for the ploy can become a trap. So in this respect, anyway, Rich shares the equality feminist concern about 'difference' I have discussed. Nonetheless, for her, all eventually rests on the female body: it is therefore a tactic that she describes above. What the final road to equality is for her, then, we cannot know.

Rich is also known for her controversial proposal of a 'lesbian continuum'.[35] Her proposal is that all women are lesbian, insofar as they want to identify with other women, though this does not mean they must *be* lesbians. Indeed, for not suggesting this, she has been attacked. For her, compulsory heterosexuality maintains female subordination as it demands that women identify with men. So strong is the institution that it has not been asked, or has been asked only by a few, why the mother–daughter bond does not lead to a primary identification with women instead.

For Rich, there is a sense in which women lead double lives, though this does not mean in any way consciously living a lie. Lesbianism is hidden from us, 'written out'. However – and this is the general pattern of her thought – Rich does make it clear that while she is opposed to heterosexuality, by this she means compulsory heterosexuality, as it exists now.[36]

Diana Fuss has noted that Rich seems to see compulsory heterosexuality as in some way concerned with men, that is, all men.[37] Indeed, she regards homosexual men as implicated in it, and thinks it serves their interests. Fuss is decidedly tart about the fact that the alliance Rich wants is not one of gays and lesbians, but of all women. This I rather think returns me to my comments on what feminism is. Does Rich's stance emerge from the fact that she supports, wishes to advance, *all* women? Alternatively, does it relate to a wish to further the interests of women, *alone*? There is nothing in either stance that rules out feminism. On the contrary, I am inclined to suggest that they describe it well. Neither rules out a stance antithetical to gay or black men. I do not think feminism can be defined in a way that avoids this. For me, and many others, this means there will be people called feminists of whom we think ill. This is something feminists have to face. Whoever thought it could be different?

There is though an aspect of Rich's work that suggests she can be impugned on this ground. She is frequently concerned to point out the ambivalences in women, the ambiguities women face. But she does – and she is not the only such writer – take an essentialist, or at least universalist, view of men. And yet, Rich's poetry is not, has never been, what this last comment suggests.[38]

I have read Daly and Rich, like other authors I address, anew. More than some whom I discuss, I have read them afresh. I do not see them as I did when I began this book; I regard them as far more nuanced, less prone to charges of essentialism, than I did then. Though of course I know that my reading could be wrong. As cultural feminism is a powerful school, and will endure, I interpret them via a major commentator, Linda Alcoff, now.[39]

Alcoff addresses what has become a major problem for feminism, in various ways: the concept of woman. It is obviously a central problem. Throughout this book we have seen the consequences of taking the notion for granted, without qualification: without understanding that 'a woman is not all we are'.[40] But Alcoff's concern springs from the philosophically more radical point that an emancipatory practice allegedly built on experience founds itself on a constituency constructed by the practices of man. Woman's 'experience', her 'interests', are constructed – and construed – by the very social order within which she is oppressed; in this version, by men. It is poststructuralism's woman of whom we speak here, I believe. Though Alcoff's point is rather that poststructuralist feminism and cultural feminism form the two major suggested answers to the problem posed above.

Cultural feminism meets the challenge by asserting that only women can say what 'woman' is; can describe women; can say how they are to be valued. As women have been insulted, degraded, and wrongly depicted by men, so the cultural feminist will redress this. Not only into the balance but outweighing male thought comes the cultural feminist view:

> [construing] woman's passivity as her peacefulness, her sentimentality as her proclivity to nurture, her subjectiveness as her advanced self-awareness . . . . Cultural feminists have not challenged the defining of woman but only that definition given by men.[41]

Alcoff is saying here that while cultural feminists have decided on a pre-emptive *definition* of woman, the problem for poststructuralists is whether we can arrive at a definition of *woman* at all.

Poststructuralists, that is, say that we mimic misogyny when we try to do this. But if we do not, if we cannot 'define . . . characterize . . . or speak for women', even after allowing for differences among and between us, then there can be no politics of gender or sex. Feminism has lost its constituency, its grounding, and its *raison d'être*.

This is a position without hope. For some while, various writers, including Alcoff, have been working on a third way. But I shall leave both that and poststructuralism, to reappraise cultural feminism with reference to her work.

Like Grosz, Alcoff addresses Daly and Rich. As she says, they are different writers in almost every way. She notes Daly's warnings against biological determinism, but adds that she seems to hold an essentialist view of men. Further, in Alcoff's reading, Daly's view of what women 'really' are is linked to their sex. I find the point logically convincing, though I do not read Daly that way.

Given my affection for Rich, I wish that Alcoff's quotations from *Woman*, on the female body, did not ring so very true; that there did not seem, there at least, to be a strong determinist streak. As neither writer is a biological determinist, how can that be? Alcoff explains:

> they reject the oppositional dichotomy of mind and body that such a reductionism presupposes. The female essence for Daly and Rich is not simply spiritual or simply biological – it is both. Yet the key point remains that it is our specifically female anatomy that is the primary source of our identity and the source of our female essence.[42]

I believe this judgement rests on an assumption made in default of a feasible alternative, though the final sentence can be read in two ways. The first says of these writers, they believe and *assert* that our anatomically female bodies are constitutive of almost all else. The second suggests that those who hold women to have some overriding factor in common, must believe that to be of the body. This is not 'determinism', apparently, but it is a powerful statement of what woman 'is'.

I agree with Alcoff that cultural feminists demarcate, and strongly, male and female traits, but that they are not all explicitly essentialist. So I argued, with respect to Daly and Rich, above. They are not essentialist thinkers, in my view. Alcoff tends to hold that an essentialism can be inferred from the project of building a feminist culture. That seems to me to take the point of what we have in common, and its consequences, too far.

I said earlier that there was no consensus on what a woman-culture might be: for Mackinnon, who is not being totally unfair, it is about making quilts.[43] Whatever we think it is, we do not need innate qualities to make cultural artefacts, to build 'cultures'. Rather, such a culture or cultural space might shelter the non-innate 'good woman'; 'good woman' qualities might have to be innate to survive outside.

Alcoff sees an emphasis on benign female character, even where strict essentialism is not involved, or on any innate characteristics whatsoever, as simply wrong. First, it is wrong because research and inquiry have proved those characteristics do not exist. (Though as we have seen, there are feminist replies to that.) Second, it is politically wrong because:

> To the extent cultural feminism merely valorizes genuinely positive attributes developed under oppression, it cannot map our future long-range course. To the extent that it reinforces essentialist explanations of these attributes, it is in danger of solidifying an important bulwark for sexist oppression: the belief in an innate 'womanhood' to which we must all adhere lest we be deemed either inferior or not 'true' women.[44]

I find this argument compelling. While I retain my reading of Rich and Daly, I do so with Alcoff's views in mind. How these authors should be read, what they offer politically, then remains unclear. Though I would tend to my earlier views and suggest that Alcoff's warning, while important and true, applies to the possible effects of these writings, if misread. Were her points to be applied to Collard, I would simply agree.

'Strong' cultural feminism, then, is heterogeneous. It is undoubtedly a sex or gender difference school, but not, *pace* Alcoff, necessarily a celebrator of difference. It has insofar as we can tell from these writings, no real purchase on 'equality' in the forms I have discussed; and if we were to assume it did, no means to attain it. I shall leave the school there, and move to its gentler variant, to 'weak' cultural feminism – if so it should be viewed.

Notes

1 See Chapter 7, where 'weak' cultural feminism will be discussed.

2 Many prefer not to use the term gender now. I simply note that, here.

3 Adrienne Rich, *Poems: Selected and New, 1950–1974*, 1975, p. 234.

4 For a discussion of the terms, and a concern similar to mine, see Kathy E. Ferguson, *The Man Question: Visions of Subjectivity in Feminist Theory*, 1993, p. 81ff.

5 Or rather, that *was* so. Increasingly 'essentialist' is used as if it meant universalist.

6 Elizabeth Grosz, 'Conclusion: a note on essentialism and difference', in Sneja Gunew (ed.), *Feminist Knowledge: Critique and Construct*, 1990, p. 334; see also Ferguson, *The Man Question*, p. 80ff.

7 Gloria Hull et al. (eds), *All the Women Are White, All the Blacks Are Men, But Some of Us Are Brave*, 1982.

8 Clearly the two senses are related in some way. I have thought it best to separate them here.

9 Mary Daly, *Gyn/Ecology*, 1987; Daly, 'Foreword' to Andrée Collard with Joyce Contrucci, *Rape of the Wild*, 1988; Collard with Contrucci, *Rape of the Wild*; Adrienne Rich, *Of Woman Born*, 1986.

10 Hester Eisenstein, *Contemporary Feminist Thought*, 1984, pp. 115, 134–5.

11 Daly, 'Foreword', p. 21.

12 Ibid., p. 28.

13 See Mary Daly's *Beyond God the Father: Towards a Philosophy of Women's Liberation*, 1991 for a different view.

14 Daly, *Gyn/Ecology*, p. xi.

15 Debates on genital mutilation continue, a main point being that 'outside' commentators ignore the members of the population concerned who oppose and resist the practice.

16 Audre Lorde, 'An open letter to Mary Daly', in Cherríe Moraga and Gloria Anzaldúa (eds), *This Bridge Called My Back: Radical Writings by Women of Color*, 1983, pp. 95–6.

17 Collard with Contrucci, *Rape of the Wild*.

18 Ibid., p. 8.

19 Ibid., p. 83.

20 Ibid., p. 87.

21 Ibid., p. 106.

22 Rich, *Of Woman Born*.

23 Biologism would of course be 'materialist', too. What I mean here is that Rich does not, at this stage, appeal to a womanly culture to derive the link, but to experience derived from familial groups.

24 Rich, *Of Woman Born*, p. 14.

25 Ibid., p. 33.

26 Ibid., p. 34ff.

27 Ibid., p. 37.

28 Ibid., p. 55.

29 Matriarchies apart. She does not, I think, quite accept that there is evidence they existed. Nor is she sure that there is even some form of longing for an archetype of Woman.

30 Rich, *Of Woman Born*, p. 73.

31 Ibid., p. 182.

32 Ibid., p. 185.

33 See the discussion of Collard earlier in this chapter.

34 Rich, *Of Woman Born*, p. 252.

35 Adrienne Rich, 'Compulsory heterosexuality and lesbian existence', *Signs*, 1980.

36 Ibid., p. 648ff.

37 Diana Fuss, *Essentially Speaking*, 1989, p. 48.

38 Rich, *Poems, passim*.

39 Linda Alcoff, 'Cultural feminism versus poststructuralism: the identity crisis in feminist theory', in Micheline R. Malson et al. (eds), *Feminist Theory in Practice and Process*, 1989.

40 Elisabeth V. Spelman, *Inessential Woman*, 1990, p. 188.

41 Alcoff, 'Cultural feminism', p. 297.

42 Ibid., p. 300.

43 Catharine Mackinnon, 'Difference and dominance', in Katharine Bartlett and Rosanne Kennedy (eds), *Feminist Legal Theory*, 1991, p. 86.

44 Alcoff, 'Cultural feminism', p. 104.

7

Woman's Kindness: Cultural Feminism's Second Face

'Strong' cultural feminism, we have seen, comprises a variety of types of work and thought, the unifying factors being an emphasis on gender difference, and the revaluing of women's activities and traits, by patriarchy debased. So it is neither monolithic as a 'school' nor celebratory alone. It is often called essentialist; however, it is only by inference that this can be said of its major figures, Daly and Rich.

I turn to a form of feminism that could also be called cultural, in its celebration and promotion of what it believes to be female characteristics, values, and beliefs. I call it 'weak' cultural feminism here. It is not to me essentialist, perhaps not even universalist, in its views. The main distinctions between it and its 'strong' counterpart are these. First, the qualities in question can – though not for every writer – also be held by men, and second, they could be deployed to make a better world. They might not be so used by women only, or in abstraction from the qualities of men. This grouping then is not separatist, as 'strong' cultural feminism has tended to be.

I implied above that the cultural feminist project had no connection with equality with men in any way in which we could conceive of that term. 'Weak' cultural feminists, however, are, I think, frequently concerned with equality. Though it is complementary difference, and therefore the possibility of androgyny, that is at issue in their work, not equality of the sexes as such. In my view, that is because of the general failure to theorize the concept and to see that such an interrogation is required.

I call these thinkers cultural because of the traits (values, attitudes, and modes of thought) involved, and the context in which they are said to emerge. Briefly, they comprise an orientation towards caring, in relationships with others, and are derived from women's role in mothering: their source is the private realm, hearth and home, and women's activities there. (This I have on occasion inferred.) So there could be said to be a 'culture' here in a dual sense, comprising both beliefs and character, and a context from which they spring.

I do not say this is the only possible source of women's traits, and our society's only female 'cultural space'. First, as I noted in Chapter 6, despite the wide currency of 'cultural feminism', theorists are by no means agreed on what a culture of women would mean. Second, just as I have spoken of our society only, to avoid the idea of a female culture worldwide, so there can be societal 'subcultures'. Third, clearly there are various arenas in which beliefs and values might be adopted or change: the family, and the private realm – not necessarily identical – are but two.

Most 'weak' cultural thinkers are, I believe, philosophers, including Sara Ruddick and Virginia Held.[1] Some are psychologists. I am going to concentrate on the work of the latter, though I shall address some of the philosophical writing that has sprung from their work. In psychology, Deborah Tannen has remarkably described differences of speech and behaviour between children of different sexes, and between women and men. I shall not describe her research in detail here. Briefly, while it initially concerned linguistic misunderstanding in general, coming by interest and demand to focus on misunderstanding between the sexes, Tannen's work clearly endorses the words of women in the conversational exchanges it relates.

I give priority to an empirical psychologist, Carol Gilligan. She, like Tannen, finds sex, or gender, differences emerging from her research. Or so she believes. Is she a writer of difference?

Corinne Squire's classification of feminist psychologists does not include Gilligan among the 'woman-centred' group[2]. She appears to take method, 'idealisation of femininity', and some form of essentialism, as this school's brand. Yet she sees Gilligan as the major test of a fraying of the line dividing that from her 'humanist egalitarian' school. Some writers, like Mary Joe Frug, could rest this kind of point simply on certain ambiguities concerning the status of 'female moral thinking' in Gilligan's text.[3] Squire, rather, follows Judy Auerbach et al.'s argument that Gilligan believes in complementary difference.[4] Though she also endorses the second meaning of androgyny given above, and thinks it will eventually occur, yet, this argument runs, her belief in such qualities ties her to difference.

I have my doubts; but this analysis possesses a certain strength. How long do we wait for the qualities to combine, and androgyny to occur? It is true that both this argument, and one that notes inconsistencies and ambiguities in Gilligan's text, have to contend with her early statement that 'The different voice I describe is characterized not by gender but by theme.'[5] For one line of defence against charges of difference, indeed essentialism, could lie in the observation that it is difficult to be consistent in wording when discussing matters such as this. Though there is an obvious counterattack. Gilligan, precisely because she is a psychologist employing empirical methods and writing a research report, should not have let those inconsistencies occur.

We could however more simply ask why a text that sets out, elaborates on, the comment I have quoted above very early indeed, on its penultimate page talks of the different languages the sexes employ, in the sense that words held in common mean different things: even though these 'languages' of responsibilities and rights interact. And on that page Gilligan adds:

As we have listened for centuries to the voices of men . . . so we have come more recently to notice not only the silence of women but the difficulty in hearing what they say when they speak. Yet in the different voice of women lies the truth of an ethic of care.[6]

There is then a problem of interpretation that moves beyond considerations such as, does Gilligan, by for example *'women* say. . .', mean, '20 per cent *more women than men* say . . .'?[7] The ambiguities and inconsistencies in *Voice* are more substantial than that.[8]

Before returning to Gilligan's text, I shall address various issues raised by her work and commentators, and certain questions I believe we must ask of any work like hers. The first stems from the fact that this is a celebration in part. That is, 'strong' cultural feminism can be seen as concerned with something called 'woman' or 'womanhood', which potentially at least forms a unity in character and characteristics, oppressed and devalued by, but also, standing in opposition to, the patriarchy: men, and the structures of domination they have made. 'Weak' cultural feminism, as discussed here, illuminates aspects of a character, or of characteristics, I shall call womanly; it is partial in the sense that it is an aspect of woman it values and reclaims. In that it is, in theory, of the two schools the nearer to conventional inquiry, and the more precise in its claims, it raises the question: and what evidence is there for the existence of these traits?

The next topic Gilligan and certain commentators, in particular Annette Baier,[9] bring to mind is this: what is being postulated, what celebrated? Above, I mentioned 'values, attitudes, and modes of thought' as aspects of a culture. But they are not the same. Which of these constitutes a 'different voice', in the discussion addressed here? We will see what Gilligan thinks she found. I am going to suggest that she located something else – possibly more than one thing.

Gilligan's work has stimulated a massive debate in various disciplines including philosophy, psychology, and law; and at various levels within them. The more theoretical and philosophical address the nature and desirability of a female 'ethic of care'. The debate is almost entirely based, I believe, on her first and best-known text, which I discuss now.

Gilligan: 'the truth of an ethic of care'?

Gilligan's famous study, *In A Different Voice*,[10] is the product of her graduate research into the psychology of moral thought. Her work, and responses to it, led to a massive debate on the possibility and desirability of a female ethic of care. There is an irony in that, for it springs from her second-choice topic, the first concerning males. She had hoped to investigate the responses of young men facing the Vietnam War draft, which was by then no longer a 'bankable' theme.[11] She chose, rather, to study the expressed views of women having abortions: abortion was by then a 'live' issue and one that could reasonably easily be researched, given its legalization in 1973. She found, she said, that women had a less universal and abstract, more relational and contextual mode of thought, and more specifically of moral reasoning, than men's.[12] However it is not only the stated finding, but its interpretation, that is crucial here.

Gilligan is one of a number of academic women who, in the 1970s, began questioning sexism within their field. Most male and some female psychologists, have, she says, modelled the 'human', the desirable, the normal, on the male. Not that they have erased difference. They have noted and interpreted the gender differences that they have found. But in their work, women have been devalued and misread.

Gilligan does not, I believe, think this intentional. Sex differences[13] have in her view consistently been found. This is not true for all fields of psychology; and as she shows, where differences appear they do so at varying ages. Further, psychologists not infrequently see them as socialized.[14] However, she notes a strong tendency to construct one measure of performance, and take the male score on that measure as the norm.

David McLelland, whom she is discussing here, says 'male behavior'. I have preferred 'score'. Neither term is ideal: we speak of tendencies, and averages, not 'all women' and 'all men'. But it is easier to speak as if we mean the latter, just as it is easier for me to say 'women', and 'we', at numerous points in my text. I would expect polarized male and female responses to be found in (observed) group behaviour, and personal interviews, more than in written 'tests'. There will be more social pressure to fulfil stereotypes at work. So Gilligan's field may be among the most likely to locate sex differences, or to suggest that they exist.

To accept findings but deny their interpretation has been a fairly standard approach for feminist psychologists, though some have sought instead to show that sex differences do not exist. The latter would say either that the studies in question could not count as proof (they were too small to be acceptable or could not be replicated), or that the data had been misread: difference had been 'found', where there was none.

Thus Gilligan is not typical of feminist psychology. She does, though, represent one important type of response to extant work in a male-dominated field. And her work is increasingly influential, both within psychology and far beyond.

Gilligan would not reject an ethic of justice – the more abstract, less 'contextual and relational', approach hinted at above – for an ethic of care. And Squire, we saw, does not regard her as unequivocally a proponent of 'strong' difference, or a cultural feminist as commonly viewed. Yet the reasons for her massive following among supporters of difference are easy to see. Her various works more or less coincide with the rise and ascendancy of cultural feminism, described above. The character of her work lends status and legitimacy to the ideas of those who think similarly, but can 'prove' nothing.[15]

From previous feminist psychology, Gilligan reviews the writing perhaps best known and most discussed: the varying interpretations of women's attitudes to success. McLelland had found that men wanted success and feared failure. Matina Horner argued that women feared success. This was said to stem from a conflict between the 'women' they had been taught to be and the achievement they had learned to seek. For Horner, expected success, 'especially against men, produces anticipation of . . . for example, threat of social rejection and loss of femininity'.[16]

This last point, which has been noted by writers in other fields, rings true to me. Georgia Sassen, however, responded in a 'cultural feminist', or 'difference', way – a response clearly approved by Gilligan – suggesting that the conflict might instead be caused by

> a heightened perception of the 'other side' of competitive success, that is, the great emotional costs at which success achieved through competition is often gained . . . an underlying sense that something is rotten in the state in which success is defined as having better grades than everyone else.

She argues in support of this interpretation that success anxiety was found only when a person could not succeed unless another failed. Success of this kind would entail another person's loss, do them harm.[17] But this argument could equally well support Horner's view, in that success anxiety disappeared where rivalry would not be present and the assumed reactions of men would not affect how a woman behaved. Nor, then, would a violation of 'the womanly', or feared retaliation, play a part.

I am for other reasons sceptical of benign difference interpretations of findings like these. Horner's explanation, like Jeane Kirkpatrick's comments on female politicians quoted below, stems from a discriminatory society where men are advantaged, perhaps doubly; not all men, but the men against whom the women studied might compete. The realistic comment is surely this. Women do compete, but conventionally, they compete for men. Certainly, they are expected to. For Kirkpatrick

> A woman who becomes an engineer not only does not gain points on the male status ladder . . . or on the female hierarchy, she can lose points for inappropriate behavior. And politics has been deemed inappropriate for women. A woman entering politics risks the social and psychological penalties so frequently associated with nonconformity. Disdain, internal conflict, and failure are widely believed to be her likely rewards.[18]

To paraphrase Kirkpatrick, achievement in a 'man's world' brings no recognition in that; 'failure' as a 'woman'; and a singularly wounding attitude towards a woman who has broken gender's laws. Knowledge of such reactions seems to me to explain the pattern of female game-theory play which Virginia Sapiro found. Women playing women were at least as competitive as men playing men; women playing men were the least so; and the change when playing men was most marked, the more successful (in status, occupation) a woman was.[19] It was as if such women felt a need to make amends to men, placate them, for their achievements elsewhere.

Gilligan's reaction to Horner differs greatly from this. She asks why men will support, pursue, a 'rather narrow vision of success'.[20] This is a version of a common feminist charge that extant literature tends to 'take men as the norm': take their behaviour for granted and query women's. A major feminist riposte, as we see here, is to query men's.

Gilligan's main focus of study is moral learning and development: her mentor Kohlberg is her main object of attack. An immediate problem of (counter-)analysis is posed by the fact that Kohlberg's major empirically based study concentrated on boys. In his six-stage scale of development in moral judgement other groups rarely rank high, and these include women, 'whose judgments seem to exemplify the third stage . . . morality . . . goodness . . . helping and pleasing others'.[21]

Gilligan is not concerned to show that empirically Kohlberg was wrong, attitudinally a sexist. Rather she is angered by the double devaluing of what she too thinks is 'a different voice'. Women's role of taking care of others is devalued by an individualist society; and a morality that is based on the avoidance of harm, a direct relationship to others, and resolving a dilemma in context, has been devalued too.

She further believes Kohlberg faces a paradox in that the traits of caring that have marked women as 'good' also mark them as morally 'low'. She believes this has come about because the idea of what is mature has been taken from men and 'reflects the importance of individuation in their development'.[22] Many feminists will feel in some way sympathetic to Gilligan here: a strong reaction occurs when men speak of 'good women'; the alarm bell rings.

I turn to the central argument. Men presented with a moral dilemma are said to think in abstract terms of justice; women in concrete notions of care. Women think of relations and relationships, men of rules; or at least, those are what women and men, respectively, put first. Women's thinking is 'contextual' and 'relational', men's not. Men are universalist, that is, they will apply universal moral principles without regard for the 'concrete other'.[23] Women are non-universalist in that they will bear in mind other persons concerned as *particular persons*, and their objective will be to avoid doing them harm, whatever other moral rules intervene.

Before further explaining this belief, I point to a problem associated with it, which emerges from Gilligan's account of Kohlberg's research, in particular the famous 'Heinz dilemma' he poses his subjects, which she employs to assess his work.[24]

The dilemma is this.[25] A woman is dying. She can be saved only by one drug, which her husband cannot afford. The pharmacist will not lower the price. 'Should Heinz steal the drug?'[26] In the instance Gilligan recounts, two eleven-year-old children, 'Jake' and 'Amy', were posed the problem.[27] They were not, on the surface, sex-stereotyped in conventional ways.

It is, apparently, clear from the answers that Jake is confident. He is following Kohlberg's trajectory in the sense of heading for a 'higher score' when older.[28] He is interested in, and deploys, logic, while 'aware of [its] limits', in particular I suppose applied to morality, where an answer may be 'right' but cannot be 'correct'.[29]

And what does he reply? Heinz should steal the drug. He should, whether he loves his wife or not,[30] for people are individuals and irreplaceable. The judge would approve;[31] would nonetheless rightly find him guilty; should impose a light sentence given the circumstances involved. A male morality does not then necessarily entail obeying rules and laws; appeal to a higher principle, at the topmost level of moral judgement, overrides that.[32] Nor though is it the case that when taking such a decision, men do not consider the consequences for others. So what is the gender difference here?

There is an apparently obvious, massive difference in confidence, and style, and train of thought, though Gilligan seems to me right to say 'impression'. Amy is less confident and definite in her response. She also appraises and describes the problem differently. One way of describing her response – though probably an over-complimentary one – would be to say that she broadens its parameters. She is, says Gilligan, the more relationship oriented, an example being that 'she considers the values of the wife's life in a context of relationships . . . "if she died, it hurts a lot of other people and it hurts her"'.[33] She does not want either the theft or the death, and tries to find a way out. For example, the pharmacist could be made to see that he should give the drug away. (However, this 'interview' is clearly a process of retreat into lack of confidence in face of an interviewer who either did not understand, or could not respond. For Amy explores possibilities to that point, and then stops.)

She would 'score lower'. Other aspects of her persona, says Gilligan, belie this. She feels secure, and thinks she knows a lot about the world. It is, Gilligan comments, 'a different world'. Her idea that the problem could be solved by its fuller representation – the pharmacist is I suppose the main example here – follows. Once we have understood this, we can see that she is not 'naïve or . . . immature':

> [her] judgments contain the insights central to an ethic of care, just as [his] . . . reflect the logic of the judgment approach.[34]

I note Gilligan's point, and turn to an area where she and I would have more in common: her views on the interview itself, and what we can infer from that. (My remarks are the more extra-contextual, and not only because she is the better able to respond to the internal dynamics of the case.)

My first comment does spring from the interview, from the opening words of Jake's self-portrait.[35] These do not necessarily show confidence. We have all heard answers like this and known the insecurity that lies beneath bravado: such speech is not confined to boys and men. Let us assume however that Jake is the more confident generally, and relaxed as he approaches the questions.

Educational research shows us that boys are taught to foray, girls to conform. We would expect a girl and a boy to look for the right answer, but a boy to be more confident that he knew it, and a girl to be concerned to please: the process would be more 'teacher-dependent'[36] in Amy's case. Research data like that have not changed; they have been confirmed in recent times. They include also the finding that boys are expected – encouraged? – to speak, and girls, not. Indeed I learn that Gilligan's recent work shows a general decrease in confidence in girls, presumably as compared to boys, as well as to their previous selves, though when rather older than Amy.

In this kind of situation I would expect the interviewer, unwittingly, to intimidate a girl more; to be more likely to be seen as 'authority'. Presumably knowing that she is 'wrong' in the eyes of the questioner, whom she faces with more difficulty, Amy 'retreats'; not from her view, but from her ability to reason for it. Gilligan too sees the dynamics of power at work here, though misunderstanding concerns her more; of the interview, she says: '[it] takes on moral dimensions of its own, pertaining to the interviewer's uses of power and to the manifestations of respect'. If we see it like this, she adds, then we also see that Amy is answering a different question: not, '*should* Heinz steal the drug?' but, 'should Heinz *steal* the drug?'[37] This leads to various forms of speculative inquiry I cannot consider here; the meanwhile, it may explain Amy's answers; it cannot buttress an edifice of assumptions about female thought.

Gilligan's major study is her work on abortion.[38] Certainly it and what she derives from it are the parts of *Voice* most frequently discussed. The importance of the topic lies for her in the fact that it may overcome '[women's] reluctance to speak publicly in their own voice, given the constraints imposed on them by their lack of power and the politics of relations between the sexes'.[39] I do not see why abortion could do that better than any other topic on which women were interviewed alone, unless the idea is that a combination of the 'interview space' and the relative autonomy given women by the then US Law sets them free to speak.[40]

I can more readily accept that abortion is an issue that brings us to the brink of the 'good' and 'bad' woman problem; for Gilligan, a 'conflict between compassion and autonomy . . . virtue and power'. Women are presented with a choice: that is, she says, rare. It is a choice that requires that moral reasoning be applied to a matter within the sphere that has been 'reserved' for women – pregnancy, natality – yet over which they have almost always had no adequate control. Given what a woman is thought to be, what her life's work is often assumed to be, and what I suppose most of us have at some time thought our lives would entail, it is a momentous decision to make.

(It is a wretched one, too, made worse – Gilligan does not touch on this – by the surrounding social and political climate. I do not know whether in the US then, there was massive anti-abortion propaganda inducing guilt.[41] It would seem likely. That Gilligan ignores such factors could add to the charges of essentialism that have beset her work.)

The study involved twenty-nine women, diverse in age, ethnicity, and class. They were referred to Gilligan; there was no one reason for agreeing to take part. Of the women, twenty-one chose abortion, four to bear the child.[42] There were before (during the decision, therefore first trimester) and after – more than a year after – study phases. Various circumstances suggest that among this group, conflict would be greater than normal. But then they are not presented as representative of women thinking about abortion; the findings, Gilligan says, 'pertain to the different ways in which women think about the dilemmas in their lives'. If that was what she intended, then by choosing abortion *and* interviewing a non-random group, she loaded the dice.

In considering the issue of abortion,[43] women saw the resolution of moral problems as associated with conducting relationships with responsibility and care. So, for Gilligan, a different logic from that of justice underlies their ethic. The former is 'a formal logic of fairness'; a 'psychological logic of relationships' backs the 'ethic of care'.

A distinct model of development can be devised, stemming from the usage of 'selfishness' and 'responsibility' by the women studied here. It begins with a primary concern for the self, and moves to a phase where responsibility for others is emphasized. Then is perceived the problem of 'the confusion between self–sacrifice and care' inherent in the womanly ideal. The insight of the third phase is that the self-other distinction hides interdependence.[44] This will lead to the form of judgement shown below.

A 'care' form of judging

> remains psychological in its concern with relationship and response but becomes universal in its condemnation of exploitation and hurt … the fact of interconnection informs the central, recurring recognition that just as the incidence of violence is in the end destructive to us all, so the activity of care enhances both others and self.[45]

An adequate model of development in moral reasoning and thought must, says Gilligan, include, not ignore, what her abortion study has demonstrated: 'the . . . *feminine* voice' [italics mine]. Only then can we understand maturity – in men as well.

The debate that has been sparked off by Gilligan's work has not been eased by the ambiguity of words like 'caring' and 'care'. Selma Sevenhuijsen's suggestion that there is a twofold, mainly separate debate, one carried out by social and public policy researchers, one by theorists and philosophers, takes us forward.[46] For we would expect policy experts to deal with the activity of 'caring', institutionalized or not, in the sense of providing facilities and carrying out (mainly household) tasks for a person or persons who are no longer capable of doing so. Then 'carers' are people who do this task, for pay, or for reasons of consanguinity, or relationship by marriage; if paid, personally hired or paid by the state or a charitable organization, though, there may be 'charitable' workers who are unpaid.

Hence also 'community care', empty slogan though it has become. Not even at its origin was this the activity of 'caring' as employed above, but, carried out with sympathy and/or empathy. Rather, it was to comprise semi-institutional 'care' within the wider community, that is, wider than that of the old mental hospitals from which patients had been flung. If a moral philosopher were to discuss whether we owe a duty to such people, would that be a contribution to the debate on 'the politics of care'? I think not. But why not?

My view that the debates are distinct derives from the line I draw between action and emotion in the instance of 'care'. I am not saying they are always separate; but they are not automatically linked. I have then, possibly arbitrarily, decided to call the 'Gilligan (etc.) debate' the debate on the politics of care, leaving the social policy debate aside. I examine the former debate below.

First I return to the 'policy debate'. Its vocabulary bears its assumptions about the character of 'care'. Early in 1994 I noticed an advertisement for a researcher into 'care and its users'. This may be unusual in its own field. I cannot imagine it being said openly in the area of what I shall call 'caring woman'. Though of course there are those connected with the caring woman who *use* her care, and who use *her*. Whatever meaning this kind of language has in social policy, for the more cynical elements in what I have called the politics of care debate, it should sound an alarm.

The 'care' debate, to which I turn, is the less easy to characterize, in part because of its broad character and wide appeal, in part because of the emotions its terms may arouse, and in part because of the ambiguity of those terms. A social policy researcher will know what a carer is, and be able to present a conference paper saying, for example, 'X per cent of carers are aged over 55', or, 'Y per cent of carers are men'. A feminist theorist or moral philosopher copes, whether they know it or not, with the association of and disjuncture between the many meanings of 'care'.

What I mean here is that 'care' and 'caring' can, and in everyday language I think do, connote an emotion: a positive one, though not one that is easily defined. It might be more correct to say 'connote emotion'. Or possibly we speak of more than one emotion here. We might for example say, 'A cares for B', or, 'A cares whether B passes or fails', or, 'A cared greatly about the Gulf War'. 'A', we may say, 'is a caring person', 'the problem with A is that they care too much'; many possible examples come to mind. In debate, however, the politics of care has come to connote something like the social policy usage 'women are the carers in our society', or a claim about the social genesis of attitudes,[47] or a near-essentialist view of women yet again. I am concerned about the linking of care as an emotion with the 'care' we pay others because of the ties of, say, consanguinity, whether we actually 'care' for them enough or not.

But this kind of muddle would happen anyway. A taxonomy that would avoid it is not going to emerge. Gilligan is saying more than that care, however we happen to define it, occurs. She is postulating a female[48] approach to moral issues based on caring *qua* emotion: 'an ethic of care'.

Has Gilligan demonstrated that the approach exists? Brabeck, among others, would say no: Gilligan's method is flawed.[49] The samples are inadequate; the all-female sample for the central abortion study cannot establish a 'female voice'. We do not know the numbers who answered in a particular way. And we do not know (a problem not unique to Gilligan) how comparably the interviews were carried out. All must be read through quotations and Gilligan's interpretations of them. I have indicated my own unease at this, less directly, above.

However, there is a dilemma for the researcher here. Precisely the kind of research that might tease out a different voice will tend to suffer from this kind of flaw.[50] And Gilligan herself said that she could make no generalizations on the basis of the data she had.[51] But that begins to sound like a prudential comment. I think, as do critics like Brabeck, that she is trying to say more than she can on the basis of the evidence she has.

Brabeck further points to the problem that in general 'sex difference' studies locate very few differences. Though as she says, empirical work can only find, and show, the extant, and what can be inferred from that (though I think we can include the latent here). She turns to Gilligan's contribution to what *ought* to be, summarizing the view of what *is* of Freud and others:

> women are the more compassionate sex; affective concerns are more influential for them than for their male counterparts; they are more concerned about specific contextual moral choice, than universal principles.

There is, thinks Brabeck, an 'intuitive appeal' to comments like this. Perhaps, she says, the difference is a 'mythic truth', which can illuminate and reveal. If we employ the work of Kohlberg *and* Gilligan, 'Justice and care are then joined.'[52]

'Mythic truth' makes sense to me, though I am not sure I could defend that. Something in Gilligan speaks to me that I may not be able to defend, and certainly cannot prove, but to which I attest. Many of us have, I believe, heard the 'different voice'. Or rather, we have heard (some) women speak 'in a different voice', though to my mind there are various voices and they occur for more than one reason.[53] I hear them all – for a reason I do not fully understand – when I read, or ponder, Gilligan.

There is the 'hesitant' voice. We may not only have heard it in (young) women; there are (young) women in whom we have not heard it; it may be our socialization that makes us believe it has something to do with *women*. Alternatively, there is the voice we have forged: though it is not hesitant, exactly, then. *Or* – a note on which I shall end – there is the voice of the silenced.

Baier has heard a 'voice'.[54] She has asked in the light of Gilligan's work whether women moral philosophers write differently, and finds that they do; there she hears the voice.[55] (Though I believe Baier to be concerned with topic, style and attitude enter in.) I am not going to pursue this interesting piece, but mention a line of inquiry to which it leads me, concerning a voice I think I have heard. The notion is that many women philosophers write, and teach, differently, in that they reject the adversarial approach characteristic of (male-orientated) philosophy; are more concerned with engagement and sympathetic readings.[56] (I have met the point in connection with literary criticism too; it is in philosophy that I have 'heard' it.)

This 'voice' is not unproblematic, for me; hence my threefold division, above. The tentative voice – not gendered but, it seems, mainly female – is only on rare occasions the voice of charm. It is more, perhaps, the voice of the wary.

But that is one voice. The main 'voice' some feminists have forged may consist in a style of argument, in large part. It also contains an idea of what relationships between people should and could be. It is reminiscent of the different way of living early radicalism postulated, at least as evinced in Piercy's speech quoted in Chapter 4; and the early movement aims of, say, equality of consideration for all. (I do not imply a relativism that says all views are cognitively or morally equal.)

So I suggest that this is a voice some women have *made*, based, it may be, on the movement's founding views. I do not mean it is inauthentic to these women, or to any men who may adopt it, or insincere. I do think it is far from Gilligan's suggestion. It may be, or may have produced, what Baier notes.

The third voice, not simply tentative but stumbling, 'deformed',[57] is to me the voice of the silenced. That voice relates to the dark side of care, as shown by, among others, Tronto and Flax.[58]

The source of the voice, or ethic, for Gilligan, is unclear. However, as has been said, it would be strange were it not thought to be connected in some way with the home. While for men

> The male world of work . . . requires a *certain* kind of 'universalist' outlook . . . an adherence to procedures that abstract from personal attachment, inclination, concern for particular others.[59]

Therefore men's thought might come from the public realm (though we need not assume that this is Gilligan's point); women's from the private. The association of women with the home and with care has worried more than one writer. Tronto, for example, has commented on the difference between a feminine and feminist analysis of caring; and at the extreme, at the way in which care can be seen as the ethic of those who indeed serve.[60]

The suggestion is that to endorse too strongly a major interpretation of Gilligan's view is to endorse women's subjugation also. The danger, at minimum, is to honour oppression. Or as Flax says, of texts extolling motherhood:

> Our upbringing . . . often encourages us to deny the many subtle forms of aggression that intimate relations with others can evoke and entail . . . . Perhaps women are not any less aggressive than men; we may just express our aggression in different, culturally sanctioned (and partially disguised or denied) ways.[61]

For Gilligan tends to ignore power relationships, and pathology within the family. She sees women as benign; she tends to reduce women's oppression to the failure of others to perceive the validity of a radically particularized,[62] and yet universal, moral voice.

I speak here as if a difference existed and the problem were its endorsement, or not.[63] In fact, as we have seen, empirically, Gilligan has been more or less definitively disproven. However, interesting points of inquiry and critique remain. For example, Gilligan both looks at women only, and at ones facing a dilemma that is likely to bring an emotive, personal, and 'care' response. What if she had been able, as she wished, to interview young men who faced the Vietnam draft? Might they not 'lapse' into what we have so far called contextual thought? But then, why do we regard one form of thought as 'universalist' and another as 'contextual'? Why is caring linked with the latter? Must the former be cold?

Pursuing this I address feminist views on impartiality and justice, in somewhat skeletal form. One approach is to claim justice for women (in the sense of equal treatment with men), with no suggestion that it had been denied hitherto because the system by which it was dispensed was irremediably flawed. (Indeed of course if this were the view, there would be little point in making the claim.) Another is precisely to allege such a flaw, and make the concomitant allegation that women could not, or could not without very great difficulty, and in unusual circumstances, obtain justice or judicial redress. Therefore the system of justice should be, at the minimum, reformed or, perhaps more likely, overhauled. It would, however, still be a system we would recognise, akin to the one we know.

The next approach goes far beyond the others. It indicts not only the system of justice. It suggests that the concept itself is man-made and/or irremediably male. (Along with this would come a concept of the woman, or the female, as better.) It makes enormous sense to construct or employ, here, something like Gilligan's view. So that 'justice' indeed becomes 'male'. Thus, again, the massive popularity of Gilligan, and the many-faceted debate her work has spawned.

A problem in discussing 'care', to which I have alluded above, is that its many meanings confuse the debate. In considering Gilligan, and the 'care ethic', I read and reread a variety of classic and newer works, to find that while certain commentators held points in common, no overall coherence emerged. This may be because while at one level the debate could be said to be over,[64] in one sense it may only just have started. The semantic problem to which I speak may have blinded me to the enormity of the philosophical task ahead: a point made by Lawrence Blum.[65]

I do though want to discuss wording now. Almost every writer seems to mean something different by 'caring'. And yet perhaps because of the link between care and taking care of others, perhaps because Gilligan's point about relationships, and others' about contextuality, have been relentlessly repeated, there is one meaning they tend to miss, which is for me the most obvious one of all, and bears no relationship to nurture, insofar as I can tell, nor any to 'woman' or 'man'. It consists quite simply in the capacity to care very deeply and very strongly indeed, characteristically, interestingly enough, about fairness and justice.

It is justice to which I turn. I said that some feminists decided against the notion because they received no justice; 'justice' was flawed. In a more radical move, the system of justice became man-made, or male, and in the most extreme versions of this form of thought, the very concept of justice becomes so. But what feminists, like many others, also say is this: that 'justice' is contextual, and relative, that judges think in context; we can take the point further and say that their allegedly universalist way of thought is formed in a context. And further, that universalism itself is the product of a context. But that I leave aside.

The suggestion that both modes of thought are in a sense universalist, both, also, contextual in character and formed within a context, has I think a certain truth. What I do not know is whether that truth can only be found by mingling different types of analysis, as those who employ the debate's findings have tended to do. I do tend to think that it would be valuable to separate the question of whether women are different from the question of whether we believe our society values certain characteristics, such as the ability to care, highly enough.[66]

But they are currently separable only in part. Indeed, some direct participants in the debate may not have mingled the various approaches enough. For I do not really think we can discuss valuing, let alone deploying, characteristics, unless we have some idea of their possible source. Obviously we then face the problem of the nature of such traits, and whether they can endure. I have raised problems like the nature and durability of 'gendered' attributes, the danger for women of postulating the innate, at various points in this book.

I have tended to dismiss complementary difference. Yet an aspect of Gilligan, the notion of conjoining 'male' and 'female', in the form of 'justice' and 'care', appeals. And then Mackinnon calls me back:

> when you are powerless, you don't just speak differently. A lot, you don't speak. Your speech is not just differently articulated, it is silenced. Eliminated, gone. You aren't just deprived of a language . . . you are deprived of a life out of which articulation might come.[67]

For when I recall this chapter, when I hear of 'care', I shall see Amy, struggling for the 'right' answer, the one that would please, as a woman should: and finding none. And I shall remember her losing her 'voice' as she tries to stand firm.

We will meet Mackinnon again, and hear her speak of the silenced. For her a 'woman's voice', as depicted here, is born of and tainted by oppression, confined beyond the power of words to express.

I turn to a vision of a polity transformed, for the sake of, among others, women: in the works of Young, who would give political and social voice to the unheard. She seeks, at least in part, to bring hitherto hidden, and suppressed, voices and bodies into the public arena, and even the realms of power.

Notes

1 Sara Ruddick, *Maternal Thinking*, 1990; Virginia Held, 'Feminism and moral theory', in Eva Kittay and Diana Meyers (eds), *Women and Moral Theory*, 1987.

2 Corinne Squire, *Significant Differences: Feminism in Psychology*, 1989.

3 Mary Joe Frug, *Postmodern Legal Feminism*, 1994, pp. 40–9.

4 Squire, *Significant Differences*, p. 92; Judy Auerbach et al., 'Commentary on Gilligan's *In a Different Voice*', *Feminist Studies*, 1985, p. 154.

5 Carol Gilligan, *In a Different Voice*, 1982, p. 2. New edition published in 1993. My references are to the first edition, which critics cite.

6 Ibid., p. 173.

7 This is a hypothetical example of a common problem in reports of empirical results.

8 See also Bill Puka, 'The liberation of caring', in Mary Jeanne Larrabee (ed.), *An Ethic of Care*, 1993, pp. 224–6.

9 Annette Baier, 'What do women want in a moral theory?', in Larrabee, *An Ethic of Care*.

10 Gilligan, *Different Voice*.

11 Mary Jeanne Larrabee, 'Introduction: gender and moral development', in Larrabee, *An Ethic of Care*, p. 3.

12 Gilligan, *Different Voice*, passim.

13 I employ 'sex' here not to imply biological causation or even association, but to make it clear that while gender expectations may play a part in research at all its stages – and probably do – the findings concern biological females and males.

14 Gilligan, *Different Voice*, pp. 8–9.

15 Frug points out that they have greatly influenced feminist difference lawyers: *Legal Feminism*, p. 37.

16 Gilligan, *Different Voice*, p. 15, citing David McLelland, *Power: The Inner Experience*, 1975, p. 81, and Matina Horner, 'Toward an understanding of achievement-related conflicts in women', *Journal of Social Issues*, 1972.

17 Gilligan, *Different Voice*, p. 15; Georgia Sassen, 'Success anxiety in women', *Harvard Educational Review*, 1980, p. 15.

18 Jeane Kirkpatrick, *Political Woman*, 1974, p. 23.

19 Virginia Sapiro, 'Sex and games: on oppression and rationality', *British Journal of Political Science*, 1979, passim.

20 Gilligan, *Different Voice*, p. 15.

21 Ibid., p. 18; L. Kohlberg and R. Kramer, 'Continuities and discontinuities in childhood and adult moral development', *Human Development*, 1969.

22 Gilligan, *Different Voice*, p. 18ff.

23 This term is Seyla Benhabib's. Benhabib, 'The generalized and the concrete other', in *Situating the Self*, 1992.

24 Gilligan, *Different Voice*, pp. 25–39, 49–51.

25 Joan Tronto, *Moral Boundaries: A Political Argument for an Ethic of Care*, 1993 also focuses on the 'Heinz dilemma', giving a valuable analysis I shall not replicate here.

26 This is Kohlberg's wording; Gilligan, *Different Voice*, p. 26.

27 The dilemma is not simply presented to the subject, who is then left to ponder it. There are a series of exploratory follow-up questions. This could lead to endless problems, of course. Ours is that we have no records of what occurred.

28 Here I loosely paraphrase Gilligan. Jake's future cannot be known.

29 Here I have changed the phrasing considerably.

30 This answers a prompt.

31 I have here obliterated a link which seems to show a lack of logic, unhappy to interpret too far where the original, which I do not know, is involved. (This study has much to show us about problems of interpretation, relevant far beyond this chapter.) I have tended otherwise to follow Gilligan's account.

32 See Tronto, *Moral Boundaries*, pp. 64–8, for the context of Kohlberg's framing of the dilemma.

33 Gilligan, *Different Voice*, p. 28.

34 Ibid., p. 30.

35 Ibid., p. 33.

36 Or teacher-surrogate; such as an interviewer.

37 Gilligan, *Different Voice*, p. 31.

38 Ibid., 1982, pp. 70–127.

39 Ibid., p. 70.

40 The decision whether or not to allow abortion has now been thrown back to the individual states. The Court currently possessing a liberal core, it may be assumed that this will remain.

41 So close to its legalization, we would expect that.

42 There were two miscarriages; two women could not be located for the second interviewing round.

43 I am following Gilligan closely here.

44 For an account of the development model Gilligan proposes, see Mary Brabeck, 'Moral judgment', in Larrabee, *An Ethic of Care*, pp. 34–7.

45 Gilligan, *Different Voice*, p. 74.

46 Talk at the Joint Political Studies Association/British Sociological Association Gender Conference, London School of Economics, February 1992.

47 I have in mind Ruddick, *Maternal Thinking*, 1990, and Okin in her later work; though Okin's claim is perhaps less clear.

48 I do not forget her point about a non-gendered theme, but begin to see it as outweighed.

49 Brabeck, 'Moral judgment'; Tronto, *Moral Boundaries*.

50 The all-female sample is an exception to my comment.

51 Gilligan, *Different Voice*, p. 2.

52 Brabeck, 'Moral judgment', p. 48.

53 Nor are they heard only when women speak.

54 Baier, 'What do women want?', p. 20.

55 Ibid., pp. 19–20.

56 I do not think anyone suggests that this is true of all, or all the time; or that no men are like this. (Baier says something very similar to this.)

57 Benhabib has made a similar comment, though, with more direct reference to the context of Gilligan's work: 'Generalized and concrete other', p. 170.

58 Joan Tronto, 'Women and caring: what can feminists learn about morality from caring?,' in Alison Jaggar and Susan Bordo (eds), *Gender/Body/Knowledge*, 1989, esp. p. 184; Jane Flax, 'Postmodernism and gender relations in feminist theory', in Linda Nicholson (ed.), *Feminism/Postmodernism*, 1990, p. 55; discussed at greater length in Jane Flax, *Thinking Fragments: Psychoanlaysis, Feminism, and Postmodernism in the Contemporary West*, 1991.

59 Lawrence Blum quoted by Linda Nicholson, 'Women, morality and history', in Larrabee, *An Ethic of Care*, pp. 91–2.

60 Tronto, 'Women and caring', esp. p. 184; Tronto's position has now changed.

61 Flax, 'Postmodernism', p. 55.

62 This term is Lawrence Blum's: 'Gilligan and Kohlberg: implications for moral theory', in Larrabee, *An Ethic of Care*, p. 51.

63 See the discussion of characteristic responses to Gilligan in Frug, *Legal Feminism*, p. 38ff.

64 Its empirical part, that is, should be regarded as settled now.

65 Blum, 'Gilligan and Kohlberg', p. 64.

66 See also, though with reference to moral philosophy and moral psychology, Marilyn Friedman, 'Beyond caring: the de-moralization of gender', in Larrabee, *An Ethic of Care*, pp. 260–1.

67 Catharine Mackinnon, 'Difference and dominance', in Katharine Bartlett and Rosanne Kennedy (eds), *Feminist Legal Theory*, 1991, pp. 87, 91.

8

Socialist Feminism: from Androgyny to Gynocentrism, Equality to Difference

I am here going to chart three changes within socialist feminism over the last fifteen years. It has, I argue, moved in large part from androgyny to gender difference, and from Marxism or revolutionary socialism towards an accommodation with, if reform of, the political and social system we know now. Further it has increasingly focused on differences between groups, and not only groups of women; also demoting, or failing to mention, class. Following a preliminary discussion, I shall centre on the work of Iris Young. For Young, in any event a major writer, exemplifies these trends.

I begin by outlining what socialist feminism was, or has been thought to be, while noting that formidable problems of definition face an analyst of this school. For example, the dividing line between welfare liberalism and reformist socialism can appear thin. I am going to avoid that problem here by concentrating on revolutionary socialist feminists, and giving a fairly standard account of their views. Importantly, they mingle radical and socialist beliefs. We see this most clearly via the discussion of patriarchy and capitalism, fierce disagreement on the former concept though there has been, from the very first years. Ehrenreich, for example, says that

> Socialist feminists, while agreeing that there is something timeless and universal about women's oppression, have insisted it takes different forms in different settings, and that the differences are of vital importance.[1]

This is a protest against the radical feminist concept of patriarchy, which was then − it is said − applied equally and invariably across groups; it is also a stance that would contest developments in socialist feminism now, which extend the notion of difference beyond what any meaning of 'patriarchy' could bear. But I speak here of early and middle socialist feminism. I note that it would be wrong to speak too categorically of radicals and socialists, and over-homogenize the schools. Nor however is it possible to do more than say that views were not as clear-cut as Ehrenreich's speech, and the debate of which it is part, would suggest.

A demarcation between Marxist and socialist feminism presents a further problem: there may be no clear dividing-line, though that would depend also on the definition of Marxism and a delineation of the changes, over the past few decades, in its views. It seems fair to say that following the perception that the relationship between feminism and Marxism was fraught, marred by the primacy of capitalism and class, the distinctive socialist feminist project became the analysis of capitalism and patriarchy, and the relationship between the two.

During the 1970s and part of the 1980s there took place, within and outside Marxism, what I shall call the 'value of housework and reproduction' debate; and within socialism the 'single and dual systems' theory', the interactive or parallel analysis of patriarchy and capitalism, dispute.[2] These projects seem in retrospect to have been singularly dispiriting and debilitating. It may not be surprising that the first debate appears, as Robert Connell said, to have 'petered out in a morass of Marxist exegetics'.[3] Certainly, it failed.

Part of the problem of the Marxist-feminist enterprise, which may apply to socialists too, was that it attempted to 'fit women in' to Marxism, and in what was potentially a reactionary way. To the Marxist emphasis on production it counterposed reproduction, arguing for the importance of the latter. Specifically, it spoke of capitalism's need for reproduction of the labour force, and sought to make women key to theory by this move. For of course it is women who reproduce in the sense of giving birth. Reproduction, though, was defined far more widely than this, so that more or less everything a woman did within a traditional relationship 'reproduced' labour. This view captured an entire economy and society as ill as did Friedan's, and it ran the danger of valorizing 'women's work'.[4]

From what more general notions did socialist feminists move? Clearly, the initial concept of equality was radical in the extreme, in its ends and its means. It demanded capitalism's overthrow; the expropriation of the property-holders, the abolition of private property, and the concomitant emancipation of the proletariat; a necessary preliminary to the liberation of women (though an 'as it happens' might well be added here), and to the ending of all other oppressions. We have of course seen this kind of belief in Mitchell, addressed in Chapter 5. Firestone, also discussed there, in a sense inverted the Marxist view by making the oppression of women and children primary, and that from which all others sprang.

The discussion rested also on androgyny, though I am unsure how, the notion of an androgynous lifestyle apart, this was conceived: and of 'androgynous lifestyle' I can say only that women would enter the waged labour force. So I do not know whether sameness is entailed, though I think that could be inferred. Mitchell brought concepts such as socialization into play, to address the transmission and inculcation of gender;[5] but most Marxists have been ill at ease with a notion they regard as liberal and as lacking in historical meaning and depth.

I here prioritize the work of political theorists and philosophers, broadly defined. I am hesitant about doing that when discussing identity politics. For 'identity writers' frequently speak of representation in the sense of delineation and depiction; as distinct from notions conventionally used in politics and the law. It is as if their questions were, 'How have we spoken of women?', 'How have women been shown to be?', rather than 'How can we speak *for* women, even, for *one*?' Thus while notions of access and accountability, and so of representation, surfaced in feminism early on, and have influenced it at various points, fully-fledged accounts, and those addressing procedures outside the movement, are fairly new.

This version of the 'politics of difference' is often seen as postmodernist. That is not in fact so, though there may be a weak and contingent link. Indeed, part of the postmodernist project would be to undermine the notion of even vaguely separate categorical groups. What may be the case is that such socialist feminist writers work within a framework called the 'post modern'. Briefly, this demotes the concepts of industrial society, production, and class, emphasizes the complexity of the contemporary world, hinting at an inability to comprehend it, instates notions of consumerism, and focuses on 'style'.[6] It has emphasized the politics of groups, and specifically, categorical groups viewed as new or recent actors, *qua* groups, on the political playing field.

I do not suggest that socialist feminists necessarily hold these views, but rather that they work within their parameters. Further, though many have renounced androgyny, and are concerned with the politics of group difference, they are not automatic celebrants of the cultures the groups know. They are aware of the power that can underlie, can be connected with forging, 'identity'. So they are not 'cultural feminists' in either sense in which I have employed the term. Indeed, they may believe it dangerous to focus on culture to the exclusion of power. I do though believe that the view that many no longer want to transcend liberal democracy, have forsaken revolutionary socialism, is correct. Thus their view both of equality and of the gendered self has changed.

The acknowledgement of difference between groups entails for these writers a belief in a common, if not equivalent, exclusion of the 'variously different' from extant structures of political power, and even their writing out from the public spaces of life. But is their internal picture of these groups over-homogeneous? Do they, in particular, ignore inequality within groups? To this point I return.

Along with the flight from radical egalitarianism, and androgyny, has come a lessening of the discussion of class. I find this a difficult topic to address, perhaps because for political reasons its exclusion brings me unease. I begin with the empirical aspect, which I sketch.[7] The manual working class has shrunk, given industrial change, and there has also occurred – though analysts are divided here – a rightward shift in its party choice. But while the 'Marxism of the post modern' will note this, there are Marxists who would say there is a truer way to analyse class, whereby all who are exploited under capitalism are workers. It is a different point I want to raise here. The smaller 'working class' we now see has, *prima facie*, as much or as little right to be considered a 'group' as any other putative grouping. However, its position is not addressed.

Is that because it is thought to possess its channels of access, via for example trade unions, and links with political parties, still? Weak as those may now be? Or is it because class is a totally different kind of category and concept from the ones we will see, 'group-embodied', below? Is it, that is, not only – as a Marxist might think – politically anathema, but also conceptually incorrect, to add class to the 'list' of women, blacks, gays, the poor . . .?

There has also been a change in the concept of equality socialist feminists hold. It is less that they have turned to a liberal notion of equality of opportunity; more that they have adopted a semi-pluralist notion of equality of political influence below, and access to, the overt elite or elites. Their intent in taking this path, I assume, is to install procedures and institutions which will confer as much substantive equality as can be gained without revolutionary change. Though there are writings which suggest even less. So a faith in the attaining of radical equality, via a transcendence of the political and social institutions we know, has been lost. With it has gone, on the whole, a faith in 'sameness equality', replaced by the valuing of sex and gender difference. But alongside this has come a general turn to an 'identity' politics of disadvantaged groupings, of whom women are only one. I regard Young as an exemplar of these changes. I discuss her now.

From revolution to difference: the work of Iris Marion Young

If one thinker can be said to stand as metaphor for socialist feminism's journey from the early years, it is Young. In her essays we see the stages through which it has passed.[8] She was a major contributor to theorizing on capitalism and patriarchy, and her 'Socialist feminism and the limits of dual systems theory' will stand as a classic, if unusual, contribution to that school.[9] By 1985 Young was a humanist socialist; a mere two years later it could reasonably be asked, in the light of 'The ideal of impartiality and the civic public',[10] whether she was a revolutionary at all. She might best be seen as a radical pluralist – one who condemns many of the results of the present political system, but would modify rather than replace it – now. In Young we meet first an engagement with, a tie to, the concepts of capitalism and class, and a commitment to revolutionary socialism and androgyny feminism. Later we see a change of political emphasis and stance, towards a radical pluralism; and an engagement with difference, an adoption of the 'gynocentric' point of view.

I do not mean there is only one socialist feminist path, and that Young has followed it: this is not the only way, though I do think it a central one. And we must see Young as a pioneer. To the contrary of a notion that she reflects a trend, her first major piece is written against the general drift of analysis at the time.[11] 'Socialist feminism and the limits of dual systems theory' argues that the dual analysis of patriarchy and capitalism, attributing gender oppression to the first, economic oppression to the second, allowed Marxist economic and social analysis to remain, with gender as a minor addition. Patriarchy becomes the weaker of the two, tending to the non-material.[12] Where it is not, men and women tend to be allotted their own productive spaces, women being relegated to the family. As Young points out, not all societies know that split; and capitalism might be strengthened by such an analysis as it mirrors its own beliefs, tying women to domesticity, thus retarding the feminist cause. Moreover, the analysis ignores or obscures the oppression and exploitation of women outside the home. What is needed is a more forceful attack on Marxism; a theoretical integration that does not subsume gender and that works to prevent socialists ignoring feminist concerns. This would also overcome the tension caused by separated 'socialist' and 'feminist' work.[13]

To replace dual systems writing Young sets out not a theory as such, but conditions for it, aimed at avoiding the problems she points out. I turn to the second move, from androgyny. Young herself illustrates this in a 1990 reflection on her 'Humanism, gynocentrism, and feminist politics' of 1985.[14] I see this as crucial to the move to gynocentrism in that she was poised between 'schools', though it was humanism she endorsed. That, she explained, rebels against the feminine, overcoming gender so that all can develop fully as individuals, regardless of sex. While she saw good in gynocentrism, it was her view that its 'revaluing' of womankind might weaken the claim that men were privileged and women oppressed. For her its major tendency, and failing, was to lead women away from large-scale politics, and certainly from the crucial centres of power:[15] as I believe an ethos that valorizes women almost always does. In the current society, said Young, equality feminism was 'what the dominant culture finds more threatening'; and she sees this as helping to show the dangers of a gynocentric stance. Even where gynocentric feminists make a proposal more radical than the quest for parity with men, 'when asserted from [their] perspective it can be an objective retreat'.[16]

Despite this, Young saw much good in gynocentrism, and in 1990 she 'climbed off the fence' to its side, because of what she perceived as its ability to capture women's experience, and the analytic powers it conferred. It gave feminists, she thought, a vital purchase on oppression and its ways, and empowered them too; and it showed how what was seen as neutral was in fact male.[17] Young will never be an essentialist or universalist, or believe in 'a' culture of women: she is an analyst of difference between groups, and her major political proposals are group based. Her theoretical viewpoint remains one concerned with power. Nonetheless, she joins the feminists who distinguish between male or masculine values and institutions, which she dislikes, and their female counterparts, seen as a potential source for good.

Young's change, then, is threefold. First, she has moved from a revolutionary socialist feminism influenced by radical feminist views,[18] to a concern with the adequate political representation of the disadvantaged in the US, which omits 'class'.[19] Second, she has adopted group and identity politics, concerned with differences between groups of women (and others), though again not with those of class. Third, she has abandoned androgyny for gynocentrism; displayed in her writing by reflection on various experiences and aspects of womanhood derived from the way we live now. We see this in the later essays in *Throwing Like a Girl*. The title piece, for example, addresses gendered styles of movement, and positioning within (a) space, relating women's characteristic mannerisms[20] to their gendered state. Woman, says Young, 'often lives her body as a burden',[21] commenting also on 'The timidity, immobility, and uncertainty that frequently characterize feminine movement' and the constraints these pose and express.[22]

For Young these styles, and their implications, are not essential or essentialist in any way. Rather, she says,

> Women in sexist society are physically handicapped. Insofar as we learn to live out our existence in accordance with the definition that patriarchal culture assigns to us, we are physically inhibited, confined, positioned, and objectified.[23]

She speaks of woman's consciousness of being seen, and more, of facing physical danger, as causal in the adoption of an 'enclosed' bodily life.[24]

Young's *Justice and the Politics of Difference* does not display the trajectory I have outlined.[25] For it represents Young's later work, with the exception of the gynocentric essays just discussed, which it omits.[26] It is concerned largely with the issue of difference in the sense of difference between groups, and with those groups as political actors; and to that extent it represents what I call 'identity politics' in this book. For those concerned with the interplay of equality and group difference it is a crucial work, and I shall discuss its major theses here.

Young's book, she says, is founded on group difference – on what are normally called new social movements – for her, group based and of the Left. Thus feminist, Black, Native American, gay and lesbian movements are those with which she is concerned.[27] Various other campaigns and organizations have been called new social movements; I take it that the distinction is that Young's groupings work for the interests of, and are based on, a category of person. Though of course potential 'membership' overlaps.

Two things must be borne in mind here. The first is that while Young indeed focuses on this, she speaks strongly of the relationship between equality and individualism, and of the dangers for women of a narrow and static view of community life; she is perturbed by what she regards as the postmodern and communitarian emphases on the small. She opposes certain feminist ideals of community and face-to-face relations, not in themselves but as 'the organizing principle of a whole society'. She points to cities, problem ridden as they are, as supporting the politics of difference and as providing congenial space for 'deviants', including women alone.[28] And amidst her politics of groups she is concerned with the maintenance of individual liberty, and democratic mechanisms for participation in politics, to ensure that 'leaders' are accountable and people heard. This could in part be early radicalism come home.[29]

While Young moved from androgyny to 'gynocentrism', she is not the kind of celebrant of woman who would, in embracing difference, cast equality aside. Yet it seems crucial to ask what sexual equality means to her now, and how it might be attained. Though we must bear in mind that *Justice* is not concerned with women alone.

Justice is central to Young's thoughts, and must contribute to her view of the nature of equality, and how it is attained. I shall not outline the debate in which she intervenes;[30] instead I give her views. For Young, justice is 'the elimination of institutionalized domination and oppression';[31] crucial to her is the manner of its attaining, that is, empowerment via participation must play a major part. She opposes the prevalent view, that of distributive justice – the 'morally proper distribution of benefits and burdens' – for it tends to focus, she believes, on the allocation of social positions and material goods, ignoring the social and institutional context that helps determine this. The notion of justice should extend to other concerns, such as control over decisions like those. And she wishes to widen our view of 'distributive', adding an enabling concept of justice, giving individuals the ability to realize their capacities, groups to act together in their interest and for their cause.[32]

This concept is adopted in part in the name of the oppressed of the US. Not all those she lists are normally so viewed. They are, I think, usually groups; and groups of a certain kind. I would tend to call them categorical, though Young defines them not by the qualities of their members but by 'identity'. The distinction I draw is this. A member of a categorical group belongs to it by virtue of some characteristic they possess[33] – in fact, they may not have to 'join' – so that 'women', 'Native Americans', and 'African Americans' comprise categorical groups. But a person's identity does not necessarily derive from this.

Hovering in the background of my discussion, Young's, and Phillips's, given below, are philosophical/metaphysical writings on identity, and on the concept of the self. In Chapter 1, as a preliminary to discussing postmodernism, I insisted that my nationalities, interests and so on did not preclude an 'I', one 'self'. But I did not *demonstrate* that. Nor shall I attempt to do so here, though I raise and articulate the issue, in the context of multiple group affiliation, below. Between philosophical and metaphysical considerations of the possibility of a 'self' and what it means to have an 'identity', and the literature on identity and difference I address here, there seems to be an unbridged gulf.[34] In the next chapter we will meet a writer, Judith Butler, who tries to leap that gap, and to my mind falls.

I return to my comments on Young's treatment of groups. Further to differentiate the positions – though in a manner possibly unfair to Young – a categorical group (which might have members with no sense of categorical or group identity at all, or only of the most attenuated kind) might comprise blacks, women, or, say, single mothers on welfare. A better example might be the categorical group of people with red hair and brown eyes. For this is a 'group' no one 'joins' unless they dye their hair; a frivolous point but one that suggests the complexity of what we are dealing with here. Nor is it likely to be an identity group. The category of people who own cars made before a given year will not be, either. However, there could be a group that consisted of collectors of old cars, with which its members identified to varying degrees.

But I write as though political allocations and perceptions never changed. A category may become an identity group by becoming an interest group, or a potential one. Suppose a disproportionate tax were suddenly levied on cars made before the given year. Their owners would then have an interest in common, which applied only to them: reducing the tax. This might lead to identification with their fellow owners: and it might not. It might add to – and, for some, define – their 'identity': and it might not.

Again, the number of visible categorical groups is not static. New ones arise. And old ones fall. An obvious example stems from the tragedy which occurred in the UK, and elsewhere other than the US, when many children were born deformed, most, gravely, following the prescribing of thalidomide as an anti-morning-sickness drug.[35] For my purposes, the parents form the categorical group: they are an interest group, too. They became an organized interest group, with a possible group identity, because they brought a lawsuit and because under British law only those who joined suit could benefit.[36] It is somewhat ironic, given the topic I address, that the US legal system would have allowed a 'class action' suit instead, so that one could sue for all.

My comments could strengthen a criticism Young's group model attracts, which points out that there could be an infinite number of groups. A possible reply is to differentiate them from mere aggregates like my hypothetical car owners, or, say, the number of people on holiday at a given seaside resort; or from statistical groupings such as households with more than one child under the age of fifteen on the premises at Census time. Young's answer, I think, is that it is possible to join an organization, and for the membership to have massive meaning for one's life, but for it ultimately not to mean the same as being, say, Indian: it would not define one's identity in the same way. For her groups are not mere aggregates, nor are they to be set over and above individuals; they are in effect a pattern of relationships between those from whom they are made.[37] Do her comments adequately address the (non-trivial) possibilities of a plurality without end?

Young does instance identity groups one can leave or join, commenting on women who were heterosexual and have become lesbians, on the fact that we grow old, and so on. (This is a somewhat limited response; and 'do join' might have been a better term.) We can define the meaning of a group and group identity for ourselves, says Young – and she would not support one where we could not – or groups together can define the meaning of their identity. The latter kind of comment is one reason why Judith Butler would greet identity politics with unease. I suspect also that it would have called forth Freeman's 'Tyranny of structurelessness'.[38]

Many of course oppose groups, or, to be more precise, groups and group/identity politics as discussed here. They may believe that stereotyping of the group, or rather of its members, and hence discrimination, stems from classification itself. Further, 'in-groups' presuppose 'out-groups', and cohesion within a group is most easily achieved or enhanced by an outbreak of hostilities with another. Then, inclusion in a group implies exclusion from it; if someone can be 'defined in', they can be 'defined out'.[39] People, the final point will be, should be treated as individuals – not as parts of a category or members of a group.

I probably have far more sympathy for this as a potential hard-line stance – though I do not mean, say, banning group membership or affiliation, or the meeting of categorical groups – than does Young. But it is wrong to see her merely as a group thinker. Individual development is of crucial importance to her, and she genuinely wants individuals to be able to pursue their lives in their own way. Her problem rather is this: that groups persist. It is, she says, 'a modern myth'[40] that group attachments decline. The opposite is true. For her, justice requires not that group differences vanish, but that they be aided to remain,[41] while their oppression falls.

For Young, groups in themselves are inherently neither oppressive nor oppressed. In any event, she says, they are massively cross-cutting: there will be persons who could be members of a fairly large number of groups.[42] In a neat move she adds that individuals themselves, then, are in a sense non-unified. I am uneasy about this semi poststructuralist turn: surely there is *a* person attached to all these groups? And I do not mean 'the black one', or 'the older one', or 'the one from Brooklyn': I really do think that there is *someone* behind all that. That a person may prioritize one group or identity at a given time is another matter. Though I do not want to suggest that we always have a choice. I believe much of what we call 'choice' is constrained, and sometimes desperately so. I say rather, *some one person* both chooses and is constrained. Here again, however, metaphysical and philosophical problems enter in. What is 'a person', their attributes apart?

I move to Young's view of the politics of care debate, which, in her now classic 'The ideal of impartiality and the civic public',[43] she has considerably extended. Young argues that feminists who propose a politics of care maintain the distinction between public roles in which ideals of impartiality and reason are held key, and private relationships which require a different moral approach.[44] She believes we should extend the argument greatly, querying impartiality wherever it occurs. She assails, also, the liberal public–private split, and the relegation of women, but others too, to the private realm.

Young's opposition to the impartial stems from her belief that it is an enemy of the particular. The impartial viewpoint is reached by abstracting from circumstances; from feelings and desires; and from affiliations of any kind. But these abstractions have their, for her negative, corollaries of neglect. The particularity of situations will be ignored, one rule only being applied. Dispassion will be achieved at the cost of neglecting feeling, 'reason' being opposed to desire. And, most crucially for Young, detachment entails '[reducing] particularity to unity': the theoretically detached, allegedly taking all perspectives into account via their transcendence, 'need acknowledge no subjects other than itself to whose interests, opinions and desires it should attend'.[45] Impartiality is impossible to attain because 'reducing differences to unity' entails that a hierarchical opposition is produced, based on the valuing of the principles by which the differences are made null.[46] Here Young is making a logical point, though empirical likelihood enters in, too. Impartiality, the argument runs, by definition values the universal over the particular: for the universal is key to the impartial, while the particular defies both. But then impartiality itself becomes partial, as the universal is exalted above all.

Young here refers of course to a process of judgement. She does not mean that differences will be eradicated, or ironed out. However, the disinterest that theoretically confers impartiality can be gained only by abstracting from relationships, emotions, and so on. These still exist. They are simply 'abstracted out' from the spheres of public judgement. So for Young there is a continual bifurcation and split: classically, between private and public, female and male.

Young declares impartiality impossible. The empirical reason is this. No point of view can be uninfluenced by background, context, circumstances and events; however, a point of view so attached cannot be universal, cannot take all others equally into account.[47] But she regards it as undesirable in any event. For her, particularities should not be removed from moral reasoning. Her model is that of a dialogic community, a community of speakers, where 'participants . . . move from self-regarding need to recognition of the claims of others'.

I do not know how we arrive at this model of judgement. Meanwhile the logical outcome of Young's beliefs, I think, is that only certain particularities should enter in. Those would be relevant to the overcoming of domination. I fail to see how a system like that could be implemented, whether I thought it welcome or not. For presumably, currently, it is the interests of the dominant that enter, and remain in. How can that be overcome? Will Young's ideal simply reverse domination? Would a wager on a 'true impartial' not hold out more hope? Is there to be no judgement? Is the dialogic a non-stop train?

Young wants a civic public which will revitalize pluralism and nullify the apoliticizing influence of interest groups. Groups of all kinds, with no entrenched political access, would take part. Public forums which discuss, debate, and take decisions would be set up. The character of the public would be changed too. Citizenship has, until now, omitted those 'associated with the body and feeling': many recent thinkers still view the civic public as a forum where people leave their differences behind; Young calls for a 'public' that can show 'the positivity of group differences, passion, and play'.[48]

Feminist critiques, says Young, have shown that the allegedly impartial and universal civic public excludes, as active, women, blacks and, on occasion, the non-propertied. This might be by chance, but if not, the 'universal' itself stood and still does stand for exclusion, largely of society's bodily and affective aspects. It created a forced homogeneity of the citizens of the public realm, which remains.

Further, it strengthened the opposition of desire and reason. It supported and maintained the manner in which types of people were so associated: usually, of course, (white) men with reason, women with others' desire. We can see the association historically, in the writings of the philosophers, and the practices of the public. For fear of the desire women can inspire in men, and the ensuing wildness and disorder of the latter sex, breaking the calm conventions of contract, women have been confined.[49] These links and practices still remain.

Young knows some believe that she and similar thinkers ask too much of impartiality. They would retain it, with its imperfections, as worth while, and a worthy aim. I agree with their position, though I am perturbed and part-persuaded by her belief that to retain it strengthens oppression by making the viewpoint of the privileged a universal one. But is this not a practical objection? I do not mean that it would be readily practicable to remove the elites, but I do think that would be one emancipatory answer to Young. It might moreover be as practicable as her idea that we 'seek public fairness, in a context of heterogeneity and partial discourse'. For, as I have suggested, the dominant would have their view on that, insofar as it is not simply a modification of the system we have now.

Public has meant open. Young wants one that is. She wants a public which is both inclusive and diverse, and a private comprising not what must be hidden from 'the public' in another sense, but the place(s) from which a person can exclude others: we could perhaps say, their personal space.[50] The individual then is part of the public, and privacy is positive. No one is forced into privacy, everyone can choose it, and no topic should be barred from free public debate.

In any case public and private do not, Young points out, exist as they did once.[51] Some are allowed to keep their privacy, in that their dealings are closed to public scrutiny; others are not. Feminists and participatory democrats want much more to be made open to the people's gaze.

I move to Young's 'Social movements and the politics of difference'.[52] First I note that influenced in part by poststructuralism though Young has been, she does not construe difference in its way, that is, as exploding group membership also. Rather she seeks to promote a recognition of the heterogeneity of groups, and an acceptance that a unified polity cannot be gained. Though nor would she want it to be gained, for cultural identity would then be lost. And unification would not bring harmony, for the enemy of that harmony is not difference but the system of domination and oppression whereby some groups rule.[53]

Young notes that some oppose a rejection of the liberal humanist ideal and the view of group difference as positive. Others assert group specificity, yet want to affirm the principle that all persons are of equal moral worth. A paradox then occurs. To overcome the effects of the segregation (and therefore discrimination) to which certain groups are subject, they self-segregate. Given that among the negative aspects of difference is the virtual 'non-humanizing' of a group, one named 'different' will be seen as having nothing whatsoever in common with the 'normal', 'personed' groups. Alternatively, that group will be forced into its own exclusion. Thus there is an essentializing, and a 'freezing', of difference.[54]

This essentializing, in turn, represses difference within groups. It expresses a fear of specificity which may increase as clear essentialism of difference wanes, as the belief in, for example, a specifically black nature becomes less tenable. The politics of difference confronts fear by and about groups, fear of difference, and aims for an understanding of group difference as ambiguous, relational, and shifting. We should neither end, says Young, with amorphous unity nor split asunder. That is almost to demand the impossible, I think.

'Oppressed groups,' she says, 'seek to seize the power of naming difference itself, and explode the implicit definition of difference as deviance in relation to a norm.'[55] And as we saw her saying above, there are very many cross-cutting sources of identity, so groups can have something in common. But I retain my concern about the view, anti-humanist in its implications, that people may become but the sum of their group identities;[56] together with my logistic doubts.

The traditional political approach to difference, a traditional politics in general, defines groups as having different natures, in order to include and exclude. The difference politics Young would want would be egalitarian, would see difference as more fluid and relational, and as socially produced.

For this to happen, equality itself must be rethought. Assimilation implies what I call procedural equality; or better, legal 'sameness equality'. But difference politics would argue that equal participation and inclusion of all groups requires different treatment. Young is not, then, importing a concept of equality we do not already know.

For Young group difference alone can better politics. It can bring the hope of seeing difference as simply that, while promoting the solidarity of groups. It is not that none of the disadvantaged have succeeded under the humanist race- and sex-blind ideal. Young's point is rather that structural inequality, patterned by group privilege and oppression, remains. All must be liberated; only basic institutional changes will do this. There must be group representation in policy-making and 'an elimination of the hierarchy of rewards that forces everyone to compete for scarce positions at the top'.[57] (I agree with this last point, but I do not see how it relates specifically to the politics of difference.)

Positive group difference brings standpoints from which to criticize what has gone before; while these derive from experience, and on occasion culture, I do not think we have here the epistemic privilege(s) of a Standpoint or Standpoints.[58] Self-organization will follow. It is not that there will be no coalitions. Nor is any one type of person, any group of people, barred – in principle, I imagine – from working for a cause. But there will in Young's view (I sensed a 'probably' at this point) need to be groups that bring empowerment and voice. Though in any event homogenization, exclusion, and hierarchy could occur.

What of the justified fear of some groups; that they take a risk by even admitting, let alone claiming and demonstrating difference? Racism, sexism, and homophobia thrive. Would not the politics of difference entail a series of separate and unequal domains, for separate and unequal groups? More than one writer has commented on the dangers inherent in difference – in addition, that is, to the major strand that runs through this book – and it will continue to be a dilemma. However, there are those who cannot deny 'difference'; and there are those who fear the consequences of admitting it, for whom that has no connection with any form of organized group. Difference has its heterogeneities and separate dilemmas, too. Not all the 'different' are similarly unequal; a problem that must be addressed by advocates of the politics of groups.

Young supports equality. But she does not mean equality in allocation of resources, though she wants some redistribution of those.[59] Rather she envisages full participation in major institutions and substantive chances for all to develop and advance, given that the formal legal equality most have obtained has failed to gain them social goods.

A problem for supporters of participation is that participatory democratic theory tends towards a unified public; for Young, that can exclude, or silence, certain groups. We know who are most likely to participate and be represented: white middle-class men. There should then, she says, be specific mechanisms for representing oppressed or disadvantaged groups, together with support for and resourcing of their organizational preconditions. Holders of power would have to show they had heard the views of all, and there would be a group power of veto when an issue affected them directly – say, on reproductive policy for women, and for reservation Indians on land.[60] I see here a problem – who is to decide which policies fall under that provision? Or to which group or groups, given overlapping membership, a veto should go? If it is to the members formally representing a certain group, what of those from that group who represent another?

This kind of policy, says Young, is more just than the traditional public's. First it is more likely to assure procedural fairness, by giving voice to the previously unheard. Next, it absolutely ensures a voice, and so is more likely to ensure that it be heard. Further, it will protect against group fear of admitting difference, partly because of policy input; partly, I suppose, because the group had been legitimized. (I still see reasons for concern, for fear of acknowledging difference, here.)

Further, Young thinks, it will lead individuals and groups to ask for what is just, or rather, to frame interests and wants in those terms. For group representation would add to accountability. When different groups are participating, that is, the sectional is less likely to be able to be masked as the universal; I suppose as in, 'Our . . .' or, 'The public . . .', 'interest is . . .'.

Only social groups of the kind discussed above will be represented in this way, and of those, only the disadvantaged or oppressed. While the representation is meant to apply to government bodies, Young thinks there is no reason not to have such groups elsewhere. Finally the proposal does not imply proportional representation, though Young would not, for non-institutionalized individual representation, ban that. A group might be relatively too small or too large for proportionality to make sense. She gives the example of no seats for American Indians, or half for women: the former obviously too few, the latter more than is necessary, depriving other groups.

Immediately we see, I think, a flaw in Young's system. Emphasizing the overlapping of groups – at one point, to a massive extent – when it seemed relevant, she now speaks of 'women'. I do not want to 'bid' for half the seats for women, as it happens. However, assume there were no such seats. What if women comprise half the members of every disadvantaged group there is, but the mores of certain groups entail that they do not elect them? We see here most concretely the problem of inequality *within* groups, indicated above; though there could be many other examples of that.

Then there is the objection put by Young herself – as a possible problem, though grave – that this is a system that could never begin. How would we arrive at the relevant public? That is, the one that decided on the groups? Who would decide their rules? (That is, rules for choosing the groups.) If oppressed groups were not at this hypothetical 'constitutional convention', then how could we be sure they would be represented? And if they were, why should they need group representation?[61]

Moreover, Young speaks as if the US system were more or less democratic, when in her terms it is not. For only a body with democratic sympathies – of a certain kind, at that – would be likely to vote this system in. Then there is the question of who else might intervene. People do not lightly give away power, if they ever really do.

But by far the most formidable argument, in my view, has been brought by Phillips. It concerns how representative the members would be of the groups from which they came.[62] I take it that they are not meant, internally to each group, to be 'mirror', 'representative sample', persons. They are supposed to represent the 'views' and interests of their group.

They cannot, though, be mandated delegates. This is for reasons of group size; because they will be deliberating considerably and a process of mutual learning is supposed to be taking place; and for a reason extraneous to the group notion: that while interests may remain static, opinions and views are not carved in stone. Non-mandated representatives, however, have always posed a problem:[63] in what sense do they represent a constituency or a group? In what sense does a woman whose views are diametrically opposed to mine, speak for me?

Phillips also raises the questions of which groups we choose to represent and who is to be considered a member. For clearly a new group could emerge, and clearly there might be identity questions unresolved by Young's depiction of cross-cut membership and the occasional ability – say, when growing 'old' – to join a new group. Phillips warns against the dangers, in Young's system, of fixity and group closure.[64] But given a group system, surely there could never be closure, given first that we can never be sure that we have located all the groups, and second, that identity is something we forge all our lives.[65] Though on Young's behalf it might be said that too great a fluidity prevents political action by and on behalf of a group, which in theory at least represents the beliefs, or the interests, of those within. Is there an inevitable tension here?

These objections can I think be lodged despite Young's calling her system normative, an ideal. At the same time, it should be said in her defence that few speculative thinkers draw up a plan. Rather they forward some fertile ideas, which may take hold.

I move to a discussion of theorists for whom difference means something vastly more complex. I have dealt with doubts about the formation of oppressed groups, and their assimilation, there. There too, female sameness and difference are more at stake than here, as is the very male or female self.

Notes

1 Speech at the [US] National Socialist Feminist Conference, Barbara Ehrenreich, 1975; quoted by Batya Weinbaum in *The Curious Courtship of Women's Liberation and Socialism*, 1978, p. 6.

2 See for example Ann Ferguson, *Blood at the Root: Motherhood, Sexuality and Male Dominance*, 1989, pp. 20–32.

3 R.W. Connell, *Gender and Power*, 1987, p. 35.

4 Iris Young's 'Socialist feminism and the limits of dual systems theory', *Socialist Review*, 1980, in Young, *Throwing Like a Girl: And Other Essays in Feminist Philosophy and Social Theory*, 1990, is something of an exception to this.

5 Juliet Mitchell, 'Women: the longest revolution', in *Women: The Longest Revolution. Essays in Feminism, Literature and Psychoanalysis*, 1984; see Chapter 5.

6 Sabina Lovibond, 'Feminism and postmodernism', in Roy Boyne and Ali Rattansi (eds), *Postmodernism and Society*, 1990, p. 175ff.

7 My account applies to the UK alone.

8 Young, *Throwing Like a Girl*.

9 Young, 'Socialist feminism'; ibid., 1990. See the extended discussion and impressive interpretation of this piece in Rosemarie Tong, *Feminist Thought*, 1989, pp. 182–6.

10 Iris Young, 'The ideal of community and the politics of difference', in Linda Nicholson (ed.), *Feminism/Postmodernism*, 1990; in *Throwing Like a Girl*.

11 Young, 'Socialist feminism'.

12 Young, 'The ideal of community', pp. 23–6.

13 Ibid., pp. 28–31.

14 'Introduction', and 'Humanism, gynocentrism and feminist politics', in Young, *Throwing Like a Girl*.

15 Young, 'Humanism', pp. 88–9.

16 Ibid., p. 89.

17 'Introduction', in Young, *Throwing Like a Girl*, p. 7.

18 Young, 'The ideal of community', p. 21.

19 Remaining are 'the poor'. But more than a change of vocabulary is involved here. The omission of class is far from unique to Young, but it is rarely raised. It is however noted by Anne Phillips, 'The promise of democracy', in *Democracy and Difference*, 1993, p. 129.

20 That is, most Western women at this time.

21 Young, *Throwing Like a Girl*, p. 148.

22 Ibid., pp. 151–2.

23 Ibid., p. 154.

24 Ibid., pp. 154–5.

25 Iris Young, *Justice and the Politics of Difference*, 1990. However it contains a piece I regard as crucial in her 'political' and humanist/gynocentric changes of stance: 'Impartiality and the civic public', first published 1987.

26 The disjuncture between the two is of interest. The 'bodily' essays show the greatest transformation of her thought, 'politically' underdeveloped as yet.

27 Young, *Justice*, p. 3.

28 Young, 'The ideal of community', pp. 317–18. See also Young, 'City life and difference', in *Justice*, 1990.

29 See Chapter 5, and especially my comments on Freeman's *Tyranny of Structurelessness*, 1970.

30 It is a debate non-specific to feminism, though relevant to it. An adequate consideration is beyond the scope of this book.

31 Young, *Justice*, p. 15.

32 Ibid., pp. 19–20, 22–3.

33 I do not suggest that the shared characteristics are more than minimal, or that it is right to see them as relevant to the treatment of 'members' of the group.

34 For an essay showing the themes at their overlapping 'margins' see Anne Phillips, 'So what's wrong with the individual?', in *Democracy and Difference*, 1993.

35 Thalidomide was refused approval by the US Food and Drug Administration, so was never prescribed in the United States.

36 Though there may be extra-legal agreements to make payments to any who claim.

37 Young, *Justice*, p. 44.

38 My suggestion is not that Young is not aware of and concerned with what I shall call the 'dark side' of groups; far from it. She does though appear frequently to overlook its implications.

39 Sheila Rowbotham, 'Feminism and democracy', in David Held and Christopher Pollitt (eds), *New Forms of Democracy*, 1986.

40 Young, *Justice*, p. 47.

41 She has in mind the importance of cultural diversity.

42 Obviously for logistic reasons, if anything more than belonging by definition is required, the number of groups will be small. As I think will be 'active identifications'.

43 Young, 'The ideal of community'. See n. 29 above.

44 Here, I believe, we see the gynocentrism in Young.

45 Ibid., pp. 100–1.

46 Ibid., p. 102.

47 Ibid., p. 104.

48 Ibid., p. 97.

49 Ibid., pp. 108–12.

50 Ibid., pp. 108–9.

51 I believe Young to be one of the theorists who holds a romantic and rose-tinted view of the active eighteenth-century public, and to base various proposals on that: ibid., pp. 98–9.

52 Iris Young, 'Social movements and the politics of difference', in *Justice*.

53 Ibid., p. 179.

54 Ibid., pp. 170–1.

55 Ibid., p. 171.

56 Young has in fact qualified this point. There are distinct problems involved in summarizing her work, in part, I believe, because of her exceptionally strong commitment but also because she frequently qualifies her statements nonetheless.

57 Young does not mean by this that there will be, for example, no differential pay. But it would be differently allocated. (It would also – here I feel unease – be group allocated.) It is current structural inequality she would combat: 'Social movements', in *Justice*, p. 212.

58 Sandra Harding, *The Science Question in Feminism*, 1986, p. 141ff.

59 Young does make it clear that she writes in the context of the US: 'Social movements', in *Justice*, pp. 19–20.

60 Ibid., p. 180ff.

61 Ibid., p. 190.

62 Phillips, *Democracy and Difference*, pp. 97–8, 99.

63 Mandates also create problems. But we are not concerned with the mandated here.

64 Phillips, *Democracy and Difference*, pp. 96–7, 99–100.

65 I am grateful to Marian Sawer for discussing this point.

9

The Postmodernist Challenge

Postmodernism and poststructuralism[1] comprise feminism's third difference: a difference *within woman*. Some see this as a difference between individual women: I tend to think it means a 'difference within', the fragmentation of, the self. Both are relevant to feminism's project; I see the second, some view both, as antithetical to its cause.

Postmodernism challenges both equality, and 'difference' as employed so far: as sex or gender based, and as existing between female groups. Rather than attempt to define it fully, I single out aspects crucial to feminist thought. I discuss in turn postmodernism's rejection of 'grand narratives', and its relativism; *différance* and deconstruction; and the 'death of the subject'. I begin with the grand narrative.

Postmodernists proclaim the end of, an end to the validity of, all-embracing ideologies and world views which proclaim Truth. They renounce all such belief systems, also called totalizing: they do not assail Marxism and liberalism, the two great political 'world views', alone. However, given their frequently vexed relationship to feminism, I shall speak to those, though not in detail, here.

These two ideologies have characteristically not aided women; or rather, in the feminist view, not enough. Both have been said to be gender blind,[2] though in different ways. Postmodernist feminists will not consider it possible that their failure to include women is contingent, rather than necessary. I have instanced liberalism as breaking its contract, in the case of women; there, we might conclude that the flaw was contingent. We might see the writings of certain liberals, the exclusion or downgrading of women, as examples of the 'theoretical special pleading' of which Hodge speaks.[3] Then liberalism might have been a grand narrative to which feminists could adhere, because of the commonality among persons key to its thought. If we think of grand narratives as what Harding would call 'the one true story', we can imagine such a narrative in which women could play a full part, and which feminists could endorse.

Yet postmodernism has aided feminism by renouncing such narratives, many would say. For it admits of no narrative that automatically subsumes women, relegates them to second place. The problem with this argument is its corollary: it admits of no narrative that puts women first. Indeed, it allows none that proposes the equality of women, let alone one that might bring it about. For its relativism would give equal standing to an argument that women should remain oppressed. This is a strange alliance for feminists to make.

Postmodernism speaks of 'texts'. This stems from its literary-philosophical connections and its pressure towards the literary and imaginative, and relates to its interpretive strategy: we 'read the world' as though it were a text. A major critique of postmodernism, related to this, has been that there is within it no room for the real world, that the 'text' is indeed all we (are allowed to) have. If there is a truth, we cannot reach it, or even approximate to it. On a reading both sympathetic to and critical of postmodernism, by Flax, there can be no representational idea of the truth.[4] We cannot directly apprehend the 'real'.

Postmodernism, then, is an idealist school. At least, it is in its epistemology, its notion of knowledge. Does postmodernist ontology, its notion of being, also tend to idealism? Is the 'real world' an illusion?[5] Joan Scott, the writer I discuss first below, does not think that. She does not, that is, believe that we have the text alone, that there is no world except, or outside, language. There is no consensus on this point concerning Jacques Derrida, whose writings inform her work.[6]

Postmodernism's interpretive strategy includes the relativist view that there can be no privileged reading of a text. No one interpretation, that is, betters another, in any way. From the very beginning of the second wave, feminists have confronted an issue of 'privileged reading' in that much of non-liberal feminism, in accord with its founding views, attempted to avoid generating a theoretical or political elite. The intention was that women would reach the ideas of liberation both together and in their own way, though – a cynical point, but one that must stand – it was nonetheless assumed what their conclusions would be.

There is a 'privileged reading' that runs: 'women are oppressed (subordinated, subjugated, unequal, disadvantaged in relation to men . . .)'. Anyone who does not think something like that, or has no interest in advancing the cause of women – in whatever way, in whatever sense – is not a feminist. This is a fairly minimal definition, many will think. I use it to clarify the notion of a 'privileged reading', and to suggest there must be one, for feminism to make its claims. Clearly this denies the validity – the equal validity? – of a 'reading' that says, 'It is men, not women, who are oppressed.' Then feminism must violate postmodernist tenets, or it cannot speak.

Given its relativism, postmodernism need not legitimize oppression, in order to maintain it. It does not forbid a group to claim or proclaim equality. But nor does it allow it to justify that. If any comment is as good as another, and all descriptions are equally near to the real, then those who seek to better their condition are lost. Why some feminists nonetheless endorse postmodernism, we will see below.

I turn to *différance* and deconstruction. I offer a brief account, giving a more detailed definition when I turn to Scott. I have already said that *différance* is not difference as normally defined. I simply gesture to its connotations, here. Among them are the interplay of differences, of meanings, in a text; and also, displacement, openness, and 'deferral'. The results of a technique informed by *différance* can never be final. As there is no privileged reading now, nor can there be. So the readings move; they do not move onwards, but they move on.

Deconstruction, informed by *différance*, opposes hierarchies by addressing a dualism, such as 'nature–culture', 'female–male'. The technique, it is said, disrupts the very terms of the dualism; and in the case of equality–difference, of the surrounding debate. It exposes the dualisms of our culture – man–woman, culture–nature – as no mere binary forms. For they are, it is argued, implicated one with another; and – for Derrida, at least – they are hierarchical. Their relationship of interdependence is also one of inequality: for example, woman is dominated by man. Exposing this, it is said, we subvert it.

I am not going to offer an example of deconstruction here, except for that which I outline when discussing Scott. There are various reasons for this. An important one is that very few deconstructionist writers employ Derrida's exact technique. Important, too, is the quality of the explanation given by Scott. There is little point in mimicking her. I turn to postmodernist views of the 'subject', that is, of people like us. Or not.

Some feminists view postmodernism as engaged in the disruption of what are seen as essentializing and universalizing concepts like 'woman' and 'man'. But they concentrate on differences between groups of women, as if postmodernism specifically licensed that and there had been no warrant for it before. These differences may 'restore the hyphen' that sometime socialist-feminists renounced. This usage of 'difference' is not, despite its ubiquity among 'postmodernist' writers, itself postmodernist at all. That it is so seen, I think, results from the postmodernist proclamation of 'the death of the (universal, human) subject'. This appears to be construed in two ways. In the first – which would I suppose support these feminists' view – a unitary white male rational subject who is history's subject abdicates his role. And the different groups and voices come in; not into history, but into political play. In the second, however, the notion of *any* unitary subject, and more, any possessed of autonomy and agency, falls.[7]

This second view, paradoxically, leads some to regard postmodernism as offering a solution to the problem of 'woman'. For Chris Weedon, it possesses a better concept of female 'nature' than other options: radical feminism's appeal to an unchanging essence of woman, liberal feminism's aim of making women like men, and humanist Marxism's concept of a 'true human nature'.[8] These are all examples of the 'universal human subject' whose death we have seen announced.

For Weedon these schools are essentialist, in that they posit a human, a personal, 'essence'. Liberalism believes in a rational consciousness; much radicalism, in a 'womanhood'; humanist Marxism, in a true human nature which we strive to (re)gain. Weedon rejects 'essence', and so, all these views: they represent the 'subject' that has gone. She further rejects the idea of the socially constructed person, unable to change, possessing no agency: in a way, not a 'person' at all. The poststructuralist self is fluid, according to Weedon. But how strong is her contention? How far does fluidity extend? What, amid the flux, remains of the self?[9]

Whether such fluidity and fragmentation is a barrier to equality depends in part on our views of how that might be gained. What is clear is this. It challenges both the idea of 'women' as an undifferentiated, or even unified, group, and the notion of groups of women. Is its challenge stronger? How far is 'woman' split? Is there a unitary self? What are the political implications for feminism of this explicitly sundering stance?

I shall try to answer that below. First, however, I discuss Joan Scott, a writer explicitly concerned to disrupt the terms of the equality–difference debate. Then I counterpose 'group' and 'category' identity politics to postmodernist fragmentation, and show the dilemma they pose for emancipatory movements and groups. For that I refer to lesbian and queer theory, via Judith Butler's work. For such writing shows the dilemma I point to in acute form.[10]

I discuss two very different postmodernist writers here, yet reach the same basic conclusion as to their relevance for feminism, and the meaning of their stance. But that awaits.

The downfall of equality/difference?: Joan Scott

I turn to Scott's well-known demolition of the terms of the 'equality–difference debate' as conventionally perceived.[11] I begin with her explanation of deconstruction, following Derrida and writers associated with him. It is, in her definition, the study of 'the operations of difference in texts, the ways in which meanings are made to work', and has 'two related steps, the reversal and displacement of binary oppositions'. These steps show how apparently dichotomous terms are in fact related, mutually dependent: their seeming opposition is a construct. Deconstruction reveals this.

Scott focuses on *Sears*, a sex discrimination suit against Sears Roebuck brought by the Equal Employment Opportunities Commission in 1979. Here I want to discuss her use of poststructuralism[12] to interrogate the case. First I note that she comments, of 'equality–difference':

> A binary opposition has been created to offer a choice to feminists . . . . In fact the antithesis itself hides the interdependence of the two terms, for equality is not the elimination of difference, and difference does not preclude equality.[13]

Here a crucial, if disputed, point is well explained, and elements of poststructuralism, as defined by Scott, are neatly shown. That is: here we have an example, in equality versus difference, of the kind of binary opposition mentioned above. And here we have a statement, admittedly, rather than an argument, but, a persuasive one, that the opposition is false, and masks our understanding. The allegedly opposing terms of equality and difference, we see, do not necessarily form a simple antithesis at all.

I expand that point. In the sex equality–difference debate, we have, I said, an axis at the poles of which were these two terms; feminists could be seen as occupying one of the two places, though I tended to think there was a continuum along which they could be ranged. I further singled out the way the terms, used in opposition, failed to conform to their standard use, but suggested that the importation of 'same' might not solve the problem, and its implications were unclear.

For Scott, equality–difference is, or rather has become, a binary opposition of the type nature–culture, woman–man. It is, I interpolate here, therefore different from the others she cites in being (seen as) a simple oppressive artefact; and as having been called strongly into question, even as *socially* real, by those outside the postmodernist school.[14] But I return to Scott. Her contention is this. Equal versus different is a false dichotomy. Deconstructed, it becomes a pairing of inter-implicated terms: equality and difference can co-exist. An example of feminist use of deconstruction will demonstrate this point; I proceed to that.

Before further discussing Scott, I note that we can accept much of what is said here without agreeing fully with her. 'Equality–difference' as antithesis has perplexed many. We do not need a deconstructive technique, or any aspect of poststructuralism, to say that we thought equality was counterposed to inequality, sameness to difference. That these may be inter-implicated, that equality and difference may be related, is another matter: again it does not require a specialist technique to ponder points like these.

Further, Scott's final point, while indeed emerging from her method, is I suggest exactly what a poststructuralist interested in a notion like equality would make. That is, the conclusion is predetermined: it is not argued for or through. It remains unclear to me, is not shown here, that 'difference does not preclude equality'. I turn to Scott's use of her interpretive strategy in a discussion of *Sears*.

Scott regards *Sears* as an example of the importance of language, and what its study can reveal, and of discourse. Discourse is a structure of statements, beliefs. Words do not comprise institutions, however, insofar as power resides in knowledge – knowledge confers power? – 'organizations and institutions . . . words . . . constitute texts and documents to be read.'[15]

Sears concerned the relative underemployment of women at certain levels within the firm. In this case, equality did not face difference in the way we would expect. While Sears indeed pled difference, and so lack of fitness for or interest in the relevant posts, the EEOC (Equal Employment Opportunities Commission) did not plead sameness/equality: ability to carry out the occupations, and interest in doing so. The case has proved fertile ground for commentary, for that reason. What might not unfairly be asked is why it should be seen as any test of 'equality–difference'. Why choose *this* case?

'Difference' arguments were made, it is said, both by Sears and by their feminist expert witness, Rosenberg. However, the plaintiffs' feminist expert, Kessler-Harris, was, says Scott, a 'difference feminist' too. The distinction seems to be that Rosenberg argued a strong, Kessler-Harris a more nuanced, case. She argued for a greater historical variation in employment patterns than Rosenberg gave; suggested that economic considerations overrode the strong socialization Rosenberg adduced; and argued that 'choice' could not be offered as proof when hiring methods militated against the work being chosen by women.

Rosenberg seemed to believe that women both accepted the norms they were taught, and had a choice; while Kessler-Harris forwarded a more relational view, of an interplay among socialization, family, economy, and waged work. Further, if contradictorily at first sight, Rosenberg argued a 'multi-causal' case whereby the situation at Sears did not necessarily show discrimination in that there existed many possible reasons for women's under-representation there.[16]

While I have called them difference feminists – as many commentators do – either could in fact be construed as an 'equality' feminist, though that is no part of Scott's case.[17] Indeed what makes them both 'difference' feminists for Scott, I assume, is simply that they believe sex differences exist. But equality feminists – I include 'sameness' advocates – do not necessarily say that women and men are the same, when for example job selection is concerned, now. Rather they say that such differences as exist are irrelevant or can be overcome. Though in a law court, for tactical reasons, they would downplay such views because of the major framework and assumption – that 'like be treated as like' – within which they plead.

Rosenberg's testimony seems not to have been essentialist. She postulated an ideology of domesticity; of the prime importance, for women, of the domestic: an ideology furthered by the state. So far, this is reminiscent of Friedan: here returns the 'mystique'; here are differences, wrought by learning, that can be overcome. It occurs to me that what *Sears* demonstrates wonderfully well is that the law might not even accept that, but require 'like for like', *now*. So it would work against or even pre-empt change, in a case like this.

It is difficult, therefore, to see *Sears* as being about, fought on the grounds of, sameness–difference as conventionally construed. Publicity about the case gave the impression that the plaintiffs pled sameness, when this was not so, and the adversary system forced them to move nearer to that type of argument than they might otherwise have done. But this is certainly not a conventional instance of the debate.

Kessler-Harris encountered problems of courtroom procedure – and, we must assume, imputed untruth – because her evidence was historical and statistical, the testimony therefore inferential where certainty was required.

That is, Kessler-Harris was unable to say 'yes' or 'no', but rather, 'on the whole', and 'at certain times'.

Scott continues to illustrate the problems facing both historians, in particular Kessler-Harris, the more nuanced, given their form of language and argument, and that preferred by the Court. In the Court's finding for Sears on the grounds of sex differences, says Scott, 'Difference was substituted for inequality, the appropriate antithesis of equality . . . [quoting Schor]: "[the judgment][18] essentializes difference and naturalizes social inequity".'

I have simplified Scott's account to make it more accessible to newcomers to the field, or more palatable to non-believers, of whom I am one. I summarize her argument and conclusion. The testimonies of Rosenberg and Kessler-Harris, and their reception, show us what the powerful favour and what they do not. They accept categorical dichotomous statements, as given by Rosenberg. (That is so, I take it, when they agree with the given views.) They reject Kessler-Harris's more varied and nuanced 'difference among women' statement of belief. And we can see the way in which what the law, in the shape of a court, 'accepts' was used against Kessler-Harris, while Rosenberg was spared.

There is no doubt that Scott has conveyed the climate in which one way of presenting evidence can be accepted, and one, in effect, ignored. I do not believe this shows that the court is a 'text' or – to be more faithful to Scott – that a court case is best studied by being read as though it were a text. Again, I could not see how the 'reading' involved a deconstruction of equality and difference; if the answer is that they were shown to be related, given the particular nature of the testimony, the counter-argument is clear, if glib. The testimony was indeed 'particular'; or so Scott says. I also could not see why we should need a technique called deconstruction, a theory called poststructuralism, to understand a legal case. Certainly, I see no need of that technique, to give this account of *Sears*. It is not Scott's interpretive ability that I call into question now, but the method she says she employs. But then, it could also be said that much of the method – as opposed to the underlying theory in its extreme form – is not new.[19]

For Scott,

> The alternative to the binary construction of sexual difference is not sameness, identity, or androgyny. By subsuming women into a general 'human' identity we lose the specificity of female diversity and women's experiences.[20]

Postmodernists anyway reject the generalized human, but as we have seen, others do too. Does Scott's point contain an essentialist view of men? Further, does it suggest more than what I argue has already been shown by empirical research, that is, variability *within* a sex? If so, does it say more than that women are individuals? I believe that is true, and should be said. But it is not poststructuralism's aim to conclude that.

My comments on method do not ignore the fact that Scott, too, is an empirical researcher. But she is not an empiricist. That is, her analysis is explicitly interpretive and theoretically informed. However it goes further; attacking 'equality versus difference' she says:

> It . . . suggests that sameness is the only ground on which equality can be claimed . . . as long as we argue within . . . [this] we grant the current conservative premise that because women cannot be identical to men in all respects, we cannot expect to be equal to them. The only alternative . . . is . . . to insist continually on differences . . . as the condition of individual and collective identities . . . as the constant challenge to the fixing of those identities . . . as the very meaning of equality itself.[21]

I want here to note again the individualism latent in this emphasis on 'differences': certainly it is the only sense I could make of them as 'the very meaning of equality'; that we are not here dealing with any form of categorical identity, nor of universalism. And that despite the reference to collective identities, a reference qualified by Scott herself. Poststructuralism does not employ the terminology of individualism. But what else can 'differences as the . . . meaning of equality' *mean*?

Scott argues next for 'the utility of certain arguments in certain discursive contexts'; what I would call an 'apt for the moment' approach. So that at one time, in one context, feminists might want women's traditional work valued, and at and in another, might aim for what have been regarded as men's jobs. There is obviously something appealing, if risky, about the suggestion that we play our cards as we see fit, though Scott I think means rather that we may have little choice. That is, we will be constrained, but not overall; rather issue by issue, case by case.

Scott ends by saying that 'power is constructed on and so must be challenged from the ground of difference'. We would all I think like to have written that. But its meaning is unclear. How do we gain equality – for that is what Scott wants – via both constructive (comparable worth) and disruptive movements, always entailing claims on difference's grounds?[22]

Scott is in part a follower of Michel Foucault, who has been interpreted both as saying that more or less absolute power controls us, and that interstices allow struggle. Scott is on what might be called the conservative side here, emphasizing the difficulty of change.

It may be, then, that this piece, while pointing to a way forward, is pessimistic in the extreme. If so, it is unfair to burden it with more pessimism. However Scott does seem to suggest – rather magnificently – that our position is one of constant opposition, negativity, and refusal. I move to a writer who believes we can do more, though refusal of a different kind is one of her major motifs.

'Being' a lesbian: Judith Butler and gender's end

Here I address Butler's challenge to the notion of one gender identity; indeed, an identity at all. This challenge is both made to and centred on the category of lesbian, though the 'heterosexual matrix' is Butler's main focus of attack.[23] It is launched despite her acceptance of 'lesbian''s connotations of oppression. I take it as a challenge to the ideas of identity politics, therefore. She regards her project as political, and I shall take it so.

In *Gender Trouble*, as elsewhere,[24] Butler is concerned to analyse the fragmentation of identity. She begins by attacking major assumptions that have historically grounded the feminist cause and its claims; and some would say still do. For her, within them we encounter fundamental dilemmas of which I shall address one (which stems from other, prior dilemmas). That is the question of 'woman': whether 'she' can be regarded as some form of unified subject or not.

At this stage I leave Butler's more strictly philosophical dilemmas aside, though I note an immediate concern. How can we be constructed by the very powers against which we rebel, but simultaneously, via which we seek freedom?[25] I move to her pondering the possibility of a politics of identity: the politics therefore of a certain kind of difference: and so, the issue that interests me most.

I first take Butler's argument that 'woman' and 'women' no longer connote an identity:

> if one 'is' a woman, that is surely not all one is . . . gender is not always constituted coherently or consistently in different historical contexts, and . . . intersects with racial, class, sexual, and regional modalities of discursively produced identities.

So, for her, gender cannot be 'separated out'. But for her use of 'discursively produced', and the apparent impossibility of detaching gender (whose production and maintenance seem to be one way: has the gendered no agency?) this is a story we have heard before. Indeed, black women have made the point time and again: as did Spelman when she said, 'though all women are women, no woman is only a woman'.[26] The reiteration may well be a sign of the difficulty they have met, whose name is racism. Has no one listened? If they have, have they *heard*?

If I have understood what follows, a political problem arises from the fact that a fixed subject, 'woman' – in particular, heterosexually viewed – might nullify feminism's goal of women's political representation.[27] The 'woman' to be represented, once defined, might exclude many. Worse, 'women' might be able to be defined, 'constructed', only within the context of gender relationships as they stand. So a 'coherent and stable' subject of representation could exist only within heterosexual norms. I believe this to be a variant of a point made on non-postmodernist grounds, which concerns the difficulty posed by the formal political representation of any categorical group, as exemplified by Phillips's response to Young.

I move to the conclusion of *Gender Trouble*, where identity politics is addressed. As Butler says, it tends to presuppose an identity which already exists and so is able to construe its interests and act in accordance with them. For her, on the contrary, 'there need not be a "doer behind the deed," . . . the "doer" is invariably constructed through the deed'.[28] Here the self constructs the acts, the acts the self, with their interaction 'all that there is'. This is not then any form of self we have so far seen. Is it one we can even imagine?

Just as we might ask this, Butler recapitulates the problem she posed before. What she calls the identity categories presumed essential for feminism to be able to *be* an identity politics, she says, 'simultaneously limit and constrain in advance the very cultural possibilities that feminism is supposed to open up'.[29] If we see our identity as an *effect*, as produced, as acted upon, then agency is possible as it would not be were identity categories fixed. Though this requires that identity is neither utterly determined nor, as it were, floating free. For Butler, we do not try to gain a foothold, establish a knowledge, outside the produced identities. We struggle by taking part in them, and acting along their lines.

How, then, do we disrupt them? Butler has talked of deconstructing sex, sexual preference, and gender. She believes that parody can disrupt. Drag and cross-dressing, for example, have been attacked as a degrading mimicry of women. For her,

> As much as drag creates a unified picture of 'woman' . . . it also reveals the distinctness of those aspects of gendered experience which are falsely naturalized as a unity through the regulatory fiction of heterosexual coherence. *In imitating gender, drag implicitly reveals the imitative structure of gender itself – as well as its contingency.*[30]

and

> the parody is *of* the very notion of an original.[31]

Butler uses 'parody' powerfully here. Normally we assume that what is parodied is the original, *an* original: the parody is in a sense a tribute to that. We can imagine many examples of parodies of plays, poems, and people. These rely on the existence and our knowledge of what is parodied, or the point would be lost.

If my last sentence read, 'our belief in the existence of an original', as it legitimately, without postmodernism, could, it would more nearly approach Butler's point. For her, drag imitates what is itself akin to imitation: a performance. That performance is gender. Because it is an imitation, because – here I depart from Butler – of its fragility, it shows the non-necessary character of gender, too. What is being parodied in drag is 'woman', the notion of original womanhood, of a unitary gender. When a man dresses like a woman as drag dressers do, he is not parodying women at all.[32] Thus Butler 'reads the text' of drag, and makes it an act of liberation from the gender trap. Or so I suggest. For her its primary use might be to expose the myths about heterogeneities of sex and sexual preference that compulsory heterosexuality brings. It would nonetheless cast light on the notion of 'gender' as normally employed; and could be used to point to the myth that heterosexuality is homogeneous, also.

Butler's points about 'imitation' can be redescribed as follows. 'Being a woman' entails appropriate behaviour. For a (properly socialized) biological woman, it is unclear how self-conscious the activity, in certain of its facets, is. Here Butler's '"doer" . . . invariably constructed through the deed' can help us, if only by reinforcing that uncertainty, understand an interplay of gender and the gendered that we cannot quite pin down. For while heterosexuality may not be homogeneous, to an extent the presentation of woman is.

For 'Agnes', a male-female transsexual,[33] that may not have been true, for Agnes had to socialize herself in order to be viewed as a woman, but nonetheless, had a choice. For her, learning to 'be a woman' – to stand, walk, talk, and giggle like a woman, to behave 'appropriately' in the presence of men – required observation and imitation. In my redescription she takes the role of the drag dresser, who also has a choice. Via them we see that biological women are 'imitating women'; over-homogenizing woman; chaining themselves, if perforce, within gender's bonds. Drag can satirize, and expose, that: it may even highlight the way many, perhaps most, women learn to be so. Further, the disjuncture between those whose imposture and play illuminate 'normal heterosexuals' and the latter's fixity, even as they perform their gender role, may be an important part of Butler's case.

This is a difficult and complex analysis. But again, I do not see why we need a particular technique to make it. It may not be immediately intuitive, but it has I think been said in various ways, of which 'The story of Agnes' is only one.[34] However, Butler's comments on gender are insightful, if problematic. Her political project is not. Lost from her version, I think, are agency and oppression. At least, that would seem to be so for the woman drag 'exposes'. But not only for her.

Consider lesbian and gay 'identity politics', and think about the consequences of not only coming out, but joining a group. Think also about the debate about 'deconstructing the gay identity';[35] that is, whether to assimilate or not. Butler knows the problems involved. In 'Imitation and gender subordination'[36] she addresses the view that lesbian and gay identities should be affirmed because they are threatened by homophobia. Perhaps the most interesting and worrying of her counter-arguments is this. While gays and lesbians are indeed

> threatened by the violence of public erasure . . . the decision to counter that violence must be careful not to reinstall another in its place . . . . Is it not a sign of despair over public politics when identity becomes its own policy, bringing with it those who would 'police' it from various sides.[37]

I can see the danger pointed to here. I can also see what we would normally call the tension between 'individual' and 'group'. And I have heard the voices that say what Butler knows – but whose implications, it seems, she would rather not accept[38] – that lesbian and gay are categories of pride, and of oppression. They are a life and a remembrance; to speak of 'playing'[39] is to forget that to be gay has led to massive persecution, and great violence: at its extreme, to Hitler's death camps.[40] I suppose the lesbian equivalent has been historically, may be still, a disproportionately 'private' life, of hidden grief.[41]

I do not suggest that Butler brushes such issues aside. She does however seem – though the complexity of her style of argument does not help a reader – to want to renounce certain of their implications. Most radically, she wants to renounce 'identity':

> There is no volitional subject behind the mime who decides, as it were, which gender it will be today . . . gender is not a performance that a prior subject elects to do, but gender is *performative* in the sense that it constitutes as an effect the very subject it appears to express.[42]

On what, then, can Butler's politics be based? Can there *be* a 'politics'? Who would enact it? We have seen Butler renounce the '"doer" behind the "deed"'; of this, and its corollaries, Benhabib says:

> If we are no more than the sum total of the gendered expressions we perform, is there ever any chance to stop the performance for a while, to pull the curtain down, and only let it rise if one can have a say in the production of the play itself? *Isn't this what the struggle over gender is all about?*[43]

For her, it is possible to curb aspects of identity politics, attack heterosexist power, without renouncing the idea of a self. Moreover – and Butler knows this – without a self, what can be the authority of a text? Yet there can be little doubt that there is no self here; that 'it' is a series of roles, which may not even be a 'sum'. Then, what status has Butler's work? So entrapped, none.

But this is not all Butler says, nor is it the only type of point she makes. I turn to her views on feminism and postmodernism,[44] and certain of feminism's concrete concerns for which the issue of the subject is key. She notes, as I have said above, the necessity to speak for, politically to represent, women; she believes that within the US system, a politics of identity is necessary for that.

However, she says, a second necessity is entailed by the first. Once 'the category of women is invoked as *describing* the constituency' for which feminism speaks, then its content will be contested. Will 'women', for example, be defined as childbearers? Might there be an invocation of female virtue? Surely, factions will emerge. And

> all women are not mothers; some cannot be, some are too young or too old to be, some choose not to be, and for some who are mothers, that is not necessarily the rallying point of their politicization.

Now Butler, as we have seen, rejects identity politics which constrain, in the manner of the forces they oppose. Her answer here is to maintain the disagreements between women, together with a permanent openness of the overall term. That is, she says – and I am tempted to agree – to give true agency.[45] (Though as we have seen in arguments on essentialism earlier in the book, total openness entails a political risk.) Certainly I do if the aim is to safeguard the individual – a problematic notion for Butler and yet, I believe, one for which she stands.[46]

We might say again, we have heard this before. Here I cite the discussion of women, as childbearers or not childbearers, for all the different reasons a woman might be unable, might not want, to give birth. I suggest that Butler is talking about individual agents of the kind to whom I am inclined to refer. There are moments in Butler when her language and her analysis fail to mesh, and I argue that this is one. Such moments are near-fatal to her endeavour. It may be that this problem is not hers alone: that postmodernism in general can exceed its grasp, and waver, when forced to confront the 'real'. Its language cannot encompass the 'real world'. Postmodernism collapses in the face of a political need.

If there is but an imposed 'woman' and a fictive self, if Butler's writing is a mix of modes correctly seen, as Patricia Clough suggests, as 'a literary reality', there may be no problem here.[47] But then, why does Butler raise the point at all? Clearly because there are aspects of this world she wants to change, and so – to be crass; a satisfying way of dealing with post-modernism, though not ideal – there has to be a world to change.

In Chapter 8 I spoke of philosophical/metaphysical discussions of the concepts of the self and of identity; and noted that between them and writings on group and identity politics there was a massive gulf. Butler engages in such discussions, and moves on to address the problems of an identity politics,[48] and of political representation as normally conceived. Then she faces the gulf, and leaps. And she falls.

It is open to Butler to say that I have misunderstood her points: that she speaks solely of imposed categories and identities.[49] But if we move beyond that to the project of political representation within whose boundaries she must speak, I think we ask: what does she say here that transcends Phillips's critique of Young? For there it is said that group representation of women is a problem, in that the chosen women may not represent others. That argument assumes a heterogeneity of women such as the one to which Butler speaks. It is an argument she does not surpass. No postmodernist technique produced it, and none was required.

Further to this, there are I believe moments – for example the preliminary discussion of identity politics and feminism, above – when Butler's non-self was never that. That and her discussion of her lesbianism in 'Imitation'[50] make me see her as an individual and an individualist. After all, who did get up on the stage at Yale, in 1989, to 'be a lesbian'? This individualism, apparently denied, is what she shares with Scott.

In *Bodies that Matter*,[51] Butler reflects on misunderstandings *Gender Trouble* brought about: for example, the notion of the performativity of gender evoking 'a figure of a choosing subject – humanist – at the center of a project whose emphasis on construction seems to be quite opposed to such a notion'. Reflecting on the issues of agency, power, and of choice versus determinism, that occur, Butler provisionally concludes that 'The discourse of "construction" that has for the most part circulated in feminist theory is perhaps not quite adequate to the task at hand', which is, for her, the '[linking] of the question of the materiality of the body to the performativity of gender'.[52]

As her critics ask, if gender is constructed, who constructs it? For does not construction require one who constructs? Butler seems to see this as a semantic problem only. Her reply is in effect a reprise of her proposal that there is no pre-gendered self:

> Subjected to gender, but subjectivated by gender, the 'I' neither precedes nor follows . . . but emerges only within and as the matrix of gender relationships themselves.[53]

There is a sense in which I find this non-problematic: but it is not Butler's sense. I shall 'translate' it, and the questions it addresses, to explain why. Butler is trying to answer a critique that supposes an either–or she sees as a product of our language use: if we are acted upon, our gender 'made', there is someone or something that makes it; if though gender is something we enact, why call it constructed?

This is a version, I think, of a far older argument; and I read Butler's answer, in part at least, as addressing it. I see her, that is, as concerned with the relationship between structure, or culture, and agency; as pointing to the parameters within which we act, and within whose limits we are born. Specifically, most of us are not born free of sex and gender; of the sex-gender system which exerts so strong a policing effect, yet leaves us 'free' to act at various places within its parameters at any one time.

Many of us could, with varying amounts of unease, accept these points, though we would want some hope of breaking the cycle of enactor and enacted, the fusion of doer and deed. However, Butler goes further, renouncing an externality that is, or produces, essence or construct. She replaces acts by acting, the material by 'materialization'. Then all becomes process, and all is in flux – though process and flux are, as before, constrained – to the point where, it seems, the body itself is in question. Here again, a subject with agency, who would resist the norms of gender, is produced by those very norms. For her, at this point, the choosing subject ends.[54]

I am moved to ask simply, why? To revert to an earlier way of discussing such matters: are all feminists, all who rebel against their 'assignments' of gender and sexual preference, the products of 'inadequate socialization'? If not, cannot we – while clinging to the notion of a material world – take something like Butler's view and yet retain elements of agency and choice? Moreover if we totally renounce the latter, as it seems Butler has done,[55] are we not even more deeply trapped than was suggested above? There is a science fiction story whose characters are doomed to repeat the same ten minutes' actions for all time: the terror is that they know it. This is not Butler's world, but it could be.

It may be apt to deploy postmodernist views against Butler. We are not at liberty to read her as we would wish.[56] By what authority can she say that? What authorial privilege can she claim? None. It is an old, and not wholly satisfactory, tactic to use the arguments of relativists to deny their claims; to say, but if all views are equal, then so is yours.[57] There are occasions to use it. And there comes a time to range Butler's belief system against her, even though (or perhaps, because) she deploys similar tactics herself.[58]

I turn to a black feminist, bell hooks. Hooks is both intrigued and perturbed by blacks' relatively – indeed, very – low interest in post-modernism, though she is perturbed by aspects of postmodernism, too. She believes it could militate against racism. It could prevent the stereotyping whereby to be black is to be associated with concrete experience only, debarred from critical and abstract thought. However, despite its status as the voice of heterogeneity and the decentred self, it has ignored blacks.[59]

Postmodernism would of course 'deconstruct' the black identity. Hooks sees this kind of move as relevant to liberating struggle, but also views identity politics, while racism prevails, as crucial for blacks. And she is wary of a critique of the subject that emerges just as the subordinate might become subjects, too.[60]

Hooks sees value in postmodernism's attacks on essentialist thought, given the imposition, by whites and blacks, of 'a narrow, constricting notion of blackness'. She believes the heterogeneity of black experience will thus be more readily seen. Though while the idea of essence must depart, the 'authority of experience' and of a 'privileged critical location' must remain.[61] It should be added that hooks regards the privileged critique as valid in certain circumstances alone.

I find plausible her view that postmodernism could erode the fixity identity politics is thought to bring, and indeed requires. Without it, she believes, there will remain a dated and over-homogenized view of what the black experience, of what it is to be black, is. Though here I meet a problem I have stated before, perhaps better called a doubt. Is postmodernism really required for an understanding of the dilemma involved? For it is a dilemma and hooks I think does not lightly embrace one side.

Many white feminist writers – sometimes I think, the vast majority – have embraced postmodernism, though mainly of an attenuated kind. But others have struck back.

Nancy Hartsock, for example, has asked why a cognitively relativist world view has sprung up at exactly the time when 'the previously silenced had begun to speak for themselves'. Why is it at this precise moment that the notion of the subject, and the possibility of the truth, becomes suspect?[62] Eisenstein points out that the 'Enlightenment' so scorned by postmodernists had emancipatory beliefs not yet extended to women.[63] While according to Hawkesworth,

At a moment when the preponderance of rational and moral argument sustains prescriptions for women's equality, it is a bit too cruel a conclusion and too reactionary a political agenda to accept that reason is impotent, that equality is impossible . . . . In a world of radical inequality, relativist resignation supports the status quo.[64]

Finally there has been a chorus of 'we must be able to say "women" ("woman")'; and it is for that reason that Spivak said, '[we] take a stand against . . . essentialism . . . *strategically* we cannot'.[65]

Despite the difficulty of some of the material here, I think we can grasp the challenge postmodernism poses for the equality–difference debate(s). Both Scott and Butler attack sameness; both, categories of difference, and identity, as conventionally understood. One can nonetheless see Scott as forwarding a feminist project, though I think we might have to ask, on what grounds? What female constituency does she address? Butler is more problematic, given the possibility that she may, despite her own comments, not believe in anything outside 'the text'. Where Scott 'deconstructs' towards individualism, and so towards liberal or libertarian viewpoints she would not endorse, Butler wavers between that and a combined sundering and determinism by which agency is denied. Then feminism too is renounced. Though that is not Butler's view.

Postmodernist techniques can alert us to the dilemmas of categorical identities acting as political groups; though I suggest such methods are not essential for the task. My insistence on this point derives from the difficulty of coming to terms with writing like this: my encounters with 'full postmodernism' remind me of learning several languages at the same time. If there is an easier mode of analysis and expression, it should be used: for the sake of efficiency and because postmodernist language intimidates all but a few.

These are not my only grounds for perturbation. I share the views of the critics I mentioned above. Postmodernism is frequently regarded as a recipe for stasis, if not indeed paralysis: and I believe that.

Next I discuss the 'legal challenge': a challenge to sameness-equality and difference, even though it is concerned with gaining equality (or so I would argue) before the law.

Notes

1 I shall on the whole use the terms interchangeably here, speaking mainly of postmodernism. For a persuasive objection to an over-homogenous use of either, see Judith Butler, 'Contingent foundations: feminism and the question of "postmodernism"', in Judith Butler and Joan Scott (eds), *Feminists Theorize the Political*, 1992; and Jane Flax, *Thinking Fragments: Psychoanalysis, Feminism, and Postmodernism in the Contemporary West*, 1991, p. 188ff.

2 In the non-complimentary sense of the term, which is normal, now. See Susan Okin, *Justice, Gender and the Family*, 1989, pp. 10–13 and *passim*: her term is 'false gender-neutrality'.

3 Joanna Hodge, 'Women and the Hegelian state', in Ellen Kennedy and Susan Mendus (eds), *Women in Western Political Philosophy*, 1987, p. 144.

4 Flax, *Thinking Fragments*, p. 199.

5 On the relationship between ontology and epistemology see Elizabeth Frazer and Nicola Lacey, *The Politics of Community: A Feminist Critique of the Liberal–Communitarian Debate*, 1992, esp. pp. 183–4.

6 A writer who abominates postmodernism but supports Derrida is Christopher Norris. See for example *Uncritical Theory: Postmodernists, Intellectuals, and the Gulf War*, 1992.

7 Linda Alcoff, 'Cultural feminism versus post-structuralism: the identity crisis in feminist theory', in Micheline R. Malson et al. (eds), *Feminist Theory in Practice and Process*, 1989, p. 297.

8 Chris Weedon, *Feminist Practice and Poststructuralist Theory*, 1989, p. 33.

9 See also Flax, *Thinking Fragments*, pp. 218–19; and Jane Flax, *Disputed Subjects*, 1993, p. 100ff.

10 So do the writings of blacks. My problem has been the relatively small number engaged with the field. I give the views of bell hooks below.

11 Joan Scott, 'Deconstructing equality-versus-difference', in Marianne Hirsch and Evelyn Fox Keller (eds), *Conflicts in Feminism*, 1990.

12 This is her term.

13 Scott, 'Deconstructing', pp. 137–8.

14 See my early chapters, and especially Chapter 10.

15 Scott, 'Deconstructing', p. 136; here Scott summarizes Michel Foucault.

16 Ibid., p. 139ff.

17 See Sondra Farganis, *Situating Feminism*, 1994, for an account that suggests this was indeed an equality–difference case; though that is not Farganis's point.

18 Scott notes that Schor was not discussing this.

19 See Peter Dews, *The Logics of Disintegration*, 1987, p. 11ff. Dews is concerned with theoretical predecessors; but methodologies are entailed.

20 Scott, 'Deconstructing', p. 143.

21 Ibid., p. 144.

22 Ibid., pp. 145–6.

23 Judith Butler, *Gender Trouble: Feminism and the Subversion of Identity*, 1990, *passim*; see for example p. 5, p. 151 n. 6.

24 Judith Butler, 'Imitation and gender subordination', in Diana Fuss (ed.), *Inside/Out*, 1991; Butler, *Bodies That Matter: On the Discursive Limits of 'Sex'* (1993).

25 I have departed radically from Butler's wording here, using a far less complex vocabulary.

26 Elisabeth V. Spelman, *Inessential Woman*, 1990, p. 187.

27 In conventional terms; Butler sees no point in not using political institutions, and the law, as they stand.

28 Butler, *Gender Trouble*, p. 142.

29 Ibid., p. 147.

30 Ibid., p. 137.

31 Ibid., p. 138.

32 Or rather, he is showing there are no 'women' to parody.

33 Howard Garfinkel, 'The story of Agnes', in *Studies in Ethnomethodology*, 1967.

34 Ian Craib, *Modern Social Theory*, 1992, pp. 186–7; Susan Bordo, 'Postmodern subjects, postmodern bodies', *Feminist Studies*, 18(1) 1992.

35 R.W. Connell, *Gender and Power*, 1987, pp. 231–4, 282–4.

36 Butler, 'Imitation'.

37 Ibid., p. 19.

38 I base this view on the opening of, and various passages in, Butler, 'Imitation'.

39 Strictly speaking, Butler is concerned with gender as a 'performative utterance': a highly specific philosophical term with its own technical context. But she employs 'play', 'perform', and 'act' sufficiently often to license my words.

40 Butler's final chapter on queer theory, in her most recent book, does move towards redress of such an interpretation of her work. I have been unable to analyse it here. *Bodies That Matter: On the Discursive Limits of 'Sex'*, 1993.

41 Nadya Aisenberg and Mona Harrington, *Women of Academe*, 1988, comment that they knew their interview groups included lesbians, but none so identified herself; p. xii.

42 Butler, 'Imitation', p. 24.

43 Seyla Benhabib, *Situating the Self*, 1992, p. 215.

44 Butler, 'Contingent foundations'.

45 Ibid., pp. 15–16.

46 See the opening section of Butler, *Bodies That Matter*; and Butler, 'Imitation'.

47 Patricia Clough, *Feminist Thought*, 1994, pp. 154–5.

48 Though that is not how she puts the point.

49 In a sense, the option is not open to her. We have seen that when looking at 'texts'. But of course more or less all postmodernists do.

50 Butler, 'Imitation'.

51 Butler, *Bodies That Matter*.

52 Ibid., pp. x–xi, 1.

53 Ibid., p. 7.

54 Ibid., pp. 6–16.

55 Ibid., p. 15; there is, however, I think an ambiguity in 'a choosing subject' here.

56 Ibid., pp. ix–x: I refer to her reactions to (the manner of) a critique.

57 That is, their view that all views are equal.

58 Butler, 'Contingent foundations', p. 14.

59 bell hooks, *Yearning: Race, Gender and Cultural Politics*, 1991, pp. 23–5.

60 Ibid., p. 26.

61 Ibid., pp. 28–9.

62 Nancy Hartsock, 'Foucault on power', in Linda Nicholson (ed.), *Feminism/ Postmodernism*, 1990, p. 163.

63 Hester Eisenstein, *Gender Shock: Practicing Feminism on Two Continents*, 1991, p. 112.

64 Mary Hawkesworth, 'Knowers, knowing, known: feminist theory and the claims of truth', in Micheline Malson et al. (eds), *Feminist Theory in Practice and Process*, p. 351.

65 Gayatri Spivak, 'Criticism, feminism and the institution', in Sarah Harasyn (ed.), *The Post-Colonial Critic*, 1990, pp. 11–12; also quoted in Chapter 2.

10

The Legal Challenge

Carol Bacchi and Catharine Mackinnon have explicitly attacked the terms and the terminology of the (gender) 'equality–difference' debate.[1] They focus firmly, in the main, on sameness/equality, difference, and the law. Given their concern to improve women's position relative to men's, they might be thought equality feminists, problematic though they would find the word. Mackinnon, I believe, thinks it so mainly because of the 'sameness' and therefore 'difference' connotations it has held until now. It may be that Bacchi does too: that is not always clear.

Mackinnon is a lawyer whose work emerges from the strand of feminist theory influenced by critical legal thought, though her view is very much her own. Bacchi, an historian, approaches equality–difference via the law. She addresses the 'sameness–difference' version of the debate on women's advance; and in her work, as in the lawyers', this stems from the classical definition of equality, and longstanding legal doctrine, that 'like be treated as like'. This notion, and the framework that surrounds it, she and Mackinnon reject.

These authors reject essentialism and universalism. They differ in the focus of their work. Mackinnon emphasizes sameness–equality and difference as parts of a system of domination and power, ideas created and disseminated by that system obfuscating the brutal realities of social life. Bacchi, in contrast, comments on the effects of the characteristics of men, or men stereotypically viewed, being taken as the standard and the norm; her analysis tends to terminate there. For example she discusses, though rarely in detail, the way in which occupational arrangements assume a 'worker' is male: to allow for separate female needs would be to make exceptional provision; to cater for men is normal. While Mackinnon would agree, that would be but part of her view.

Bacchi clearly opposes many aspects of the economy and society we know, her dislike relating both to the secondary position of women and to the treatment of certain men, but her full view is latent. Mackinnon, in contrast, forwards an analysis of the origin of gender oppression: in terms of patriarchy and the eroticization and sexualization of power. A better way to explain this might be to say that (hetero?)sexuality has become intertwined and infused with domination, until domination is what it is. Hence, perhaps, Bacchi's willingness to rely on the state and its legislative enactments, and Mackinnon's aversion to working via its provisions and powers. Not that Mackinnon can avoid this. But then, she has argued that women must work with various institutions and belief systems they can neither 'trust . . . [nor] control'.[2] Here she is not alone among feminists of the critical legal school.

These writers' challenge poses a problem of classification. If feminism can be analysed in terms of equality/sameness and difference, how do we name those who *prima facie* reject both? How can I suggest they work for equality? If they can be shown to do that, should they be termed equality feminists? I turn to these issues, and others, through a consideration of the texts.

Bacchi and sameness

Bacchi challenges equality–difference as a correct or even tenable axis in feminist debate, and for women's advance. Her contention is not that the true antithesis is between sameness and difference, equality and inequality. Rather, women have been forced into conceptualizing equality as sameness, and claiming it on those grounds, which is detrimental to their cause.

So if Bacchi is an equality feminist, she is not a sameness one. She wants parity or potential parity of the sexes in, for example, occupational provision and reward. However, she seeks less an identity of treatment in every respect than particular treatment for women; though she would not so phrase the point. Bacchi wants working conditions, which she emphasizes, changed to accommodate women's needs, though not theirs alone.

Here, I capture Bacchi's main theme. But I also omit what makes her difficult to assess. That is her insistence that she speaks of stereotypes: 'male' and 'female' rather than woman and man; and has in mind also the needs of men. Her policy discussion, however, tends to cast stereotypes aside and prioritize what she regards as women's needs. Rather than single out divergences as they occur, I shall follow her major train of thought.

Bacchi clearly seeks not radical equality, but a semi-liberal kind, attained under the legal and governmental systems we know now. She believes women are disadvantaged, or she would not intervene in the debate as she does. Nonetheless, she is an exemplar of the point that the feminist notion of radical equality has been in large part lost, as her aims show.

Her policy proposals would, like certain liberal feminist goals, require massive change. But her analysis suggests only ameliorative acts. For we do not find here attacks on hierarchy; on the notions of 'worker' and 'employer'; or on the current form of the state. Rather she insists that working conditions must be improved, and other provisions necessary to a humane society be made. We can infer that employers, and those in governmental office, are responsible for these. We also, though, have to infer what they are. That must depend on the likeness of the sexes, and the extent to which each can be regarded as a unitary one. Bacchi is not totally consistent here. Assuming that differing attributes and needs of men and women are involved, we are left not knowing – except when a legal case she discusses can illuminate the point – what or how great they are; or how they might be met.

This leads to a vagueness about what is required. If we are thinking of a workplace and occupation designed equally for women and men, we could imagine various changes from what I take it is the norm. I do not know enough about all-female factory assembly lines, say, to be able to tell. But I assume they meet women's needs as little as men's meet theirs. We could want crèches in the legislative lower houses, and women's lavatories in upper houses, and courts;[3] and their equivalents elsewhere. Or we could go further than this, and propose more flexible working hours. But more flexibility must surely be for all. That women bear children is not good enough reason to change hours for them alone. Though I admit, I speak here as both an equality feminist, and as a woman who rears no child.[4]

Bacchi's answer would be this. We should 'include women in the rules by which social standards are set', that is, to order society for *human beings* in such a manner that difference is both taken into account, and seen as irrelevant.[5] This says no more about exact provisions. Nor does it say what differences Bacchi thinks there are. It does show that the fact of sex difference, and women's being viewed as 'the different', is Bacchi's motive force.

For Bacchi, then, the debate refers to a situation where traditional sex roles favour men, and 'women' are seen as 'the problem'.[6] Women must conform; not men, or society, change. 'Why', she asks, 'should it matter if women are the same as or different from men?', here importing a cultural-feminist form of argument: 'why does the economic system reward competition and penalize caring?' But the point is not pursued. As she also attacks the debate for leading us to ignore differences between groups of women, and the power and hierarchy 'sameness and difference' mask, her exact stance is unclear.

I make no attempt to summarize the mass of case-law in Bacchi's book. Instead I single out major cases and issues where equality and difference, or rather, 'equal' and 'different' *treatment* feminism, have clashed. The first is the US debate on paid pregnancy leave. 'Equal treatment' advocates, who oppose it, are concerned lest employers use the suggested added cost to avoid hiring women. 'Special treatment' proponents invoke 'difference'.[7] On occasion, the disputants seem less to argue with one another than to talk past.

The legal background to the 'equal treatment' approach is the classic dictum that '"likes . . . [are] treated alike"': the '"similarly situated"', the '"same"'.[8] Feminist lawyers faced judgments invoking 'difference' as a reason to uphold the status quo of unpaid leave, without re-employment rights. To cope with these, equality lawyers argued that pregnancy was like other conditions: subsequent EEOC (Equal Employment Opportunities Commission) guidelines stated that pregnancy and natality should be treated *'like any other temporary disabilities'* [italics in original].[9] For then they could be viewed as 'the same' as inability to work as a result of illness, and benefit paid.

The well-known case of *Geduldig* v. *Aiello* upheld state disability insurance which excluded pregnancy-related disabilities in a normal pregnancy, whatever that means. The court explained that the insurance divided people into 'two groups – pregnant women and non-pregnant persons – . . . the first group . . . exclusively female',[10] therefore no sex-based discrimination, none based *on sex alone*, occurred. Given such judgments, certain feminists campaigned for a change to the Civil Rights Act. The Pregnancy Disability Amendment of 1978 held that pregnant women 'shall be treated *the same for all employment-related purposes* . . . as other persons . . . *similar in their ability or inability to work'*. [Italics in original][11]

Existing law had been extended; a major problem remained. Extant disability provisions would have to include pregnancy; no new provisions had to be made. Feminists divided on whether to seek more, and further cases intensified the equal and special treatment split.

I view this divide as simultaneously tactical or pragmatic, and ideological; its tactical components relate to a US ideological tradition of individualism and lack of state welfare, and the extent to which the latter is disliked. Thus feminists' tactical decisions are made within an ideological framework to which they may or may not adhere, but of which they must take note. So a lawyer who sought equality but did not believe in sameness, might still choose to argue that.

'Equal' feminists argue that employers would be swayed against women by the cost of benefits, and that other workers would oppose preferential treatment for some. 'Special treatment' advocates hold maternity cover to be an easier short-term goal than welfare for all, and point out practical problems – such as certification – of the 'disability' view. Further, equality feminists point to the danger of difference in judgments like *Geduldig*, while special treatment advocates think women will never gain equality of opportunity until pregnancy can be accommodated in a normal pattern of work. Both approaches are tactical to an extent, and both make sense. This is in part a time-frame division: do not risk arguing difference *now*, against, if we sell the pass on pregnancy yet again, we may never get working lives more suited to us.

One dilemma here may stem from the American context alone.[12] The 'certification problem' arises because pregnancy is not an illness. But it also emerges because of a relative lack of welfare provision in the US, of the kind that the UK and Australia know. How equal are US women, given, and in relation to, a relative lack of provision? Is a malnourished pregnant woman 'ill'? If so, how ill? The less the general scope of mandatory care, the more perturbing the question becomes.

Bacchi supports pregnancy and natality leave, and birth-time leave for partners. Her policy should, she says, be viewed not as catering for women, but implemented because 'the system must acknowledge that people have children'. How does this 'include women in the standard'? Does Bacchi mean that the women who bear children are *people*? While her policy would redress the result of *Geduldig*, her wording does not. There would be *people* who were pregnant, and people who were not. Then her words approach the reason why, and the way in which, liberals have in theory justified equality through the years: via a commonality of personhood. Does Bacchi endorse this? I think not. Yet surely she means to say here, 'must acknowledge that childbearers are people', so adopting the liberal view. For she would refuse the possibly more radical, for a feminist potentially fraught, outlook which says that *people* 'have children': including men.[13]

Bacchi turns to protective legislation. She supports protective laws, but again does not want them to rest on 'difference', which may be acknowledged, but, must never be allowed to hamper women. How would Bacchi answer a charge of special pleading? Her response – her major argument, never fully spelled out – would be that society has been made for men. There is no fair and just reason why this should be so. Society must be made for women too. And – a point latent in Bacchi – to deny that is to fail to see that it is possible to talk about men's differences from women, as well as women's differences from men.

The dilemma here is to earn a living in an unsafe job, or risk having none. The question is whether both a fair living and safe working conditions can be gained. Bacchi's answer, based on the Australian experience, seems to be that where a government will improve conditions for all, they can.

This evades various issues. What do we do when a government will improve conditions for *nobody*? Or for none of the groupings most at need? What happens if it changes policy, or a new government comes in? The American lawyers' dilemma, and split, may be more understandable, and more intractable, than Bacchi thinks.

Talking of protection from reproductive hazard, Bacchi – while again wanting women 'included' – says that if women are people (as I would say), if *workers* are people and not some abstraction, then we must have 'the recognition of heterogeneous attributes'.[14] I strongly support this. It is not clear that Bacchi should, as it could lead to differentiations between women which she would not want. For how then could we include 'women' in the standard? A further comment by Bacchi reinforces this doubt.

'Most jobs', she says,

have been designed for the average man, who by some peculiar quirk of fate, tends to be a white male undergraduate aged 18 to 23. This means that many jobs are unsuitable for most men and women.[15]

This is a crucial point. It undercuts much of what Bacchi says: 'drawing attention to women's sex-specific characteristics' will not help fight the combined ageism, racism, and sexism involved here, together with the emphasis on the 'able-bodied' which we can infer. On the contrary, danger lurks in invoking sex-specificity before the law.

Sears is considered a major equality–difference case. I shall address it briefly here. To the charges that women were under-represented in the better-paid selling jobs and that there was a pay differential in other fields, Sears pled difference, and won.

For Bacchi, *Sears* illustrates feminism's problem concerning the meaning and utility of 'woman'. Does this, she asks, have a 'transhistorical meaning' of any value? Is there a 'female essence' which is benevolent?[16] I want to put her questions in another way. Is 'woman' ahistorical? Or is she constructed by power, place, and time? If the former, is her nature valuable, her essence kind?

Sears decided women were different: that legitimized their virtual exclusion; women could enter the market as it was, or stay out. Bacchi would 'change marketplace rules to make them more humane and more responsive to people's needs'. *Sears* she regards as proving that 'reducing social analysis to discussions about women's sameness to or difference from men deflects attention from general social problems' such as those exemplified by market norms. Feminists should, she thinks, study how economic arrangements affect behaviour, rather than seeing women as 'the problem' yet again, leaving the system untouched.[17]

Certainly women will fare ill in an inhuman market. (Some say that is what markets are.) But women have also fared ill in movements to combat inhumanity: so, a major part of Second-Wave feminism began. Earlier I named the tenets I think we must hold before taking the view that to, say, vary the market, necessarily benefits women as a group; let alone that we should eschew the logical step of working for women only, in favour of a revolution that, should it happen, might not help us.

It is unlikely that Bacchi wants this. Yet what she does want amounts to it. If she wants all the changes she suggests, then surely only a revolution could bring them about? Or rather: if she wants a 'truly humane society', will not that entail revolutionary change?

I return briefly to *Sears*. Part of the problem, it is suggested, lay in the company's ethos and the nature of the work. Employers, says Bacchi, should change their culture so that women will join their firms.[18] Rather than emphasize a difference, and bar women from employment because of it, she believes we should ask 'why aggressive and even unethical sales techniques are approved and rewarded'.[19] Thus we approach cultural feminism, via a suggestion of superior female qualities and values, once more. Now to ban or change commission sales is not to 'include women' rather than accept the 'male standard'. Many women work on commission. Does that make matters better? And what of saleswomen we find aggressive? At least as aggressive as salesmen?

Mary Joe Frug's doubts go further. She suspects that 'the warrior image of the commission sales worker' forwarded by Sears was a ploy, and of the behaviour of saleswomen she adds: 'Trying to sneak past department store cosmetic counters . . . reminds me that women who work in those locales could easily be described as "aggressive", "outgoing", and quite informed.'[20]

Bacchi knows the dangers of 'womanhood' but does not want women to surrender difference for sameness.

> [S]etting equality *against* difference makes it difficult to question the nature of the equality which is on offer . . . seeking out sameness and differences diverts attention from the conditions which produce the norm . . . . The project of feminism . . . is to learn from the encounter with 'female' values and 'female' experience and to extend the lessons to society at large.[21]

This resembles cultural feminism. Feminism, Bacchi continues, will forward the idea of human relationships which are interdependent, not hierarchical. Here she cites Gilligan's later work wherein 'male' and 'female' 'voices', ways of reasoning and judging, 'ethics of justice and care', would combine.[22] By whose standard would we then live? Can it really be said to be equality that Bacchi seeks? Are women to be advanced via difference, after all?

I end by noting that for Bacchi there is more at stake than a denial of human needs by failure to 'include women' in society's norms. This is shown clearly by her comment on Mackinnon's stand on women and the draft. Mackinnon, she says, at least sees that the real point is whether we agree with US foreign policy or not.[23] But that is precisely what is not the *feminist* point. It cannot be, unless there is a secure theoretical linkage between feminist and other views, so that feminism's aims of the advancement of women are tied to them.[24] Even that may not be guarantee enough, that women not lose again.

Mackinnon and power

> Gender is an inequality of power . . . . Only derivatively is it a difference. (Catharine Mackinnon, 1987)[25]

To grasp Mackinnon's thought, we must understand the way she employs the terminology of sex and gender, and the fact that she retains the distinction more or less throughout her work. I shall therefore explain her terms, even though I am in part repeating a well-known and widespread use.

Men and women are different sexes. That in itself does not constitute a strong dichotomy, for sex is a continuum. The true social dichotomy is gender. I am, it happens, a woman born, as most people called a woman are. I could have been assigned a 'sex' at birth, perhaps to ensure that the social order, gender based, is not threatened. There is no doubt of my gender: I am female. That does not mean I conform to the requirements of my automatically ascribed gender in every respect. However, I should. By such expectations, I am judged. That is true of us all.[26]

The value of Mackinnon's position is this. It maintains gender as a dichotomy which, while generally tied to sex, is more flexible than that suggests, as might be – though this I infer – the power relationship sex both expresses and entails. To accept this we must also accept that not all men are dominant, not all dominate. As Mackinnon says, men can be raped, men can be 'feminized'; I think that means they will have known the wounds of gender. They may even be de-gendered; they have I suppose been 'unmanned'. For as women differ in their status, so do men in their power.

I move to the origins and character of male domination. I find Mackinnon's account difficult to understand, perhaps because sexuality and power interact and I do not know which is prior.[27] For her, (hetero?)sexuality[28] is key to male dominance, though it expresses that dominance too. The relationship of dominance and subordination, in which the relationship between the sexes consists, is sexual; sexuality is both a relationship of dominance and subordination, and an expression of that.[29] When I ponder this I understand it at the 'gut' level at which I understand 'pornography silences women'. Analysing it is difficult in the extreme.

It follows from the logic of Mackinnon's sex–gender division that she speaks of sexuality as institutionalized now. Further, not all men and women are as they 'should be' – though the overwhelming majority are – nor need they be. For the dichotomy we face is gender. Thus the notion that in effect heterosexuality must cease is not present here,[30] though obviously a 'good relationship' would be rare. I take this position as akin to Firestone's, though with more emphasis on sexuality as such.

Though heterosexuality is emphasized, Mackinnon sees homosexuality also, as involved: 'the structure of social power which stands behind and defines gender is hardly irrelevant, even if it is rearranged'. She dismisses the idea that lesbianism can solve the problem of dominance in that 'women remain socially defined . . . in relation to men'. For her, it is possible that 'sexuality is so gender marked that it carries dominance and submission with it, whatever the gender of its participants'.[31] Yet while sexuality cannot be a woman's, given the forces that define what a woman is, there are 'truly rare and contrapuntal glimpses (which most people think they live almost their entire sex life within)'.[32] These aside, equality within sexuality demands radical political change. Again I am reminded of Firestone's view of equality in love. Like Firestone, Mackinnon, amid the squalor, holds out hope.

Gender is a social construct, the persona that overlays biological distinctions, such as they are. What Mackinnon adds to previous such analyses is this. Gender is a hierarchy, not a difference. Society, polity and economy are a hierarchy, within which one gender rules. Relationships between the sexes are then relationships of power; 'gender differences' are the expression, and the product of the exercise, of that power.

Just as not all men have equal power, so women are not equally likely to be subjected to the excesses of domination: Mackinnon points to black women's greater danger of being murdered or raped.[33]

So gender is enmeshed in power, and gender 'differences' stem from and express that power. When we emphasize difference we fall into a trap, for we are diverted from thoughts of hierarchy and power. Pornography has a major, indeed key, part in this. For it is pornography which 'turns sex inequality into sexuality and . . . male dominance into the sex difference'. It 'makes inequality into sex, which makes it enjoyable, and into gender, which makes it seem natural'. Pornography as a commodity turns inequality into '"speech", which has made it a right . . . [pornography is] cloaked as the essence of nature and the index of freedom':[34] we see the full analysis of this in *Only Words*, discussed below.[35]

And difference 'is the velvet glove on the iron fist' of women's domination by men.[36] Again, not all men. Women's subjugation, men's aggression, has no biological base:

> Men who do not rape women have nothing wrong with their hormones. Men who are made sick by pornography and do not eroticize their revulsion are not under-evolved.[37]

The problem concerns, rather, how society is structured now. Mackinnon then is not only not an essentialist – that is, a biological or other determinist – she is not a universalist in the conventional sense of the word. She applies neither kind of analysis to women or men.[38]

Nor is Mackinnon, in her view, an advocate of either (sameness) equality or difference; it is a dichotomy she rejects. Though obviously, she does not regard her position as unrelated to the law as it stands. Legal categories, for her, are derivative of the power that underlies, and constructs, social reality and our views of that: a power veiled and masked. Hidden is the problematic distribution of power implicated in the hierarchy that is gender. So we think and act in terms of false classifications like equality and difference. Within the conventional approach to sex equality, 'equality is an equivalence . . . and sex is a distinction', so that the whole idea of sex equality becomes a contradiction in terms. For, 'the words "equal to" are code for, equivalent to, the words "the same as" – referent for both unspecified'.[39]

These views do not entail that she renounce a quest for women's advancement via the law. First, the truth about 'equality' and 'difference' is not totally hidden (this I infer). Second, as we have seen, she does not believe that because some institution or system of thought is inimical to women, we should refuse to engage with it. And of course we cannot. That would mean defeat. For where and with what conventions could we work?

For Mackinnon, unequal treatment of women is worse treatment. If we accept this; if we also see that 'equal', 'same', and 'different' discussions serve to hide the face of power, then we will know that there is no moral question or dilemma left. The point is, rather, whether a given issue is a gender question or not. Of course by this Mackinnon means that not to bid for the advancement of women is to commit oneself to inequality; inequality as normally defined. When she speaks of a 'legal mandate of equality', and says it must be made meaningful, she is using 'equal' in its conventional sense. There is no doubt that it is equality Mackinnon seeks, though I think she works for its preconditions, now.

Mackinnon comments of the US Abolitionist Movement that the time came when the only relevant question was how slavery could be brought to an end. Group difference(s) had finally ceased to be at issue. Speaking of women she adds: 'The moment when one's particular qualities become part of the standard by which humanity is measured is a millennial moment.'[40] She awaits the time when group difference becomes an irrelevance in the case of women, unillusioned though she is as to the extent of African-Americans' advance.

For Mackinnon, then, there is a sense in which much that has been said by writers in the 'narrow', more usual version of the 'equality–difference' debate is beside the point. Both sameness/equality and difference pleas are artefacts of male domination, but so is the fact that we think in terms of sameness/equality and difference, too. The situation is not simply that we are in effect being made, in the courts and elsewhere, to argue for equality via sameness, to meet a rebuttal that asserts difference. We *believe* what we are saying and doing; and the categories in which we think, the words we use, are politically harmful and wrong. Male domination has patterned our very thoughts and words; it has reduced us to real and metaphorical silence; to real, and semantic, inefficacy: so it has moulded our lives.

It is not Mackinnon's argument that either of these positions (which she together calls the 'difference approach', with its two halves) is nonsense, but that they are not ours. The views are structured and created; they emerge from dominance by men. They are not just beliefs that happen to be held, nor do they emerge from women's unmediated experience. Though Mackinnon does not believe we face an ideology so all-embracing that it cannot be overcome.

My view that Mackinnon was an equality feminist, leaning towards sameness, stemmed from the general character of her discussion in 'Difference and dominance'[41] and her views on the US draft. While I outline that, it is now on her discussion of pornography, with which I end, that I would base my claim.

The first path to equality, given Mackinnon's analysis, and within the society she depicts, is to be the same as a man. The second is to be different, to ask for special protection, in some areas of life. But they are *one* approach. Its two parts arise because men are the measure. The 'difference approach' lets the law make women conform to the world men have made. Its 'sameness' strand seeks parity with men as the world is now; 'difference', (re)valuation of the female gendered self.

Mackinnon does not argue that this dual approach is useless. On the contrary, she believes it has forwarded the crucial issue of how to obtain for women what they should have within the realms of men, while holding to what good has been developed under oppression. Prioritizing the 'sameness side' of this, she comments: 'Its guiding impulse is: we're as good as you. Anything you can do, we can do. Just get out of the way.'[42] She adds that it has gained women more than a little in terms of access to employment hitherto restricted or denied. The armed forces are an example.

Mackinnon opposes drafting women, but also men. Nonetheless she says:

> The issue . . . has presented the sameness answer to the sex equality question in all its simple dignity. . . . As a citizen, I should have to risk being killed just like you. The consequences of my resistance to this risk should count like yours.[43]

Here she pays qualified tribute to sameness, as she does to difference; to Gilligan, whom she does not however endorse. The special treatment approach, she says, has not obtained compensation enough, and neglects the issue of power. Further, whatever it gains, it attests the 'nature' and character born of oppression, which for her cannot be good.[44]

It is not Mackinnon's view that women have produced, say, no valuable art, but that much of it is what men have allowed. To take pride in such activity is to act, she thinks, as if we had reached equality now. This could, though she does not say so, help lull women in their servitude. In any event, how can we know what is truly ours? And what of the political work omitted while cultural work is done?

I end this part of my discussion of Mackinnon with a statement emblematic of her strength and force, which admirably summarizes her view of the limitations of women's lives now, and gives a fair if general idea of what she seeks.

> I say, give women equal power in social life. Let what we say matter, then we will discourse on questions of morality. Take your foot off our necks, then we will hear in what tongue women speak. . . . We would settle for equal protection of the laws under which one would be born, live, and die, in a country where protection is not a dirty word and equality is not a special privilege.[45]

This is far from the dreams of early radicalism; but just as far from the way we live now.

I turn to Mackinnon's most controversial work, which resurged explosively in 1993, and in the UK in 1994, with the publication of *Only Words*. That is, of course, her battle against pornography and those who produce it or who uphold the latter's rights.

Mackinnon and Andrea Dworkin have campaigned long and hard for civil anti-pornography measures.[46] These allow an individual to sue: they do not ban pornography, as 'ban' is normally understood, though one provision could amount to that.[47] Mackinnon may have inclined towards civil law to avoid giving power to the state, though she sees civil suits as more empowering to women, despite the courage needed to give evidence, and the problem of proof, that she depicts. Her attempted laws were the Minneapolis and Indianapolis Ordinances.[48] The Ordinance passed by the Indianapolis legislature[49] was ruled unconstitutional, in *Hudnut*, by the District Court of Appeal. However, said the Court,

> we accept the premises of this legislation. Depictions of subordination tend to perpetuate subordination. The subordinate status of women in turn leads to affront and lower pay at work, insult and injury at home, battery and rape on the streets . . . 'pornography is central to creating and maintaining sex as a basis of discrimination'.

The Court found that the Constitution's First Amendment guarantees of freedom of speech and expression must override these harms. But the harm argument was accepted. This ruling was therefore, I believe, a massive inroad even in defeat. Mackinnon would disagree,[50] though her discussion shows that it is exploitable on women's behalf.

To say that the ordinances did not ban pornography is to omit one proviso which would, should the plaintiff win, amount to a ban: 'traffickers' could be sued on behalf of all women. A furore, cries of 'censorship', ensued.[51] According to Ferguson, were that clause deleted,

> the law would create the right to sue anyone . . . for being involved in the production or use of a pornographic item which is actually used to coerce a woman. In this way, it is *an actual harms suit*, similar to a suit brought against a toy manufacturer or distributor that is shown to cause *actual harm* to children. [Italics in original][52]

I suspect that so long as 'trafficker' and 'production' remain in the proposal, accusations of censorship will continue, despite the analogies shown here. But I also see a strength in Mackinnon's argument on the difficulty of proving individual harm.[53] I turn to issues of free speech, equal protection under the law, 'procedural' and 'substantive' equality, and the vexed question of civil rights, reviewing these in the context of Mackinnon's *Only Words*.[54]

> [T]he word starts out to free thought and ends by enslaving it. ([Justice] Benjamin Cardozo, 1926)[55]

We saw the attempt to provide legal redress against pornography fall when it collided with the US Constitution's First Amendment and its entrenched and paramount right of free speech. In *Only Words* Mackinnon puts the following case. First, the Amendment is raised above the 'Equality Amendment', the Fourteenth, which guarantees 'equal protection under the law'; for freedom of speech and expression takes precedence. But this is not always so: 'obscenity', child pornography, and 'fighting words' are not protected under the First Amendment. Mackinnon then queries the basis on which this is decided, these are defined, and pornography or spoken insults to women found exempt. She ends by looking to a society where equality is no mere shell of a 'right', and silence is no oppression.

Before returning to Mackinnon's text I discuss two issues that may hamper our understanding of her case. The first is the question of rights,[56] which I shall discuss in relation to the Amendments cited here.[57] Mackinnon is making two separate arguments about these. The first is that one right wars with another, and freedom of speech wins over equal legal protection: let us say – though this is not quite the same thing – that equality and freedom are pitted one against the other, though with freedom the more highly placed. Given this, equality becomes a formal and not a substantive right, and one that is not attained.

But for Mackinnon and her supporters the situation is worse, as there is an important sense in which free speech is a formal right too, at least for most. Money and power grant privileged access to a 'right' of public free speech, which would become substantive only when it could be roughly equalized for all. Otherwise my entrenched right to say 'I live under an unjust regime' is empty as against the powers of the regime to control the media; to limit the distance at which I can be heard, and the chance that people will listen. Nor do the powerful need to exert such controls. The known or assumed side-effects of contradicting *their* speech will decide what is 'heard'. Thus two constitutional rights are implemented only in the letter, if that; certainly not in their spirit as we might think it to be. And so for Mackinnon there are, especially for women, rights which are – as pornography is alleged to be – *only words*.

Second I address the issue of 'silencing'. Many speak of women's silence: Gilligan, who has more or less nothing in common with Mackinnon, yet speaks, we have seen, of 'the silence of women [and] . . . the difficulty in hearing what they say'.[58] My readers may find the notion of silencing easy to grasp. I did not. Indeed, for some while I thought that because women actually 'spoke', and more importantly, some had massive public access to the ways of disseminating speech, the whole idea was wrong. I changed my mind about six years ago, before I began working on this book, as I reflected on what I had seen and experiences I had known. Though I speak of silencing by day-to-day devaluation – in meetings, in 'conversation', by advertisements – which I could not until then name, rather than by pornography, however defined. I believe there is a link, as all modes of silencing concern the way women are represented and perceived. But I am unable to argue further than that.

Mackinnon contrasts the framing of the US law and its interpretation,[59] resulting from 'the lack of an equality context in which to interpret expressive freedoms', with the situation in Canada under its Constitution of 1982, and its Supreme Court's

> [defining] equality in a meaningful way – one more substantive than formal, directed towards changing unequal social situations rather than monitoring their equal positioning before the law.[60]

and

> projecting the law into a more equal future, rather than remaining rigidly neutral in ways that either reinforce existing social inequality or prohibit changing it.

It was a Canadian case, *Butler* v. *Regina*, that strengthened attacks on Mackinnon. Butler, owner of a pornography store, was prosecuted for obscenity, and appealed on freedom of expression grounds. LEAF (Women's Legal and Educational Action Fund) argued that if the community protection aspect of the obscenity law applied to harm to women, the law was constitutional in promoting equality. The Supreme Court found the obscenity provision constitutional on sex equality grounds.[61]

It is not, says Mackinnon, the case that in the US equality cannot overcome First Amendment rights: there can be 'a "compelling state interest"', as in a judgment of 1983.[62] However, that did not address free speech, the possible infringement of which various of her critics cite as reason to oppose her proposed laws, and the Canadian law as defined in *Butler*.

As we have seen in *Hudnut*, free speech enters into the argument as a consequence of the idea that pornography is speech, or expresses a view. However, that judgment also says that pornography harms women in general, and in a very wide-ranging way indeed, as 'Depictions of subordination tend to perpetuate subordination.' Therefore it sets freedom of speech against equality. For legally, pornography is 'only words'. Her other arguments apart,[63] Mackinnon comments that speech is related to, in effect owned by, wealth and power.

That 'the most speech' in the sense of the greatest access to publications, media of various kinds, and the ability to gain attention for one's views, indeed belongs to the already dominant, is fairly clear. That free speech is subject to market values is argued by, among others, Susanne Kappeler and Russell Jacoby, neither of whom believes in censorship as normally understood: both would opt for critique.[64] For Kappeler supporting 'freedom of expression' is not the same as supporting freedom; rather it is 'to hold a political opinion in favour of the status quo', one that is anathema to her. But she cannot take either side of the 'censorship' debate. The liberal side for her is not a matter of leaving decisions to the individual, but of abdicating responsibility 'in the name of those individuals who stand to gain from it: pornographers and their clientele'.

Stoltenberg stands with Mackinnon; he makes a similar point to Kappeler's though very differently phrased:

> The First Amendment protects *those who have already spoken* . . . women and blacks . . . have been systematically excluded from public discourse by civil inferiority, economic powerlessness, and violence.[65]

These points seem so clear to me that I am hard pressed to look at arguments against them. I do not think there *are* counter-arguments that hold. But that may be because long before pornography became an issue, before I thought it silenced women, indeed before I let myself see and say that women *were* silenced, I believed speech was neither equal nor 'free'. However, there is a gap in Mackinnon's argument, and I show it here:

[the Constitution-framers'] posture to freedom of speech tends to presuppose that whole segments of the population are not systematically silenced, socially, prior to government action. If . . . this were a non-hierarchical society, that might make sense. *But the place of pornography in the inequality of the sexes makes the assumption of equal power untrue.* [Italics in original][66]

Now Mackinnon talks of poverty, and race; she is no kind of essentialist, but at this crucial stage she asserts that pornography is the key to an inequality that is also an imbalance in freedom. The judgment in *Hudnut* gives her leeway to do this. Yet the discussion of the apparent clash of rights concerns hierarchies other than dominance by men. Now and then, in the debates on pornography that have occurred so frequently over the last years, a voice intrudes and asks that we speak of class: and is passed over. And I feel an unease. Though I understand that the massive number of feminist battles that await should not lead us to fight none.[67]

Freedom of speech seems so greatly and systematically imbalanced as less to clash with equality than to be an inequality itself. (It will link with other inequalities, of course.) So we may have, as perhaps Mackinnon is saying above, not freedom ranged against equality, so that by working for 'equality' we endanger 'freedom', but a series of inequalities. We could say: until we reach equality, we cannot speak of freedom. That is a dangerous position, but it grows the more appealing as we ask what freedoms the disadvantaged possess. Mackinnon thinks we face a difficult choice, but she believes risk must be balanced against risk, as 'Women will never have that dignity, security, compensation that is the promise of equality so long as . . . pornography exists as it does now.'[68]

For Mackinnon and others,[69] pornography silences women. We saw in Chapter 7 how humiliating a process silencing is, how it devalues and subordinates us. We can imagine a continuum from a failure to listen to, to hear, women, of the kind of which Gilligan speaks,[70] to the deserts where the truly silenced live.

Mackinnon has led us through the degradation of the body and the wastelands of the heart. Precious little tolerance has she been shown by those who speak of freedom. Yet she ends, as for now do I, with a vision of understanding:

> In a society in which equality is *a fact, not merely a word*, words of racial or sexual assault and humiliation will be nonsense syllables. Sex between people and things . . . real men and unreal women, will be a turn-off . . . . When this day comes, silence will be . . . a context of repose into which thought can expand, an invitation that gives speech its shape, an opening to a new conversation.[71] [Italics mine]

Notes

1 Carol Lee Bacchi, *Same Difference. Feminism and Sexual Difference*, 1990; Catharine Mackinnon, *Feminism Unmodified: Discourses on Life and Law*, 1987; Mackinnon, *Toward a Feminist Theory of the State*, 1989; Mackinnon, 'Difference and dominance', in Katharine

Bartlett and Rosanne Kennedy (eds), *Feminism Legal Theory*, 1991; Mackinnon, 'Legal perspectives on sexual difference', in Deborah L. Rhode (ed.), *Theoretical Perspectives on Sexual Difference*, 1991; Mackinnon, *Only Words*, 1994.

2 Wendy McElroy (ed.), *Freedom, Feminism and the State*, 1993, p. 53.

3 I have taken these examples from fairly standard discussions in parts of the academic literature, and in the press.

4 The conventional 'has' reminds me of property rights.

5 Bacchi, *Same Difference*, pp. xvi, xvii. Here she follows Martha Minow, 'Adjudicating differences: conflicts among feminist lawyers', in Marianne Hirsch and Evelyn Fox Keller (eds), *Conflicts in Feminism*, 1990.

6 Bacchi, *Same Difference*, pp. xv, xvi.

7 Ibid., p. 111.

8 These quotations are Bacchi's.

9 Bacchi, *Same Difference*, pp. 111–13.

10 Ibid., p. 113.

11 Ibid., p. 114.

12 Alone, that is, of the countries of which Bacchi speaks; the others are Australia and the UK.

13 Part of the concern is that men would then have 'property' in their children. For anyone to have 'property' in children is worrying to me, though I do not endorse a more collective view.

14 Bacchi, *Same Difference*, p. 147.

15 Ibid., p. 152.

16 Ibid., p. 231.

17 Ibid., p. 233.

18 Ibid., p. 241.

19 Ibid., p. 243.

20 Mary Joe Frug, *Postmodern Legal Feminism*, 1992, p. 16.

21 Bacchi, *Same Difference*, pp. 250–1; italics hers.

22 Ibid., p. 253.

23 Ibid., p. 249.

24 See in particular Chapter 5.

25 Mackinnon, *Feminism Unmodified*, p. 8.

26 There are societies where there are more than two sexes, and more than two genders. I speak here of the UK and US.

27 It is the explanation of its origins I find hard to understand.

28 Hereafter, 'sexuality'.

29 Mackinnon, *Feminism Unmodified*, p. 3.

30 I say 'in effect' because I know of no writer who suggests that heterosexuality is not an option once its institutionalization has been overthrown. See for example, Sheila Jeffreys, *Anticlimax: A Feminist Perspective on the Sexual Revolution*, 1990, p. 316.

31 Mackinnon, *Feminist Theory of the State*, p. 2.

32 Ibid., pp. 153–4.

33 Mackinnon, *Feminism Unmodified*, p. 7.

34 Ibid., p. 3.

35 Mackinnon, *Only Words* (UK edition). See also Mackinnon, 'Pornography, civil rights and speech', in Catherine Itzin (ed.), *Pornography: Women, Violence and Civil Liberties*, 1993.

36 Mackinnon, *Feminism Unmodified*, p. 8.

37 Ibid., 1987, p. 41.

38 Ann Ferguson, while noting this, believes that Mackinnon and Andrea Dworkin forward a 'form of social essentialism' which over-universalizes male and female traits: *Blood at the Root: Motherhood, Sexuality and Male Dominance*, 1989, pp. 53–4.

39 Mackinnon, 'Difference and dominance', p. 82.

40 Mackinnon, *Feminism Unmodified*, pp. 40–4.

41 Ibid., and Mackinnon, 'Difference and dominance'.

42 Mackinnon, *Feminism Unmodified*, p. 35.

43 Mackinnon, 'Difference and dominance', p. 83.

44 Mackinnon, *Feminism Unmodified*, p. 39.

45 Mackinnon, 'Difference and dominance', p. 91.

46 She is also associated with a Canadian federal law. I turn to that below.

47 I am giving a benign interpretation, close to Mackinnon's, of the ordinances she proposed; and the legally more realistic assessment of the likely results.

48 See Rosemarie Tong, *Feminist Thought*, 1989, p. 112ff.; Mackinnon, 'Pornography', p. 465ff.; John Stoltenberg, 'Confronting pornography as a civil rights issue', in *Refusing to be a Man*, 1990, pp. 142–70.

49 The other was vetoed by the Governor of Minneapolis.

50 Mackinnon, *Only Words*, pp. 65–6, quoting the Appeal Court decision in *American Booksellers* v. *Hudnut*, 1985.

51 Though not only because of that.

52 Ferguson, *Blood at the Root*, 1987, p. 221.

53 Mackinnon, 'Pornography', *passim*.

54 Mackinnon, *Only Words*.

55 Mackinnon, *Feminism Unmodified*, p. 9.

56 Rights analysis is a vast and complex field within political theory. I am not addressing that here.

57 I shall not employ Mackinnon's terms.

58 Carol Gilligan, *Different Voice*, 1982, p. 173.

59 Such as a lower court finding that nude dancing was 'protected speech': Mackinnon, *Only Words*, p. 69.

60 Ibid.

61 Ibid.

62 Ibid., p. 75.

63 I have here omitted much of *Only Words*, including graphic and distressing accounts of pornography and violence.

64 Susanne Kappeler, 'Pornography: the representation of power', in Itzin, *Pornography*, p. 88; Russell Jacoby, *Social Amnesia*, 1978, p. xviii. (Pornography is not Jacoby's concern.)

65 Stoltenberg, *Refusing to be A Man*, p. 168.

66 Mackinnon, 'Pornography', p. 486

67 Ferguson, *Blood at the Root*, p. 222.

68 Mackinnon, 'Pornography', p. 486.

69 See, *inter alia*, Susan Griffin, *Pornography and Silence: Culture's Revenge against Nature*, 1981; Stoltenberg, *Refusing to be a Man*; Andrea Dworkin, *Pornography*, 1981, *Right-Wing Women: The Politics of Domesticated Females*, 1988.

70 Gilligan, *Different Voice*, p. 173.

71 Mackinnon, *Only Words*, pp. 77–8.

11

Conclusion and Afterthoughts

[Feminism] proposes 'the individuality of each human soul . . . . In discussing the rights of woman, we are to consider, first, what belongs to her as an individual, in a world of her own, the arbiter of her own destiny . . .'. This is simply a recognition of the human condition, in which women are included. It is also the precondition for the realization of Marx's greatest ethical idea: from each according to her ability, to each according to her need. (Andrea Dworkin, 1983)[1]

My aim in this book was to introduce contemporary feminist thought, classified mainly into conventional schools but structured around equality, sameness, and difference. I have tried to extend the scope of the 'equality–difference' debate, concerned with the sameness and difference of women and men. In pursuit of that, I looked at the various concepts of equality and difference feminist theory employs, and suggested that a tension between equality and difference – variously defined – ran through feminist thought.

I did not expect to decide the equality–difference issue. One part, which concerns sex differences, could have been settled long ago, though only by those who accept certain parameters of debate.[2] However, I believe both that and other equal–different themes I have addressed will continue for the present to divide feminism, and feminist thought. Further, I am convinced that when other 'differences' have been negotiated or overcome – utopian as that thought may seem – the issue of sex-gender dominance will remain. It will be the last to be defeated. And of course it will be prevalent and important, if on occasion demoted, as other differences are thought, worked, even fought, through. That may well be why the attaining of women's equality has been called 'The longest revolution' of all.

In what way would the sex sameness–difference debate have been 'settled long ago', for those who accept conventional means of inquiry? The findings are of three kinds. First, psychological differences attributable to biological difference are virtually non-existent. Second, attitudinal differences are few in number, and normally small in size. Third, there are a variety of behavioural differences; but then we know that behaviour is more socially constrained than attitudes. I would call these 'gender'.

Further relevant points are that there is on the whole more variation within the sexes than between them, and more between national cultures than within. I take as an example scores on IQ tests, though they must be in doubt: while there is a difference between the sexes taken as groups, the important variation is between individuals of either sex. Empirical psychology can make a sameness case. Why argue difference?

To say that sex differences are not a problem, and a debate conducted as though they were should cease,[3] we must accept certain views of knowledge and reality, embodied in basic social scientific tenets and techniques. I regard these as value neutral, though I do not mean that they are always neutrally employed. And I further believe that social reality is sufficiently 'transparent', open to their methods, to be investigated and understood in a systematic way.

I do not mean such work is easy. Nor do I suggest that there is no social and political control of social science. Of course there is. There are, in addition, ideologies, and ways and theories of knowledge, that underlie 'method' in its narrow sense. They influence topics of inquiry, methods employed (to an extent, at least), interpretation of results, and conclusions drawn. At their strongest, they mould our thought, and affect what we 'see'. But they do not do so to the extent that it is impossible for us to achieve an accurate picture of the world, though they may make it very difficult indeed.

Issues like this have run through my text. We have for example seen Gilligan attacked for studying only women when she looked at abortion, and for the presentation of her results. I have commented on her failure to perceive various external factors relevant to her research. And beyond Gilligan has come the position oddly endorsed by Okin, and discussed by Harding, in an unintended echo of a point of Friedan's:[4] that 'man-made', androcentric, science cannot say whether the sexes are different or the same.

From methodological critiques of Gilligan we can learn that we do not have to allege androcentrism to point to a problem in method that might hamper our understanding of how women think. If we do say this, we must demonstrate why the problem applies only to women: if that is indeed the charge.

I shall briefly summarize that kind of attack. It is said that science and social science are too male biased, in all possible senses of the term, to be able to comprehend women. I do not believe that. All the suggestions of androcentrism, and what seem to me to be separate points about political and social control,[5] I understand. But I do not accept that they necessarily create a monolithic climate of inquiry. If they did, this debate could not have occurred.

In Chapter 2 I suggested that the turn to identity and difference politics occurred because 'sameness equality' politics had failed. The sameness case had been proven. And for blacks in the US, race had been made an 'inherently suspect classification', throwing the onus of proof on those charged with discrimination; though black women, as Kimberle Crenshaw shows, were not necessarily helped.[6] But equality even in the liberal sense had not been gained. Why then assimilate?[7] And if that is not the chosen

path, may it not be necessary to take a stand on difference? This point can
be put more strongly still: why should equality require that a group
'assimilate' to, with, those who dominate them?

Though here I point out a difference between women and blacks; that is,
between all women and all blacks, keeping in mind the overlap that ensues
and the 'difference' I must, by speaking so, ignore. It is a difference that
may crucially affect our stance on assimilation, and what that notion
means. It stems from the simple fact that separatism is not normally an
option for women, who will, eloquently though Sheila Jeffreys has put the
case against heterosexuality, tend to live in some manner or other with
men. This continued interaction may well be one reason why equality–
difference has been so perplexed and confusing a debate, and why non-
assimilation, as an idea, is odd for us. For black women of course there is
a yet more complex problem of dual affiliation, I have not been able
adequately to encompass here. It is well expressed in various writings of
hooks.

The turn to difference and womanly character, by cultural feminists or
no, has been equated with a turning away from politics, even where
political issues are still addressed. Lynne Segal is one such critic. Nonetheless she states:

> it is also true that women's values and maternal thinking can serve . . . to
> inspire women to resist destructive and oppressive forces, *especially on behalf of
> others*. Nearly all feminists today are more likely to stress the importance of
> 'women-centred' values . . . by whatever complex route and at whatever cost
> women may have acquired . . . the virtues that accompany such values.[8] [Italics
> mine]

This acceptance, qualified though it is, perturbs me; 'at whatever cost'
brings alarm. Is the suggestion that we trade, and retain virtue by
accepting oppression? Further, the importance of such 'difference' tends,
Segal suggests, to be its potential work 'on behalf of others'. This is one of
the aspects of women's condition that 'sameness equality' feminists have
sought to escape, as Mackinnon has.

But we have seen various sameness feminists turn to difference: Friedan
and Rossi most certainly, among the liberals;[9] among the socialists,
Young. Of my 'strong' and 'weak' cultural feminists, Daly moved from
androgyny, but others seem to have been 'difference thinkers', in this
sense, from the start.

I have given discrete reasons for such changes. Are they enough? Is
there no overall, overarching reason? I believe there are two. I have
emphasized the fear of difference as a tactic as a fear I share. But I suggest
there is a fear of sameness, of androgynous equality, also. My suggestion
is not necessarily aimed at the writers I discuss: it is not taken, or inferred,
from their texts. It concerns a more general aversion to 'equality', a
preference for the terms 'same' and 'different', that I sense now. Perhaps
that stems from a belief that equality feminism is indeed 'what the
dominant culture finds the more threatening' stance,[10] and a weariness at

facing the risks of that. In any event, it involves opting for difference; and I assume, 'equality in difference', if equality there is to be.

This last suggestion is yet to be argued through. It cannot adequately be theorized until those who would move to 'sameness–difference' to avoid opposing 'difference' and 'equality', nonetheless accept the evidence for a lack of differences by sex. Alternatively they could better interrogate 'androcentrism' in social inquiry, although I believe they would be left with a series of questions at best.

Further, I think it a stance not best suited to this 'difference'. Christine Littleton suggests that we see difference *'among'* women, and more, see it 'as diversity rather than division', quoting Lorde on the need to extend this to 'all human difference' (italics mine).[11] (The usage 'diversity rather than division', I suggest, attempts to overcome the essentializing which is likely to occur should 'difference' remain key.) A sameness–equality lawyer like Williams, though, should have no problem with that. The stance of such lawyers is not that all women are the same. Rather on aggregate women are – for substantive purposes – 'the same' as men.

But we can have equality of treatment without identity of treatment; a point relevant to the possibility that we can both be impartial, and take the needs of individuals – and groups – into account. I instance medical treatment. We do not expect equal 'amounts' of treatment, the same doses of drugs, identical types of medication, for different ills. Indeed, a doctor who treated differently diagnosed patients identically would be treating them *unequally*, in that there would be different results. And should the same illness, treated in the same way, progress differently, continued identical treatment would probably be wrong. An example like this does not help apostles of difference who speak in terms of groups. For it points to the problem of an endless proliferation of those.

I return to the issue of sex equality and difference, and a question I cannot resolve. Such sex differences as exist, and are not outweighed by within-sex variation, require no political-theoretical stance of equality in difference.[12] Do differences 'among women', construed for my present purpose as 'between groups', provide a better starting-point? In Chapter 2 I quoted Donald and Rattansi on findings of no, or trivial, differences between races, and in Chapter 9, gave bell hooks's concern lest 'identity politics' lead to the maintained stereotyping of blacks. Therefore, I think not. Interestingly, differences 'within woman' may, though not as its authors conceive it. That stance may stumble, unknowingly, upon the position I forward below.

For there is a case for 'equality in difference'; but not as regarded so far. It is based on a liberal view of commonality, and so it concerns the 'equality in difference' of *individuals*. Whether it makes sense for feminists to take this road depends on how much equality, and of what kind, such (fairly minimal) commonality affords. For I assume it tends to the granting of formal rights of a kind we can, after Mackinnon, call *only words*. Then this is not only based on a once emancipatory liberal moment: it might stop short of that. It could gain at best the equality within a hierarchy I discussed near the beginning of this book.

I have argued my way back to a tension between equality and difference with which I began, though, at first sight, of a different kind. But only at that first sight, for by importing the feminist endeavour I have moved the parameters of equality–difference to the issue of groups, and a group approach to inequality, again. While women remain subordinate, that move will recur. So long as only liberal feminist equality can be reached – though as I said in Chapter 3, *that* is millennial – there may also remain the issue of differences between groups.

I say 'may' because I think it possible – if unlikely in the extreme – that groups could be or become equal in a hierarchical and stratified society like ours. To employ my early analogy: were the race indeed to the swift, the battle to the strong, society and polity's heights gained on merit alone, group difference would not matter. Then we would see what kind of difference did: we would be forced to an awareness of inequality *within* groups, which I raised in Chapter 8. We might speak then, as we did before, of inequality and class. Would the struggles of feminism within radicalism begin all over again? Or would that battle have been won?

At the end of my text, I discussed challenges to the dichotomy, focused – with a major exception I discuss here – on sex equality and difference alone. I first return to Butler's critique of identity politics, in particular of the identity politics of gay and lesbian groups. I said above that I consider her to be an individualist, though her postmodernism would debar that. Here I address her views on the violence of homophobia; her recognition of that; but her counterposing to it the 'violence' of the grouping against those within.

I once thought the second use hyperbolic. It is a fairly typical postmodernist counterattack. However, the problem of the wording may rather lie, ironically given Butler's stated beliefs, in a fixity within her view of groups. For there could indeed be moments when it made sense to think that group treatment of, or effect on, the individual was 'violent' in a way that 'out-group' behaviour was not, metaphorically though Butler may deploy the term. And there could be moments when such a comment did immeasurable harm to the group's cause.

My final verdict on Butler is that she is an individualist in the liberal sense of the term. Certainly that is the kind of status she claims for herself.[13] Were she less utterly convinced that she was right to refuse to be labelled lesbian, then we might see within her what we see when we counterpose her to certain critics: a tension with broader relevance both within feminism, and without its bounds. This is the tension between the group and the individual, and given her phrasing, the end and the means, with which those who seek change have struggled for so long.

Mackinnon regards the 'sameness–difference' dichotomy as a product, and instrument of male dominance and female oppression. She believes she can explain difference and the 'difference ploy':

when we understand that women are *forced* into this situation . . . it makes a lot of sense that we should want to negotiate, since we lose conflicts. It makes a lot of sense that we should want to urge values of care, because it is what we have been valued for. We have had little choice but to be valued this way.[14]

This is an explanation only in part; and of only one kind of female behaviour. But I think Mackinnon would accept that. What concerns me is this. Mackinnon believes that sameness, difference, are one approach, and an approach dominance has both constructed and enforced. It makes tremendous sense that she would focus, if mainly by civil law, on pornography, which she sees as a key element of that. And her attack has, though it has not yet won, hit home with massive force, struck a crucial patriarchal nerve: the responses to her actions, I believe, show us that. But does Mackinnon's ending where women would gain 'equal protection of the laws . . . in a country where protection is not a dirty word and equality is not a special privilege'[15] fulfil the terms of the challenge she made to sameness/equality and difference, both of which she has criticized, though to which she has paid qualified homage, too? We are, I think, unable to say. That is, I still do not think we know what equality means for her. However the ending of *Only Words* suggests this: that Mackinnon is a thinker for whom the parameters of the good society cannot be laid down until oppression ends. For then, silence ends. And then communication, and I say, freedom, begin.

I return to the 'fear of sameness' I mentioned above: fear of the consequences of equality, as society is now, would be a better way of phrasing the point. In Chapter 7 I singled out as the major 'pre-Gilligan' feminist work the 'fear of success' debate. There I sided with Horner, who thought that women feared success, and that this stemmed from a conflict between the 'women' they had been taught to be and the achievement they had learned. For Horner, expected success, 'especially against men, produces anticipation of . . . for example, threat of social rejection and loss of femininity'.[16] Kirkpatrick, speaking of women politicians, similarly says, 'disdain and failure . . . are widely perceived to be their likely rewards',[17] while Sapiro's work showed 'successful' women the less likely overtly to compete with men.[18] The implications are clear – and grim: equality feminism's gains are far outweighed by the expected retaliation of men.

Autonomy has been conceived as a male attribute and value:[19] that may be why it is viewed as the mark of a life isolated and cold.[20] Perhaps that is why so many feminists have again come to laud a 'relational' and 'contextual' womanhood. As early as Chapter 3 we saw the costs – at a minimum, the loss of male esteem – that Rossi, in theory a leading equality feminist, would not pay. And in Chapter 4, we saw Friedan retreat. Perhaps we should not be surprised when others endorse the difference and virtues of woman, on the surface, and when controlled, so congenial to men.

When I talk, when I teach, quite often someone reminds me that matters have changed for the better during the last thirty years. Yes and no. As I prepared to write this book, Ros Coward published *Our Treacherous Hearts: Why Women Let Men Get Their Way*; the feminist anger it evoked led me to expect a decidedly different work. I quote from Coward – who thinks we are 'programmed':[21]

> Women have let men get away with it. When it came to the crunch, most made it quite clear that they didn't want conflict with men . . . . In exchange, they have ostensibly been given more power in the family by accepting a *new mythology concerning childbirth, mothering and nurturing*. But that 'gift' is ambiguous.[22] [Italics mine]

So for Coward, though 'massive advances'[23] have occurred, we have travelled a short way in thirty years. We have reacquired a Feminine Mystique.[24] I am going to turn back nearly that far, to Firestone, and to my query, in the light of her comments, whether after equality there could be love.

This query has nothing, androgynist though I believe Firestone to be, to do with the notion of an enforced sameness to come. Her vision rather is, as Michèle Barrett and Mary McIntosh have so clearly said, of flexible and changing lifestyles;[25] it would complement the comment on 'diversity', rather than 'division', made above. For Firestone, flexibility and change include the sexual: that is, of course, after the revolution has come. In the light of that vision, if we can somehow retain it; if in generally dispiriting times for those who seek change, we can maintain the values early radicalism held; do we not also maintain that equality involves the breaking of hierarchy in love? Does that endeavour strike at patriarchy's chains? Is that the sense in which feminism's is the longest road?

For I believe that feminists and feminist thought will remain divided by the various differences I have outlined. And within each form of difference – individual, group, and 'postmodernist' – the final division will be the first and the strongest: the 'difference' of sex.

That is, it will for heterosexuals.[26] Homosexuality has been addressed in this book, but not enough. There is a practical problem involved in considering the gay and lesbian literature. It like postmodernism inhabits, in the main, the literary and cultural world. Sexuality, sexual preference of any kind, finds virtually no place within my discipline of politics, foolish and impoverishing though the exclusion is. So certain writers whom I have always read, like Rich, apart, I turned to this writing late. My tentative view, which makes me deeply regret its exclusion here, is this. While gays and lesbians are of the oppressed, compulsory heterosexuality harms us all. It does so – I derive this primarily, I believe, from the writings of Butler, and other comments on camp and drag – by its insistence that a legitimate love involves what we bizarrely call the 'opposite sex'. This situation relates to equality and difference, too.

I said in my first chapter that Theory both framed and predominated over feminist thought, and I had decided to say a partial no to that. Here I have quoted Segal to the effect that 'our' virtues are valuable because used on others' behalf. There is a time to say no to that, too: a point I have made elsewhere.[27] Though my major belief, following my discussions of equality, is that it is not the place of feminists *qua* feminists to solve all the world's ills. It is in the case and the cause of women that we want to bring about a difference, as Ehrenreich used the term.[28] It is a difference for which women have died, and other women will. That should not have to be. Other costs of feminism pale into insignificance beside that.

Notes

1 Andrea Dworkin, 'The coming gynocide', in *Right-Wing Women: The Politics of Domesticated Females*, 1988, p. 190; quoting Elizabeth Cady Stanton, 'The solitude of self', p. 189, in Susan B. Anthony and Ida Husted Harper (eds), *History of Woman Suffrage*, 1970.

2 What would not have been settled would have been the tactics to be pursued to gain equality in the sense of equality of treatment, attainment, and reward; let alone how radical equality would be reached.

3 I do not mean to rule out any debate arising from belief in difference where none exists. I think we have to accept that the ensuing debate is normative and speculative; speculative in the extreme when founded 'against the facts'. Nonetheless it is possible that without an initial belief that *women* were caring, certain feminists would not have urged that our society value care more.

4 Susan Okin, *Justice*, 1989, p. 15; Sandra Harding, *Science Question*, 1986, *passim*; Betty Friedan, *The Feminine Mystique*, 1982; first published in 1963.

5 I separate them because the first, 'androcentric', point, stemming I think from an assumption of patriarchal structuring of thought, concerns a way of conducting science of which scientists may not even be aware. The second point, which can co-exist with, or be separable from, the first, makes no (necessary) assumptions about men, and concerns something that may be more transient. It can range from Soviet science under Stalin – where, for example, only one approach to genetics was allowed – to a list of areas for which research grants will be given, variable between countries at any one time. Here thought is not structured, at least not at first, but behaviour may well be influenced.

We see a 'market' example of the latter in Gilligan's own topic choice.

6 Kimberle Crenshaw, 'Demarginalizing the intersection of race and sex', in Katharine Bartlett and Rosanne Kennedy (eds), *Feminist Legal Theory*, 1991.

7 I am radically simplifying the various writings and debates within the black community, here.

8 Lynne Segal, *Is the Future Female? Troubled Thoughts on Contemporary Feminism*, 1987, p. 199.

9 Okin's turn can only really be found in *Justice*, 1989.

10 See Chapter 8, n. 13.

11 Christine Littleton, 'Reconstructing sexual equality', in Bartlett and Kennedy, *Feminist Legal Theory*, p. 41, quoting Lorde, *Sister Outsider*, 1984.

12 I say this in awareness of the vexed question of pregnancy and maternity provision in the US.

13 See the opening passages of Judith Butler, *Bodies That Matter: On the Discursive Limits of 'Sex'*, 1993.

14 Quoted by Littleton, 'Reconstructing Sexual Equality', p. 39.

15 Catharine Mackinnon, *Feminism Unmodified: Discourses on Life and Law*, 1987, p. 45.

16 Carol Gilligan, *In a Different Voice*, p. 15.

17 Jeane Kirkpatrick, *Political Woman*, 1974, p. 23.

18 Virginia Sapiro, 'Sex and games: on oppression and rationality', *British Joutnal of Political Science*, 1979, *passim*.

19 Carol Lee Bacchi, *Same Difference. Feminism and Sexual Difference*, 1990, p. xvi.

20 Gilligan, *Different Voice*, pp. 21, 48, 98.

21 Rosalind Coward, *Our Treacherous Hearts: Why Women Let Men Get Their Way*, 1992, *passim*.

22 Ibid., p. 197.

23 Ibid., p. 15.

24 Coward refers to Friedan; ibid., p. 4.

25 Michèle Barrett and Mary McIntosh, *The Anti-Social Family*, 1991, p. 140.

26 I shall speak here as if the heterosexual and homosexual constituted a dichotomy, and both were monolithic.

27 Judy Evans, 'Ecofeminism and the politics of the gendered self', in Andrew Dobson and Paul Lucardie (eds), *The Politics of Nature*, 1993, p. 187.

28 See Chapter 2.

Select Bibliography

Includes items not cited in the text.

Aisenberg, Nadya and Harrington, Mona, *Women of Academe*. Amherst: University of Massachusetts Press, 1988.

Alcoff, Linda, 'Cultural feminism versus post-structuralism: the identity crisis in feminist theory', pp. 295–326 in Micheline R. Malson, Jean F. O'Barr, Sarah Westphal-Wihl and Mary Wyer (eds), *Feminist Theory in Practice and Process*. Chicago and London: University of Chicago Press, 1989.

Ardener, Shirley, *Defining Females: The Nature of Women in Society*. London: Croom Helm, 1978.

Arms, Suzanne, *Immaculate Deception: A New Look at Women and Childbirth in America*. Boston: Houghton Mifflin, 1975.

Assiter, Alison, *Pornography, Feminism and the Individual*. London and Concord, MA: Pluto Press, 1991.

Auerbach, Judy, Blum, Linda, Smith, Vicky and Williams, Christine, 'Commentary on Gilligan's *In a Different Voice*', *Feminist Studies*, 11(1) (1985): 149–61.

Bacchi, Carol Lee, *Same Difference. Feminism and Sexual Difference*. North Sydney: Allen & Unwin, 1990.

Baier, Annette, 'What do women want in a moral theory?', pp. 19–32 in Mary Jeanne Larrabee (ed.), *An Ethic of Care*. New York and London: Routledge, 1993.

Barrett, Michèle, 'Introduction to the 1988 edition', in *Women's Oppression Today*. London: Verso, 1988.

Barrett, Michèle, *Women's Oppression Today*. London: Verso, 1988.

Barrett, Michèle and McIntosh, Mary, *The Anti-Social Family*. London: Verso, 1991, first published 1982.

Barrett, Michèle and Phillips, Anne (eds), *Destabilizing Theory: Contemporary Feminist Debates*. Cambridge: Polity Press, 1992.

Bartlett, Katharine T. and Kennedy, Rosanne (eds), *Feminist Legal Theory: Readings in Law and Gender*. Oxford: Westview Press, 1991.

Benhabib, Seyla, 'Feminism and the question of postmodernism', pp. 203–41 in Seyla Benhabib, *Situating the Self*. Cambridge: Polity Press, 1992.

Benhabib, Seyla, 'The generalized and the concrete other', pp. 148–77 in Seyla Benhabib, *Situating the Self*. Cambridge: Polity Press, 1992.

Benhabib, Seyla, *Situating the Self: Gender, Community and Postmodernism in Contemporary Ethics*. Cambridge: Polity Press, 1992.

Benhabib, Seyla and Cornell, Drusilla (eds), *Feminism as Critique*. Cambridge: Polity Press, 1987.

Benjamin, Andrew (ed.), *The Problems of Modernity*. London: Routledge, 1991.

Bettelheim, Bruno, 'Growing up Female', *Harper's*, November 1962, p. 125.

Bleier, Ruth, *Science and Gender*. Oxford: Pergamon Press, 1984.

Bluestone, Natalie Harris, *Women and the Ideal Society: Plato's 'Republic' and Modern Myths of Gender*. Oxford: Berg, 1987.

Blum, Lawrence, 'Gilligan and Kohlberg: implications for moral theory', pp. 49–68 in Mary Jeanne Larrabee (ed.), *An Ethic of Care*. New York and London: Routledge, 1993.

Bock, Gisela and James, Susan, *Beyond Equality and Difference*. London: Routledge, 1992.

Bordo, Susan, 'Feminism, postmodernism and gender skepticism', pp. 133–56 in Linda Nicholson (ed.), *Feminism/Postmodernism*. London: Routledge, 1990.

Bordo, Susan, '"Material girl": the effacements of postmodern culture', pp. 106–30 in Laurence Goldstein (ed.), *The Female Body*. Ann Arbor: University of Michigan Press, 1991.

Bordo, Susan, 'Postmodern subjects, postmodern bodies' [review of *Gender Trouble*], *Feminist Studies* 18(1) (1992): 159–75.

Bordo, Susan, 'Reading the slender body', pp. 83–112 in Mary Jacobus, Evelyn Fox Keller and Sally Shuttleworth (eds), *Body/Politics*. New York and London: Routledge, 1990.

Boyne, Roy and Rattansi, Ali (eds), *Postmodernism and Society*. Basingstoke and London: Macmillan, 1990.

Brabeck, Mary, 'Moral judgment', pp. 33–48 in Mary Jeanne Larrabee (ed.), *An Ethic of Care*. New York and London: Routledge, 1993.

Braidotti, Rosa, *Patterns of Dissonance*. Cambridge: Polity Press, 1991.

Breines, Paul, 'Marxism and the New Left in America', pp. 133–51 in Jürgen Habermas (ed.), *Antworten auf Herbert Marcuse*. Frankfurt: Sührkump Verlag, 1968.

Brennan, Teresa (ed.), *Between Feminism and Psychoanalysis*. London and New York: Routledge, 1990.

Brittan, Vera and Holtby, Winifred, 'Why feminism lives' (1927), pp. 40–1 in Maggie Humm (ed.), *Feminisms*. Hemel Hempstead: Harvester Wheatsheaf, 1992.

Brownmiller, Susan, *Against Our Will*. Harmondsworth: Penguin, 1976.

Bunch, Charlotte, 'The reform tool-kit', pp. 189–201 in 'Quest', *Building Feminist Theory: Essays from 'Quest'*. New York: Longmans, 1981.

Butler, Judith, *Bodies That Matter: On the Discursive Limits of 'Sex'*. London: Routledge, 1993.

Butler, Judith, 'Contingent foundations: feminism and the question of "postmodernism"', pp. 3–21 in Judith Butler and Joan Scott (eds), *Feminists Theorize the Political*. New York and London: Routledge, 1992.

Butler, Judith, *Gender Trouble: Feminism and the Subversion of Identity*. New York and London: Routledge, 1990.

Butler, Judith, 'Imitation and gender subordination', pp. 13–31 in Diana Fuss (ed.), *Inside/Out*. New York and London: Routledge, 1991.

Butler, Judith and Scott, Joan (eds), *Feminists Theorize the Political*. New York and London: Routledge, 1992.

Callan, Hilary, 'Harems and overlords: biosocial models and the female', pp. 200–19 in Shirley Ardener (ed.), *Defining Females: The Nature of Women in Society*. London: Croom Helm, 1978.

Callinicos, Alex, *Against Postmodernism*. Cambridge: Polity Press, 1989.

Caplan, Cora, *Sea Changes*. London: Verso, 1986.

Caplan, Pat, *The Cultural Construction of Sexuality*. London: Routledge, 1989.

Card, Claudia (ed.), *Feminist Ethics*. Kansas: Kansas University Press, 1991.

Carrier, John, *The Campaign for the Employment of Women as Police Officers*. Aldershot: Avebury, 1988.

Chester, Gail and Dickey, Julienne, *Feminism and Censorship: The Current Debate*. Dorset: Prism Press, 1988.

Clough, Patricia, *Feminist Thought*. Oxford: Basil Blackwell, 1994.

Cocks, Joan, *The Oppositional Imagination: Feminism, Critique and Political Theory*. London and New York: Routledge, 1989.

Cole, Eve Browning and Coultrap-McQuin, Susan (eds), *Explorations in Feminist Ethics*. Bloomington and Indianapolis: Indiana University Press, 1992.

Collard, Andrée with Contrucci, Joyce, *Rape of the Wild*. London: The Women's Press, 1988.

Collins, Patricia Hill, *Black Feminist Thought*. Boston and London: Unwin Hyman, 1990.

Connell, R.W., *Gender and Power*. Cambridge: Polity Press, 1987.

Coote, Anna and Campbell, Beatrix, *Sweet Freedom: The Struggle for Women's Liberation*. Oxford: Basil Blackwell, 1987.

Coward, Rosalind, *Our Treacherous Hearts: Why Women Let Men Get Their Way*. London: Faber & Faber, 1992.

Coward, Rosalind, *Patriarchal Precedents: Sexuality and Social Relations*. London: Routledge & Kegan Paul, 1983.

Craib, Ian, *Modern Social Theory*. Hemel Hempstead: Harvester Wheatsheaf, 1992.

Crawford, Vicky L., Rouse, Jaqueline Anne and Woods, Barbara, *Women in the Civil Rights Movement. Trailblazers and Torchbearers, 1941–1965*. Bloomington and Indianapolis: Indiana University Press, 1993.

Crenshaw, Kimberle, 'Demarginalizing the intersection of race and sex', pp. 57–80 in Katharine Bartlett and Rosanne Kennedy (eds), *Feminist Legal Theory*. Boulder, CO and Oxford: Westview Press, 1991.

Croll, Elisabeth, *Feminism and Socialism in China*. London: Routledge & Kegan Paul, 1978.

Daly, Mary, *Beyond God the Father: Toward a Philosophy of Women's Liberation*. London: The Women's Press, 1991, first published 1973.

Daly, Mary, Foreword to Andrée Collard with Joyce Contrucci, *Rape of the Wild*. London: The Women's Press, 1988.

Daly, Mary, *Gyn/Ecology*. London: The Women's Press, 1987.

Davis, Angela, *If They Come in the Morning*. Manchester: Orbach and Chambers with the Angela Davis Defence Committee, 1971.

Davis, Angela, *Women, Race and Class*. London: The Women's Press, 1982.

Delphy, Christine and Leonard, Diana, *Familiar Exploitation: A New Analysis of Marriage in Contemporary Western Societies*. Cambridge: Polity Press, 1992.

Dews, Peter, *The Logics of Disintegration*. London: Verso, 1987.

Dinnerstein, Dorothy, *The Rocking of the Cradle and the Ruling of the World* [*The Mermaid and the Minotaur*]. London: The Women's Press, 1987.

Di Stefano, Christine, 'Masculine Marx', pp. 146–63 in Mary Shanley and Carole Pateman (eds), *Feminist Interpretations and Political Theory*. Cambridge: Polity Press, 1991.

Dobson, Andrew and Lucardie, Paul (eds), *The Politics of Nature*. London: Routledge, 1993.

Donald, James and Rattansi, Ali, *'Race', Culture and Difference*. London: Sage, 1992.

Donovan, Josephine, *Feminist Theory*. New York: Continuum, 1992.

Douglas, Carol Anne, *Love and Politics: Radical Feminist and Lesbian Theorists*. San Francisco: Ism Press, 1990.

Dworkin, Andrea, *Letters from a War Zone*. London: Secker & Warburg, 1988.

Dworkin, Andrea, *Pornography: Men Possessing Women*. London: The Women's Press, 1981.

Dworkin, Andrea, *Right-Wing Women: The Politics of Domesticated Females*. London: The Women's Press, 1988.

Echols, Alice, *Daring to be Bad. Radical Feminism in America 1967–75*. Minneapolis: University of Minnesota Press, 1989.

Eisenstein, Hester, *Contemporary Feminist Thought*. London: Unwin Paperbacks, 1984.

Eisenstein, Hester, *Gender Shock: Practicing Feminism on Two Continents*. North Sydney: Allen & Unwin, 1991.

Eisenstein, Zillah (ed.), *Capitalist Patriarchy and the Case for Socialist Feminism*. London and New York: Monthly Review Press, 1979.

Eisenstein, Zillah, *Feminism and Sexual Equality: Crisis in Liberal America*. London and New York: Monthly Review Press, 1984.

Eisenstein, Zillah, *The Radical Future of Liberal Feminism*. Boston: Northeastern University Press, 1981.

Elshtain, Jean Bethke, 'Antigone's daughters', pp. 61–75 in Wendy McElroy (ed.), *Freedom, Feminism and the State*. Washington, DC: The Cato Institute, 1982.

Elshtain, Jean Bethke, 'Moral woman and immoral man: a consideration of the public–private split and its political ramifications', *Politics and Society*, 4 (1974): 453–73.

Elshtain, Jean Bethke, *Public Man, Private Woman: Women in Social and Political Thought*. Oxford: Martin Robertson, 1993, first published 1981.

Epstein, Cynthia Fuchs, *Deceptive Distinctions*. London: Yale University Press, 1988.

Epstein, Cynthia Fuchs, *A Woman's Place*. Berkeley: University of California Press, 1971.

Evans, Judy, 'Ecofeminism and the politics of the gendered self', pp. 177–89 in Andrew Dobson and Paul Lucardie (eds), *The Politics of Nature*. London: Routledge, 1993.

Evans, Judith et al., *Feminism and Political Theory*. London: Sage, 1986.

Faderman, Lillian, *Surpassing the Love of Men*. London: Junction Books, 1981.

Farganis, Sondra, *Situating Feminism*. Thousand Oaks, CA and London: Sage, 1994.

Ferguson, Ann, *Blood at the Root: Motherhood, Sexuality and Male Dominance*. London: Pandora Press, 1989.

Ferguson, Ann, *Sexual Democracy: Women, Oppression, and Revolution*. Boulder, CO and Oxford: Westview Press, 1991.

Ferguson, Kathy E., *The Feminist Case against Bureaucracy*. Philadelphia: Temple University Press, 1984.

Ferguson, Kathy E., *The Man Question: Visions of Subjectivity in Feminist Theory*. Berkeley and Los Angeles: University of California Press, 1993.

Fineman, Martha and Thomadsen, Nancy (eds), *At the Boundaries of Law: Feminism and Legal Theory*. New York and London: Routledge, 1991.

Firestone, Shulamith, *The Dialectic of Sex*. London: Jonathan Cape, 1971.

Flax, Jane, *Disputed Subjects*. New York and London: Routledge, 1993.

Flax, Jane, 'Postmodernism and gender relations in feminist theory', pp. 39–62 in Linda Nicholson (ed.), *Feminism/Postmodernism*. London: Routledge, 1990.

Flax, Jane, *Thinking Fragments: Psychoanalysis, Feminism, and Postmodernism in the Contemporary West*. Berkeley and London: University of California Press, 1991.

Franzway, Suzanne, Court, Dianne and Connell, R.W., *Staking a Claim: Feminism, Bureaucracy and the State*. Cambridge: Polity Press, 1989.

Fraser, Nancy, *Unruly Practices: Power, Discourse and Gender in Contemporary Social Theory*. Cambridge: Polity Press, 1989.

Fraser, Nancy and Bartky, Sandra Lee (eds), *Revaluing French Feminism*. Bloomington and Indianapolis: Indiana University Press, 1992.

Frazer, Elizabeth and Lacey, Nicola, *The Politics of Community: A Feminist Critique of the Liberal–Communitarian Debate*. Hemel Hempstead: Harvester Wheatsheaf, 1992.

Freeman, Jo, *The Politics of Women's Liberation*. New York: Longmans, 1975.

Freeman, Jo, *The Tyranny of Structurelessness* (1970). London: Dark Star/Rebel Press, 1984.

French, Marilyn, *The Women's Room*. London: Abacus, 1986.

Friedan, Betty, *The Feminine Mystique*. Harmondsworth: Penguin, 1982, first published 1963.

Friedan, Betty, *The Second Stage*. London: Sphere Books, 1983.

Friedman, Marilyn, 'Beyond caring: the de-moralization of gender', pp. 258–73 in Mary Jeanne Larrabee (ed.), *An Ethic of Care*. New York and London: Routledge, 1993.

Friedman, Marilyn, 'Feminism and modern friendship: dislocating the community', pp. 89–97 in Eve Browning Cole and Susan Coultrap-McQuin (eds), *Explorations in Feminist Ethics*. Bloomington and Indianapolis: Indiana University Press, 1992.

Frug, Mary Joe, *Postmodern Legal Feminism*. London: Routledge, 1992.

Frye, Marilyn, *The Politics of Reality*. Trumansburg, NY: The Crossing Press, 1983.

Fuss, Diana, *Essentially Speaking*. New York and London: Routledge, 1989.

Fuss, Diana (ed.), *Inside/Out: Lesbian Theories, Gay Theories*. London: Routledge, 1991.

Garfinkel, Howard, *Studies in Ethnomethodology*. Englewood Cliffs, NJ: Prentice-Hall, 1967.

Garry, Ann and Pearsall, Marilyn (eds), *Women, Knowledge and Reality*. Boston and London: Unwin Hyman, 1989.

Gatens, Moira, *Feminism and Philosophy: Perspectives on Difference and Inequality*. Cambridge: Polity Press, 1991.

Gavron, Hannah, *The Captive Wife*. London: Routledge, 1966.

Gergen, Mary McCanney (ed.), *Feminist Thought and the Structure of Knowledge*. New York and London: New York University Press, 1988.

German, Lindsey, *Sex, Class and Socialism*. London: Bookmarks, 1989.

Gilligan, Carol, *In a Different Voice*. London: Harvard University Press, 1982 (new edition 1993).

Goldfield, Evelyn, Munaker, Sue and Weisstein, Naomi, 'A woman is a sometime thing', pp. 236–71 in Priscilla Long (ed.), *The New Left*. Boston: F. Porter Sargent, 1969.

Goldstein, Laurence (ed.), *The Female Body*. Ann Arbor: University of Michigan Press, 1991.

Gould, Carol C. and Wartofsky, Marx W. (eds), *Women and Philosophy: Toward a Theory of Liberation*. New York: Capricorn Books/G.P. Putnam's Sons, 1972.

Griffin, Susan, *Pornography and Silence: Culture's Revenge against Nature*. London: The Women's Press, 1981.

Grimshaw, Jean, *Feminist Philosophers: Women's Perspectives on Philosophical Traditions*. Brighton: Wheatsheaf Books, 1986.

Grosz, Elizabeth, 'Conclusion: a note on essentialism and difference', pp. 332–44 in Sneja Gunew (ed.), *Feminist Knowledge: Critique and Construct*. London: Routledge, 1990.

Gunew, Sneja (ed.), *Feminist Knowledge: Critique and Construct*. London: Routledge, 1990.

Harasyn, Sarah (ed.), *The Post-Colonial Critic*. New York and London: Routledge, 1990.

Haraway, Donna, 'A manifesto for cyborgs: science, technology and socialist feminism in the 1980s', pp. 190–233 in Linda Nicholson (ed.), *Feminism/Postmodernism*. New York and London: Routledge, 1990.

Harding, Sandra, 'Feminist justificatory strategies', pp. 189–201 in Ann Garry and Marilyn Pearsall (eds), *Women, Knowledge and Reality: Explorations in Feminist Philosophy*. London: Unwin Hyman, 1989.

Harding, Sandra, 'The instability of the analytical categories of feminist theory', *Signs: Journal of Women in Culture and Society*, 11(4) (1986): 645–64.

Harding, Sandra, *The Science Question in Feminism*. Milton Keynes: Open University Press, 1986.

Harding, Sandra, *Whose Science? Whose Knowledge?* Milton Keynes: Open University Press, 1991.

Hartsock, Nancy, 'Foucault on power', pp. 157–75 in Linda Nicholson (ed.), *Feminism/Postmodernism*. New York and London: Routledge, 1990.

Hartsock, Nancy, *Money, Sex and Power: Toward a Feminist Historical Materialism*. New York: Longmans, 1983.

Harvey, David, *The Condition of Postmodernity*. Oxford: Basil Blackwell, 1989.

Hawkesworth, Mary, 'Knowers, knowing, known: feminist theory and the claims of truth', pp. 327–52 in Micheline Malson, Jean F. O'Barr, Sarah Westphal-Wihl and Mary Wyer (eds), *Feminist Theory in Practice and Process*. London: University of Chicago Press, 1989.

Hekman, Susan J., *Gender and Knowledge: Elements of a Postmodern Feminism*. Cambridge: Polity Press, 1990.

Held, David and Pollitt, Christopher (eds), *New Forms of Democracy*. London and Beverly Hills: Sage, 1986.

Held, Virginia, 'Feminism and moral theory', pp. 111–28 in Eva Kittay and Diana Meyers (eds), *Women and Moral Theory*. New Jersey: Rowman & Littlefield, 1987.

Hirsch, Marianne and Keller, Evelyn Fox (eds), *Conflicts in Feminism*. London: Routledge, 1990.

Hoagland, Sarah, 'Lesbian ethics and female agency', pp. 156–64 in Eve Browning Cole and Susan Coultrap-McQuin (eds), *Explorations in Feminist Ethics*. Bloomington and Indianapolis: Indiana University Press, 1992.

Hodge, Joanna, 'Feminism and postmodernism', pp. 86–111 in Andrew Benjamin (ed.), *The Problems of Modernity*. London: Routledge, 1991.

Hodge, Joanna, 'Women and the Hegelian state', pp. 127–58 in Ellen Kennedy and Susan Mendus (eds), *Women in Western Political Philosophy*. Brighton: Wheatsheaf Books, 1987.

hooks, bell, *Ain't I a Woman: Black Women and Feminism*. London: Pluto Press, 1982.

hooks, bell, *Black Looks: Race and Representation*. London: Turnaround, 1992.

hooks, bell, *From Margin to Center*. Boston: South End Press, 1984.

hooks, bell, *Talking Back: Thinking Feminist – Thinking Black*. London: Sheba Feminist Publishers, 1989.

hooks, bell, *Yearning: Race, Gender and Cultural Politics*. London: Turnaround, 1991.

hooks, bell and West, Cornel, *Breaking Bread: Insurgent Black Intellectual Life*. Boston: South End Press, 1991.

Horner, Matina, 'Towards an understanding of achievement-related conflicts in women', *Journal of Social Issues*, 28 (1972): 157–75.

Hrdy, Sarah B., *The Woman That Never Evolved*. Cambridge, MA: Harvard University Press, 1981.

Hull, Gloria T., Scott, Patricia Bell and Smith, Barbara (eds), *All the Women Are White, All the Blacks Are Men, But Some of Us Are Brave*. New York: Feminist Press, 1982.

Humm, Maggie (ed.), *Feminisms: A Reader*. Hemel Hempstead: Harvester Wheatsheaf, 1992.

Itzin, Catherine (ed.), *Pornography: Women, Violence and Civil Liberties*. Oxford: Oxford University Press, 1993.

Jacobs, Paul and Landau, Saul, *The New Radicals*. Harmondsworth: Penguin, 1967.

Jacobus, Mary, Fox Keller, Evelyn and Shuttleworth, Sally (eds), *Body/Politics: Women and the Discourses of Science*. New York and London: Routledge, 1990.

Jacoby, Russell, *Social Amnesia*. Brighton: Harvester, 1978.

Jaggar, Alison, *Feminist Politics and Human Nature*. Brighton: Harvester, 1983.

Jaggar, Alison and Bordo, Susan (eds), *Gender/Body/Knowledge: Feminist Reconstructions of Being and Knowing*. New Brunswick and London: Rutgers University Press, 1989.

Janeway, Elizabeth, *Man's World, Woman's Place: A Study in Social Mythology*. New York: William Morrow, 1971.

Jeffreys, Sheila, *Anticlimax: A Feminist Perspective on the Sexual Revolution*. London: The Women's Press, 1990.

Jones, Kathleen and Jónasdóttir, Anna (eds), *The Political Interests of Gender*. London: Sage, 1988.

Jordan, June, *Moving towards Home*. London: Virago, 1989.

Kaplan, Cora, *Sea Changes: Culture and Feminism*. London: Verso, 1986.

Kaplan, E. Ann (ed.), *Postmodernism and its Discontents*. London: Verso, 1988.

Kappeler, Susanne, 'Pornography: the representation of power', pp. 88–101 in Catherine Itzin (ed.), *Pornography: Women, Violence and Civil Liberties*. Oxford: Oxford University Press, 1983.

Keller, Evelyn Fox, *Reflections on Gender and Science*. New Haven: Yale University Press, 1985.

Kennedy, Ellen and Mendus, Susan (eds), *Women in Western Political Philosophy*. Brighton: Wheatsheaf Books, 1987.

King, Ynestra, 'Healing the wounds', pp. 115–41 in Alison Jaggar and Susan Bordo (eds), *Gender/Body/Knowledge: Feminist Reconstructions of Being and Knowing*. New Brunswick and London: Rutgers University Press, 1989.

Kirkpatrick, Jeane, *Political Woman*. New York: Basic Books, 1974.

Kirp, David L., Yudof, Mark G. and Franks, Marlene Strong, *Gender Justice*. Chicago and London: University of Chicago Press, 1986.

Kohlberg, L. and Kramer, R. 'Continuities and discontinuities in childhood and adult moral development', *Human Development*, 12 (1969): 93–120.

Kohlberg, Lawrence, *The Philosophy of Moral Development*. San Francisco: Harper & Row, 1981.

Larrabee, Mary Jeanne, 'Introduction: gender and moral development', pp. 3–16 in Mary Jeanne Larrabee (ed.), *An Ethic of Care*. New York and London: Routledge, 1993.

Larrabee, Mary Jeanne (ed.), *An Ethic of Care*. New York and London: Routledge, 1993.

Lawson, Hilary and Appignanesi, Lisa (eds), *Dismantling Truth*. London: Weidenfeld & Nicolson, 1989.

Leidholdt, Dorchen and Raymond, Janice G. (eds), *The Sexual Liberals and the Attack on Feminism*. Oxford: Pergamon Press, 1990.

Lipschultz, Sibyl, 'Social feminism and legal discourse, 1908–1923', pp. 209–25 in Martha Fineman and Nancy Thomadsen (eds), *At the Boundaries of Law*. New York and London: Routledge, 1991.

Littleton, Christine, 'Reconstructing sexual equality', pp. 35–56 in Katharine Bartlett and

Rosanne Kennedy (eds), *Feminist Legal Theory*. Boulder, CO and Oxford: Westview Press, 1991.

Lloyd, Genevieve, *Man of Reason*. London: Methuen, 1986.

Long, Priscilla (ed.), *The New Left*. Boston: F. Porter Sargent, 1969.

Longino, Helen, 'Can there be a feminist science?', *Hypatia*, 2(3) (1987): 51–64.

Lorde, Audre, *A Burst of Light*. London: Sheba Feminist Publishers, 1988.

Lorde, Audre, 'An open letter to Mary Daly', pp. 94–7 in Cherríe Moraga and Gloria Anzaldúa (eds), *This Bridge Called My Back: Radical Writings by Women of Color*. Latham, NY: Kitchen Table, Women of Color Press, 1983.

Lorde, Audre, *Sister Outsider*. Freedom, CA: The Crossing Press, 1984.

Lovell, Terry (ed.), *British Feminist Thought: A Reader*. Oxford: Basil Blackwell, 1990.

Lovibond, Sabina, 'Feminism and postmodernism', pp. 154–86 in Roy Boyne and Ali Rattansi (eds), *Postmodernism and Society*. Basingstoke and London: Macmillan, 1990.

Lyotard, Jean-François, *The Postmodern Condition*. Manchester: Manchester University Press, 1984.

McElroy, Wendy (ed.), *Freedom, Feminism and the State: An Overview of Individualist Feminism*. New York and London: Holmes and Meier, 1991.

McEnloe, Cynthia, 'The right to fight: a feminist catch-22', *Ms.*, 4(1) (1993): 84–7.

Mackinnon, Catharine, 'Difference and dominance', pp. 81–94 in Katharine Bartlett and Rosanne Kennedy (eds), *Feminist Legal Theory*. Boulder, CO and Oxford: Westview Press, 1991.

Mackinnon, Catharine, *Feminism Unmodified: Discourses on Life and Law*. Cambridge, MA and London: Harvard University Press, 1987.

Mackinnon, Catharine, 'Legal perspectives on sexual difference', pp. 213–25 in Deborah L. Rhode (ed.), *Theoretical Perspectives on Sexual Difference*. New Haven: Yale University Press, 1991.

Mackinnon, Catharine (UK edition), *Only Words*. London: HarperCollins, 1994.

Mackinnon, Catharine, 'Pornography, civil rights and speech', pp. 456–511 in Catherine Itzin (ed.), *Pornography: Women, Violence and Civil Liberties*. Oxford: Oxford University Press, 1993.

Mackinnon, Catharine, *The Sexual Harassment of Working Women*. New Haven: Yale University Press, 1979.

Mackinnon, Catharine, *Toward a Feminist Theory of the State*. Cambridge, MA and London: Harvard University Press, 1989.

McLelland, David, *Power: The Inner Experience*. New York: Irvington, 1975.

Malson, Micheline R., O'Barr, Jean F., Westphal-Wihl, Sarah and Wyer, Mary (eds), *Feminist Theory in Practice and Process*. Chicago and London: University of Chicago Press, 1989.

Manning, Marable, *Race, Reform and Rebellion: The Second Reconstruction in Black America, 1945–1990*. Jackson and London: University Press of Mississippi, 1991.

Massell, Gregory, *The Surrogate Proletariat: Moslem Women and Revolutionary Strategies in Soviet Central Asia, 1919–29*. Princeton, NJ: Princeton University Press, 1974.

Midgley, Mary and Hughes, Judith, *Women's Choices: Philosophical Problems Facing Feminism*. London: Weidenfeld & Nicolson, 1983.

Millett, Kate, *Sexual Politics*. London: Abacus, 1972.

Minow, Martha, 'Adjudicating differences: conflicts among feminist lawyers', pp. 149–63 in Marianne Hirsch and Evelyn Fox Keller (eds), *Conflicts in Feminism*. New York and London: Routledge, 1990.

Mitchell, Juliet, *Woman's Estate*. Harmondsworth: Penguin, 1971.

Mitchell, Juliet, 'Women: the longest revolution', pp. 17–54 in *Women: The Longest Revolution. Essays in Feminism, Literature and Psychoanalysis*. London: Virago, 1984.

Mitchell, Juliet and Oakley, Ann (eds), *What is Feminism?* Oxford: Basil Blackwell, 1986.

Moraga, Cherríe and Anzaldúa, Gloria (eds), *This Bridge Called My Back: Radical Writings by Women of Color*. Latham, NY: Kitchen Table, Women of Color Press, 1983.

Morgan, Robin, 'Goodbye to all that', pp. 268–76 in Leslie Tanner (ed.), *Voices From Women's Liberation*. New York: Signet, 1971.

Morgan, Robin (ed.), *Sisterhood is Powerful*. New York: Vintage Books, 1970.

Narayan, Uma, 'The project of feminist epistemology: perspectives from a nonwestern feminist', pp. 256–69 in Alison Jaggar and Susan Bordo (eds), *Gender/Body/Knowledge: Feminist Reconstructions of Being and Knowing*. New Brunswick and London: Rutgers University Press, 1989.

Nell, Onora (O'Neill), 'How do we know when opportunities are equal?', pp. 334–46 in Carol C. Gould and Marx Wartofsky (eds), *Women and Philosophy*. New York: G.P. Putnam, 1976.

Nicholson, Linda (ed.), *Feminism/Postmodernism*. London: Routledge, 1990.

Nicholson, Linda J., 'Women, morality and history', pp. 87–101 in Mary Jeanne Larrabee (ed.), *An Ethic of Care*. London and New York: Routledge, 1993.

Noddings, Nell, *Women and Evil*. London: University of California Press, 1989.

Norris, Christopher, *Uncritical Theory: Postmodernists, Intellectuals, and the Gulf War*. London: Lawrence & Wishart, 1992.

Nye, Andrea, *Feminist Theory and the Philosophies of Man*. London: Routledge, 1989.

O'Brien, Mary, *The Politics of Reproduction*. London: Routledge & Kegan Paul, 1981.

Okin, Susan, 'Gender inequality and cultural differences', *Political Theory*, 2(2) (1994): 5–24.

Okin, Susan, 'Gender, the public and the private', pp. 67–90 in David Held (ed.), *Political Theory Today*. Cambridge: Polity Press, 1992.

Okin, Susan, 'John Rawls: justice as fairness – for whom?', pp. 181–98 in Mary Shanley and Carole Pateman (eds), *Feminist Interpretations and Political Theory*. Cambridge: Polity Press, 1991.

Okin, Susan, *Justice, Gender, and the Family*. New York: Basic Books, 1989.

Okin, Susan, 'Thinking like a woman', pp. 145–59 in Deborah L. Rhode (ed.), *Theoretical Perspectives on Sexual Difference*. New Haven and London: Yale University Press, 1991.

Okin, Susan, *Women in Western Political Thought*, 2nd edn. London: Virago, 1992, first published 1980.

Pateman, Carole, *The Disorder of Women: Democracy, Feminism and Political Theory*. Cambridge: Polity Press, 1989.

Pateman, Carole, 'Equality, difference, subordination', pp. 17–47 in Gisela Bock and Susan James (eds), *Beyond Equality and Difference*. London: Routledge, 1992.

Pateman, Carole and Grosz, Elizabeth (eds), *Feminist Challenges*. Sydney and London: Allen & Unwin, 1986.

Phillips, Anne, *Democracy and Difference*. Cambridge: Polity Press, 1993.

Phillips, Anne, *Divided Loyalties: Dilemmas of Sex and Class*. London: Virago, 1987.

Phillips, Anne, *Engendering Democracy*. Cambridge: Polity Press, 1991.

Piercy, Marge, 'The grand coolie damn', pp. 421–37 in Robin Morgan (ed.), *Sisterhood is Powerful*. New York: Vintage Books, 1970.

Plumwood, Valerie, 'Women, humanity and nature', pp. 177–89 in Sean Sayers and Peter Osborne (eds), *Socialism, Feminism and Philosophy: A Radical Philosophy Reader*. London: Routledge, 1990.

Puka, Bill, 'The liberation of caring', pp. 215–39 in Mary Jeanne Larrabee (ed.), *An Ethic of Care*. London and New York: Routledge, 1993.

Quest, *Building Feminist Theory. Essays from 'Quest'*. New York and London: Longmans, 1981.

Ramanazoglu, Caroline, *Feminism and the Contradictions of Oppression*. London and New York: Routledge, 1989.

Rawls, John, *A Theory of Justice*. Oxford: Oxford University Press, 1972.

Rhode, Deborah L. (ed.), *Theoretical Perspectives on Sexual Difference*. New Haven: Yale University Press, 1991.

Rich, Adrienne, 'Compulsory heterosexuality and lesbian existence', *Signs*, 5(4) (1980): 631–90.

Rich, Adrienne, *Of Woman Born*. London: Virago Press, 1986.

Rich, Adrienne, *Poems: Selected and New, 1950–1974*. New York: W.W. Norton, 1975.

Richards, Janet Radcliffe, *The Sceptical Feminist*. London: Routledge, 1980.

Rossi, Alice S., 'A biosocial perspective on parenting', *Daedalus*, 106(2) (1975): 1–31.

Rossi, Alice S., 'Equality between the sexes: an immodest proposal', *Daedalus*, 93(2) (1964): 607–52.

Rowbotham, Sheila, *Dreams and Dilemmas*. London: Virago Press, 1983.

Rowbotham, Sheila, 'Feminism and democracy', pp. 78–109 in David Held and Christopher Pollitt (eds), *New Forms of Democracy*. London and Beverly Hills: Sage, 1986.

Ruddick, Sara, *Maternal Thinking*. London: The Women's Press, 1990.

Russell, Diana (ed.), *Making Violence Sexy: A Feminist View on Pornography*. Buckingham: Open University Press, 1993.

Rutherford, Jonathan (ed.), *Identity*. London: Lawrence & Wishart, 1990.

Ryan, Barbara, *Feminism and the Women's Movement*. New York and London: Routledge, 1992.

Sapiro, Virginia, 'Sex and games: on oppression and rationality', *British Journal of Political Science*, 9 (1979): 385–408.

Sargent, Lyman T., *New Left Thought*. Homewood, IL: Dorsey Press, 1972.

Sargent, Lydia (ed.), *Women and Revolution: A Discussion of the Unhappy Marriage of Marxism and Feminism*. London: Pluto Press, 1981.

Sassen, Georgia, 'Success anxiety in women: a constructivist interpretation of its sources and its significance', *Harvard Educational Review*, 50 (1980): 13–25.

Scott, Joan, 'Deconstructing equality-versus-difference', pp. 134–48 in Marianne Hirsch and Evelyn Fox Keller (eds), *Conflicts in Feminism*. New York and London: Routledge, 1990.

Segal, Lynne, *Is the Future Female?: Troubled Thoughts on Contemporary Feminism*. London: Virago, 1987.

Segal, Lynne and McIntosh, Mary (eds), *Sex Exposed: Sexuality and the Pornography Debate*. London: Virago, 1992.

Segal, Lynne, *Straight Sex*. London: Virago, 1994.

Sen, Mala, *India's Bandit Queen: The True Story of Phoolan Devi*. London: Pandora, 1993.

Shange, Ntozake, *A Daughter's Geography*. London: Methuen, 1985.

Shange, Ntozake, 'Some men', pp. 37–44 in *A Daughter's Geography*. London: Methuen, 1985.

Shanley, Mary and Pateman, Carole (eds), *Feminist Interpretations and Political Theory*. Cambridge: Polity Press, 1991.

Snitow, Ann, 'A gender diary', pp. 9–43 in Marianne Hirsch and Evelyn Fox Keller (eds), *Conflicts in Feminism*. London: Routledge, 1990.

Soper, Kate, *Troubled Pleasures. Writings on Politics, Gender and Hedonism*. London: Verso, 1990.

Spelman, Elisabeth V., *Inessential Woman*. London: The Women's Press, 1990.

Spender, Dale (ed.), *Feminist Theorists*. London: The Women's Press, 1983.

Spender, Dale, *For the Record: The Making and Meaning of Feminist Knowledge*. London: The Women's Press, 1985.

Spivak, Gayatri, 'Criticism, feminism and the institution', pp. 1–16 in Sarah Harasyn (ed.), *The Post-Colonial Critic*. New York and London: Routledge, 1990.

Squire, Corinne, *Significant Differences: Feminism in Psychology*. London: Routledge, 1989.

Stanton, Elizabeth Cady, 'The solitude of self', p. 189 in Susan B. Anthony and Ida Husted Harper (eds), *History of Woman Suffrage*, Vol. IV. New York: Source Book Press, 1970.

Steinem, Gloria, 'Houston and history', pp. 281–91 in *Outrageous Acts and Everyday Rebellions*. London: Fontana, 1985.

Steinem, Gloria, *Outrageous Acts and Everyday Rebellions*. London: Fontana, 1985.

Stimpson, Catharine R., *Where the Meanings Are: Feminism and Cultural Spaces*. London and New York: Routledge, 1988.

Stoltenberg, John, 'Confronting pornography as a civil rights issue', pp. 137–70 in *Refusing to be a Man*. London: Fontana, 1990.

Tanner, Leslie (ed.), *Voices from Women's Liberation*. New York: Signet, 1971.

Tong, Rosemarie, *Feminist Thought*. London and Sydney: Unwin Hyman, 1989.

Tronto, Joan, *Moral Boundaries. A Political Argument for an Ethic of Care*. New York and London: Routledge, 1993.

Tronto, Joan, 'Women and caring: what can feminists learn about morality from caring?', pp. 172–87 in Alison Jaggar and Susan Bordo (eds), *Gender/Body/Knowledge*. New Brunswick and London: Rutgers University Press, 1989.

Vance, Carole (ed.), *Pleasure and Danger: Exploring Female Sexuality*. London: Pandora Press, 1992.

Walby, Sylvia, *Theorizing Patriarchy*. Oxford: Basil Blackwell, 1990.

Weedon, Chris, *Feminist Practice and Poststructuralist Theory*. Oxford: Basil Blackwell, 1989.

Weinbaum, Batya, *The Curious Courtship of Women's Liberation and Socialism*. Boston: South End Press, 1978.

Weldon, Fay, *Praxis*. London: Sceptre Books, 1993.

Wendell, Susan, 'A (qualified) defense of liberal feminism', *Hypatia*, 2(2) (1987): 65–94.

West, Rebecca, 'The life of Emily Davison', pp. 31–3 in Maggie Humm (ed.), *Feminisms: A Reader*. Hemel Hempstead: Harvester Wheatsheaf, 1992, first published 1913.

Whisker, Brenda, Bishop, Jacky, Mohin, Lilian and Longdon, Trish, *Breaching the Peace*. London: Onlywomen Press, 1983.

Williams, Patricia, 'On being the object of property', pp. 165–80 in Katharine Bartlett and Rosanne Kennedy (eds), *Feminist Legal Theory*. Boulder, CO and Oxford: Westview Press, 1991.

Williams, Wendy, 'The equality crisis', pp. 15–34 in Katharine Bartlett and Rosanne Kennedy (eds), *Feminist Legal Theory*. Boulder, CO and Oxford: Westview Press, 1991.

Wolff, Robert Paul, 'There's nobody here but us persons', pp. 128–44 in Carol C. Gould and Marx Wartofsky (eds), *Women and Philosophy*. New York: G.P. Putnam, 1976.

Yates, Gayle Graham, *What Women Want: The Ideas of the Movement*. Cambridge, MA and London: Harvard University Press, 1977.

Young, Iris, 'The ideal of community and the politics of difference', pp. 300–23 in Linda Nicholson (ed.), *Feminism/Postmodernism*. London: Routledge, 1990, first published 1987.

Young, Iris, 'Impartiality and the civic public', pp. 57–76 in Seyla Benhabib and Drusilla Cornell (eds), *Feminism as Critique*. Cambridge: Polity Press, 1987.

Young, Iris, *Justice and the Politics of Difference*. Princeton and Oxford: Princeton University Press, 1990.

Young, Iris, 'Socialist feminism and the limits of dual systems theory', *Socialist Review*, 50–1(2–3) (1980): 169–88.

Young, Iris, *Throwing Like a Girl: And Other Essays in Feminist Philosophy and Social Theory*. Indianapolis: Indiana University Press, 1990.

Index

abortion, 51, 70, 93–4, 98–9
acceptable inequality, 31
agency, 137–8
Alcoff, L., 86–8
androcentrism, 4, 5, 161, 167n
androgyny, 14, 29, 55, 92
  Daly and, 81
  early radicalism and, 64
  liberal feminism and, 29–33, 50
  socialist feminism and, 109
  see also sameness equality
armed services, women in, 49, 50, 153
Arms, S., 85
assimilation, 119, 161–2
attitudinal differences, 160
Auerbach, J., 92

Bacchi, C.L., 24, 143, 144–9
Baier, A., 93, 102
Barrett, M., 63, 166
beauty, 69
Beauvoir, S. de, 82
behavioural differences, 14, 50, 94, 160
Benhabib, S., 136
biological determinism, 67, 83, 87–8
black identity, 139
black women, 17, 21, 161–2
Bluestone, N., 39–40, 43, 56
Blum, L., 104
Bodies that Matter (Butler), 137–8
Brabeck, M., 101
Bunch, C., 16, 63
Butler, J., 114, 116, 132–40, 164
Butler v. Regina, 156

Canada, equality and law in, 155–6
capitalism, 64, 109, 111–12
care, 77, 91, 99–100, 104
  ethic of, 39, 52, 93, 96, 99, 102
  Young and, 116
Carrier, J., 47
censorship, 154, 156
childbearing, 73, 85
  control of, 68
childcare, 35, 57, 73–4

citizenship, 117–18
Civil Rights movement, 17, 22
Cixous, H., 9
class, neglect of, 110–11
Clough, P., 137
Collard, A., 18, 82–3
communitarianism, 113
competition, 95
complementarity, 47, 50
Connell, R., 109
consciousness-raising groups, 38
Coward, R. 166
Crenshaw, K. 161
cultural feminism, 18–20, 76–88, 149
  race and, 21–2
  'weak', 91–105

Daly, M., 18, 80–2, 87, 162
deconstruction, 23–4, 127, 128
Derrida, J., 23, 127
desire, 118
detachment, 117
determinism, 72
Devi, Phoolan, 1
Dialectic of Sex, The (Firestone), 67–71
différance, 23, 126–7
difference, 29, 30, 162
  cultural feminism and, 18–20, 76–88,
    92
  between groups, 113, 119–22, 152, 164
  identity politics and, 21–2, 113
  law and, 147, 148
  postmodernism and, 23–4, 110, 127
  power and, 151
  between women, 6–7, 17, 65, 163
  see also equality/difference; sameness/
    difference; sex differences
'different and better' argument, 18, 19
different voice, 92, 93, 101–2
Dinnerstein, D., 53
domesticity, 130
domination, 117, 143, 150–1
  see also oppression; subordination
Donald, J., 22
draft, male-only, 41, 42, 153

drag, 134–5
dual systems theory, 111–12
Dworkin, A., 153, 160

early radical feminism, 14, 15–16, 20,
    62–74
Echols, A., 20
ecology, 69
education, 34, 74
egalitarianism, 65, 83
Ehrenreich, B., 25, 108
Eisenstein, H., 18, 139
elites, 54, 66
Elshtain, J.B., 53, 58–9
epistemology, 20, 126, 141n
Epstein, C.F., 14
equal capability, 13, 40
Equal Employment Opportunities
    Commission, 129, 146
equal treatment, 41, 145, 146, 163
equality, 5, 79, 82, 151
    in difference, 3, 163
    freedom and, 155–6, 157
    law and, 41–2, 145–8, 155–6, 165
    in liberal feminism, 29–33, 36, 43–4, 51,
        58
        Bluestone and, 39–40
    meanings of, 14–17
    in radical feminism, 63, 65, 68, 70
    socialist feminism and, 109, 111
    in working conditions, 144–5
    Young and, 119, 120
    see also equality/difference debate;
        sameness equality
equality of condition, 16, 30, 62, 63
equality/difference debate, 2–5, 13–25,
    162–4
    Friedan and, 33–5
    Rossi and, 36
    Scott and, 128–32
    see also sameness/difference
equality of opportunity, 14–15, 28, 30–2
eroticism, 69
essentialism, 18, 24, 77–8, 83, 88, 119, 127
ethic of care, 39, 52, 93, 96, 99, 101, 102
ethic of justice, 39, 52, 94
exclusion, 119, 148

failure, 35, 95
family, 35, 73, 74
fathers, support of children by, 55
female body, 85, 88
female values, 19, 47, 76, 77, 79, 148, 162
Feminine Mystique, The (Friedan), 13, 29,
    33–5

feminism, 25, 43, 86
    Firestone on, 69, 70
    Friedan on, 36–7
    Richards on, 36–7
    see also cultural feminism; early radical
        feminism; liberal feminism; socialist
        feminism
feminist theory, 10–11
Ferguson, A., 154
financial equality, 48–9
Firestone, S., 14, 15, 16, 64, 67–71, 109, 150,
    166
First Amendment (of US Constitution),
    154
Flax, J., 102, 103
Foucault, M., 132
Fourteenth Amendment, 154
freedom, 155–6, 157
    of speech, 154–5, 156
Freeman, J., 65–6
French, M., 34
Friedan, B., 18, 31, 33–5, 43, 162
    The Second Stage, 48–51
friendship, 66
Frug, M.J., 92, 149
Fuss, D., 86

Geduldig v. Aiello, 53, 146
gender, 41
    construction of, 133, 137–8
    power and, 149–51
    sex and, 76–7, 160
    wish to abolish, 43, 55
gender-blindness, 29
gender-neutral legislation, 53
Gender Trouble (Butler), 133–5
genital mutilation, 81, 82, 89
Gilligan, C., 38–9, 52, 54, 92–3, 155, 161
    In a Different Voice, 93–104
Grosz, E., 18, 77
group identities, 112, 113–16, 119–22, 152,
    164
Gyn/Ecology (Daly), 81, 82
gynocentrism, 111, 112, 114

Harding, S., 28, 161
Hartsock, N., 139
Hawkesworth, M., 139–40
Heinz dilemma, 96–7
Held, V., 92
heterosexuality, 16, 86, 134, 135, 150, 166
hierarchy, 32, 40, 66, 82
Hirsch, M., 8
Hodge, J., 9, 125
homophobia, 36, 135, 164

homosexuality, 150, 166
  see also lesbianism
hooks, bell, 17, 21, 139, 162
Horner, M., 95, 165
housework, 34, 35, 54
Hudnut, 154
humanism, 112

idealism, 126
identity, 6, 7, 114, 133–4
identity politics, 109–10, 114, 115, 137,
  163
  difference and, 21–2, 113
  lesbian and gay, 135–6
impartiality, 116–17, 118, 163
In a Different Voice (Gilligan), 93, 98–9
individualism, 35, 113, 116, 132, 164
inequality, 31, 33–4, 40, 151–2

Jacoby, R., 156
Jeffreys, S., 162
justice, 37, 38–9, 43, 52, 96, 99, 103–4,
  114
Justice, Gender and the Family (Okin), 38–9,
  52
Justice and the Politics of Difference
  (Young), 113, 114

Kappeler, S. 156
Keller, E.F., 8
Kirkpatrick, J., 95, 165
Kohlberg, L., 96
Kristeva, J., 9

language, 80–1
Larrabee, M.J., 105n
law
  difference and, 147, 148
  equality under, 41–2, 145–8, 155–6, 165
  pornography and, 153–4, 156
lesbianism, 6, 86, 133, 135–6, 150
liberal empiricism, 59
liberal feminism, 9, 13, 15, 20, 29–44
  difference and, 47–59
liberalism, 9, 62, 125, 127
Littleton, C., 163
Lorde, A., 20, 82, 163
love, 16, 19, 69
Lovibond, S., 43
Lyotard, J.-F., 23

McIntosh, M., 166
Mackinnon, C., 4–5, 20, 24, 88, 104, 105,
  143, 164–5
  and power, 149–57

McLelland, D., 94, 95
marginalization of women, 71–2
marriage, 35
Marxism, 72, 127
  and socialist feminism, 108–9, 112
meritocracy, 31, 32
Michael M. v. Sonoma County, 41, 42
Mitchell, J., 71–4, 109
moral issues, 98–9
  gender differences in, 38–9, 52, 96–7
Morgan, R., 1, 17
motherhood, 19, 36, 53, 68, 73–4
  Rich and, 84–5
mystique, 33, 35, 51, 78
myth, 72
mythic truth, 101

National Organization for Women (NOW),
  41
nature/culture, 74
Nell, O., 31
New Left, 16, 62, 64–5, 71
new social movements, 113
non-mothers, 85
nurture, 19, 77, 83, 85

occupational equality, 48
Of Woman Born (Rich), 84–5
Okin, S., 14, 38–9, 43, 51–5, 56, 161
O'Neill (O. Nell), 31
Only Words (Mackinnon), 153–7, 165
ontology, 20, 126, 141n
oppression, 15, 67, 70, 83, 103
  and dual systems theory, 111–12
  eradication of, 16, 62, 63
  patriarchy and, 65, 80, 81
  postmodernism and, 126
  see also subordination of women

parenting, 53, 54–5
  difference in, 57–8
parity, 15, 43, 47
parody, 134
participation, 119, 120, 121
part-time work, 51
Pateman, C., 47
patriarchy, 17, 64, 77, 83, 84–5, 108,
  112
  and oppression, 65, 80, 81
peace movements, 18
Phillips, A., 29, 40, 66, 121–2
philosophy, 102
Piercy, M., 64–5
pluralism, 24
pornography, 151, 154, 156, 157, 165

postmodernism, 7, 9, 10
  difference and, 23–4, 110
  feminist, 9–10, 125–40
poststructuralism, 23–4, 87
  see also postmodernism
poverty, 38
power, 82, 84, 112, 120, 132
  gender and, 151–2
  Mackinnon and, 149–57
pregnancy, 53, 145–7
privileged reading, 126
procedural fairness, 15, 28, 30, 31,
  120–1
protective legislation, 147, 153
psychological differences, 14, 51–2, 160
psychology, 92, 94
public/private split, 19, 35, 58, 116–17,
  117–18

racism, 17–18, 21–2, 139
Rape of the Wild (Collard), 82–3
Rattansi, A., 22
Rawls, J., 52
reason, 118
reasoning, 54, 56
relativism, 24
representation
  of groups, 121–2
  of women, 133, 137
reproduction, 67, 73, 109
reproductive technology, 67–8, 69, 70
revolution, 14, 16, 63, 67, 68, 74, 148
Rich, A., 18, 83–6, 87
Richards, J. Radcliffe, 36–8, 43
rights, 155
Rossi, A., 35–6, 57–8, 162, 165
Rostker v. Goldberg, 41, 42
Ruddick, S., 92

sales workers, 148–9
sameness/difference, 3, 4, 30, 130, 152–3,
  162, 165
sameness equality, 4, 5, 13–14, 34, 41,
  161
  Bacchi and, 144–9
  Firestone and, 68
  liberal feminists and, 28–44, 56
Sapiro, V., 165
Sassen, G., 95
Sceptical Feminist, The (Richards), 36–8
science, 28–9, 85, 161
Scott, J., 126, 127, 128–32
*Sears Roebuck v. Equal Opportunities
  Commission (Sears)*, 128, 129–30,
  148

Second Stage, The (Friedan), 31, 48–51
Segal, L., 162
separatism, 79, 162
service jobs, 69
Sevenhuijsen, S., 99
sex differences, 38–9, 42, 45, 50, 52, 54,
  160–1
  Bluestone and, 39–40
  early radicalism and, 64
  Firestone and, 67, 68
  Gilligan and, 94, 96–9
sex/gender distinction, 76–7, 149–50
sexual politics, 48, 49, 71
sexuality, 62, 74, 150
  see also heterosexuality; homosexuality
silencing, 93, 155, 156, 157
sisterhood, 17, 20, 64–6
Snitow, A., 19
social science, 39, 161
socialism, 32, 72, 74
socialist feminism, 108–22
socialization, 49, 109
  difference and, 13, 59
sociobiology, 57–8
special treatment, 4, 145, 146, 153
Spelman, E.V., 133
Spivak, G., 21, 24, 140
Squires, C., 92, 94
standpoint theory, 54, 120
stereotypes, 116, 144
Stoltenberg, J., 156
structurelessness, 65–6
structures, Mitchell and, 72–4
subordination of women, 67, 72, 86, 150,
  156
  see also domination; oppression
success, 95–6, 165
'superwoman syndrome', 49
Supreme Court, 53
surrogate motherhood, 70

Tannen, D., 92
technology, effects of on women, 69–70
Tong, R., 50, 80–1
Tronto, J., 102

unhappiness, 34
universalism, 21, 30, 77, 78, 104

'Wages for Housework', 54, 55
Weedon, C., 127–8
Weldon, F., 34
welfare liberalism, 47, 50, 55
Wendell, S., 32
Williams, W., 41–2, 43, 163

woman
  concept of, 86–7, 148
  culture of, 78, 79, 88, 91
  in postmodernism, 127, 133, 135, 136–7
  see also female values
womanhood, 19, 93, 165

Women, The Longest Revolution (Mitchell),
  71–4
work, 73, 74, 148–9
  conditions at, 144–5, 147

Young, I., 105, 108, 111–22, 162